Mad for God

Sara Tilghman Nalle

Mad for God

BARTOLOMÉ SÁNCHEZ,

THE SECRET MESSIAH

OF CARDENETE

University Press of Virginia

CHARLOTTESVILLE & LONDON

Publication of this book was assisted by a grant
from the Program for Cultural Cooperation between Spain's
Ministry of Education and Culture and United States Universities.

The University Press of Virginia
© 2001 by Sara Tilghman Nalle
All rights reserved
Printed in the United States of America
First published 2001

♾ The paper used in this publication meets the minimum
requirements of the American National Standard for Information
Sciences—Permanence of Paper for Printed Library Materials,
ANSI Z39.48-1984.

Library of Congress Cataloging-in-Publication Data

Nalle, Sara Tilghman.
    Mad for God : Bartolomé Sánchez, the secret Messiah of Cardenete /
Sara Tilghman Nalle.
    p.   cm.
    Includes bibliographical references and index.
    ISBN 0-8139-2000-0 (cloth : alk. paper)—
ISBN 0-8139-2001-9 (pbk. : alk. paper)
    1. Sánchez, Bartolomé, fl. 1501.   2. Inquisition—Spain—Cuenca
(Province).   3. Spain—Church history.   4. Cuenca (Spain : Province)—
History.   I. Title.
BX1735 .N35 2001
272'.2'092—dc21   00-044921

For my parents

CONTENTS

ILLUSTRATIONS

ACKNOWLEDGMENTS

Many individuals and institutions have helped me with this project through its various stages, and I owe them all some words of thanks. The Fulbright Hays Commission funded the research that led me to Sánchez's trial while I was still a graduate student. Years later, a sabbatical leave from William Paterson College (now University) enabled me to carry out research in the archives and libraries of Cuenca, Madrid, Simancas, and Granada. The archivists and librarians at these various institutions, particularly P. Dimas Pérez Ramírez, director of the Archivo Diocesano de Cuenca, were always helpful. Funding to write the book came from the National Endowment for the Humanities and William Paterson College, which enabled me to spend two terms at the Institute for Advanced Study, and from the University of Virginia, where I completed the manuscript. I must particularly thank Peter Onuf, then chair of the History Department at the University of Virginia, for his generous invitation to join his department for a year under ideal circumstances. Many colleagues and friends in Princeton, Charlottesville, and elsewhere have read or heard portions of the manuscript and I am grateful to them for sharing their reactions and advice with me: Ida Altman, Peter Brown, Lu Ann Homza, Eric Johnson, Lloyd and Dorothy Moote, Anne Moyer, J. H. M. Salmon, and members of the Experimenting with Historical Narrative Seminar at the University of Virginia, in particular H. C. Erik Midelfort, Anne J. Schutte, Duane Osheim, and Alison Weber. Finally, I am grateful to Régulo Algarra and Pilar Grande for their unstinting hospitality in Spain and for their enthusiasm for anything related to this project.

ABBREVIATIONS

ADC	Archivo Diocesano de Cuenca
AGS	Archivo General de Simancas
AHN	Archivo Histórico Nacional, Madrid
AMC	Archivo Municipal de Cuenca
ARCG	Archivo Real de la Chancillería, Granada
BAC	Biblioteca de Autores Cristianos
cab.	cabinete
CC	Cámara de Castilla, AGS
CSIC	Consejo Superior de Investigaciones Científicas
DHEE	*Diccionario de Historia Eclesiástica de España.* 4 vols. Madrid: CSIC, 1972.
exp.	expediente (dosier)
f., ff.	folio, folios
HIEA	*Historia de la Inquisición en España y América.* 2 vols. Madrid: BAC, 1984.
Inq.	Inquisición
leg.	legajo (file)
RAH	Real Academia de Historia
lib.	libro (book)
Proceso	ADC, Inq., leg 196, exp. 2216
RGS	Registro General del Sello, AGS
sec.	sección (department)

Mad for God

INTRODUCTION

TRUE LIFE STORIES ARE OFTEN UNTIDY, WITH OBSCURE BEGINNINGS, long silences, abrupt twists and turns, and forgotten endings. There is no record of the life of Bartolomé Sánchez, the failed farmer and wool carder of sixteenth-century Spain who is the subject of this book, except in a lengthy Inquisition trial conducted over the course of seven years, between 1553 and 1560. In this attempt to bring Sánchez and his world back into view, readers may find themselves without the usual comforts of a historical monograph. This study has no overall thesis, no highroad to historical truth, not even simple closure to the story.

Bartolomé Sánchez lived during one of the most expansive and turbulent periods in Spanish and European history. When he was born, around 1501, news of the discovery of the New World was not yet ten years old, and Spanish forces were poised to capture Naples, inaugurating over two hundred years of Spanish imperialism in Europe. At home Ferdinand and Isabella had united the various kingdoms of Spain under their crowns, conquered the last Muslim enclave in Western Europe, and forced the conversion or exile of Spain's large Jewish minority. As Sánchez grew to adulthood, mystics and visionaries held unprecedented influence in Spanish society, the kingdoms of Castile and Valencia were torn by revolts against the monarchy of Charles V, and the first reports of the Lutheran and Anabaptist revolutions began to reach Spain. Because Sánchez traveled widely looking for work around New Castile and Andalusia, he must have known quite a bit about the world beyond his village, but since he came to the attention of the authorities for his religious ideas and for no other reason, we can only speculate as to whether he knew about the discovery of the New World or was aware of Spain's sudden rise to prominence on the world stage. By contrast, we know a great deal about what Sánchez thought of the leadership of the Church and Catholic doctrine, and the heterodox religious notions he could glean from the surrounding environment.

Rather than the reconstruction of a life long ago lost, this book is an account of one man's descent into religious madness. It is part courtroom drama, part adventure story, and part debate over the nature of religious inspiration, insanity, and criminal responsibility. The issues raised by Sánchez's story are at the same time universal and specific to the cultural environment of sixteenth-century Spain: Who decides what is a genuine message from God? Who should possess certain kinds of knowledge? What goes beyond the boundaries of rational behavior? And what constitutes a crime? Most readers of this book will have some impression of Spanish history that includes aspects of the Black Legend: an intolerant society obsessed with religious orthodoxy and racial purity, which were enforced by the Inquisition, one of the most notorious of all European institutions. Recent scholarship has helped to mitigate the Inquisition's fearsome reputation, but old stereotypes die slowly. Obviously, Spanish society was far more complex than the simple assumptions of the Black Legend. Readers should realize that while most Spaniards were devout and conservative Catholics, there also existed, thanks to the legacy of Aristotelianism and Roman jurisprudence, a spirit of rationalism and respect for the rule of law that may surprise those who think that our own times have a monopoly on these things. If this seems paradoxical, readers need only reflect that the same contradictory tendencies exist in modern society: we can find a president's wife consulting an astrologer to arrange her husband's schedule and scientists who believe in the biblical account of creation.

At times, then, Sánchez's world can seem surprisingly modern, populated as it is by inquisitors who worry about the nature of forensic evidence and their retirement pensions, and physicians who believe that mental illness is caused by some organic imbalance within the body. Those same individuals, however, also believed in the twin realities of miracles and the devil's power, and were convinced that freedom of speech and of religion were incompatible with the functioning of a well-ordered society. It was a world where the spread of literacy and the availability of cheap printed books enabled powerless men like Bartolomé Sánchez to dream of things beyond what the Holy Mother Catholic Church commanded, and dreams such as his could condemn one to death.

Such, in brief, are some of the historical concerns of this book. Early in the project, I also became interested in two related historiographical problems. First, there was the challenge of postmodernism, which questions at every turn the textual, linguistic, and esthetic foundations of historical writing.[1] The postmodernist critique, or "linguistic turn," is particularly relevant to this project because of the documentary evidence on which the book is based. Virtually everything we know about Sánchez comes from one lengthy trial process. While no transcript is a completely transparent window to the past, Sánchez's trial is even more problematic than most. From a statement made by the court recorder, we know that the irrational aspects of Sánchez's behavior in court were systematically dropped from the record. The transcript, in fact, is a carefully constructed artifact that bears witness primarily to Sánchez's heterodox speech and behavior, and only secondarily to his illness. Any attempt to understand the real man must compete against the edited version of himself.

Yet when Sánchez does speak for the record, his words are irresistible.[2] It was the compelling nature of his voice that convinced me from the beginning that I should attempt to write this book in the form of a historical reconstruction, rather than as a monograph. Meeting this goal has required the adoption of writing strategies very different from those one would encounter in an academic work of history, where analysis and historiographical argument are privileged. Here, narration, description, and dialogue convey the book's themes indirectly to the reader. In the end, while remaining faithful to the historical record, this history is more self-consciously constructed than most, and some word of explanation is required if the reader is to appreciate the methods that were employed in its writing.

At the core of this book are the extended conversations between Sánchez and the inquisitor Pedro Cortes and Sánchez's own confessions, preserved as part of his trial before the Inquisition of Cuenca.[3] Normally in the tribunals of the Holy Office, the relationship between judge and prisoner was an adversarial one, but this was not to be the case in Sánchez's trial. In the interviews conducted with Pedro Cortes, Sánchez hid nothing from the court because he was convinced that he had done nothing wrong and God would protect him from harm. In fact, as God's messenger, he had a special obligation to deliver his message and to tell the truth—at least, in the beginning. I use the word "interview" rather than "interrogation" because for his part Pedro Cortes did not conduct a normal trial with the wool carder. Because Cortes was convinced that Sánchez was not mentally competent to stand trial, his primary concern was to save his prisoner's life—he did not want a judicial murder on his conscience. To this end, he spent many hours in conversation with Sánchez before the formal indictment of the prisoner in an attempt to persuade the wool carder to recant. The result is a document that records a lively debate between two individuals, each equally committed to the justice of his position.

Such lengthy conversations between a member of the lower class and his or her more literate social superior are rarely found in the sources of the time, even in court records, and full use of them is made in this book.[4] In some works of microhistory and historical reconstruction, authors have invented dialogue or speeches to take advantage of the impact that the impression of spoken language can have on the reader's imagination.[5] It is important to emphasize that all of the conversations and paraphrases of conversations that are recorded in this book originally appeared as part of the court record; by the same token, gestures, motions (walking, kneeling, etc.), clothes, props, and actions such as crying are presented as they appeared to the court recorder.

As the reader can appreciate, the skill and methods of the court recorder are an integral part of the reliability of the text. Juan de Ybaneta, the principal notary throughout Sánchez's trial, had passed the necessary examination to hold the title of royal secretary and at age thirty-five had worked for the tribunal of Cuenca for some ten years. While the court record that he produced is not the equivalent of a tape recording, it does represent what was said for the record, and it received Sánchez's approval on a variety of occasions. In the secretary's recording of testimony, the spoken language underwent some conventional modifications. Irrelevant responses were dropped, and all speech that was preserved was converted into the third person, past tense. To recover the immediacy of the court-room experience, I have restored the language to the original first person and appropriate tense, and dropped the introductory "He said that . . ." The result is direct and natural speech. Occasionally Sánchez's testimony was so gripping that the secretary forgot his own training and took down the wool carder's words verbatim, omitting to make the usual transpositions. In the notes, I point out the more important instances in which he has done so.

While all speech and actions are presented as recorded, on two occasions I have allowed myself to think for Cortes and Sánchez. I have assumed that Pedro Cortes, as a theologian and career inquisitor, knew in broad outline the history of the Spanish Inquisition and shared in its prejudices and judicial practices. Occasionally he must have reflected on his training, which I have articulated for him in order to explain something about the Holy Office from his point of view. During Bartolomé Sánchez's *auto de fe,* I have assumed that Sánchez was listening while his sentence was read aloud and that he would have reacted with dismay to the fact that the sentence made no mention whatever of his belief that he was the Elijah-Messiah. I have tried to express that dismay in the same terms that Sánchez often used to refer to his enemies.

With the ground rules for the presentation of dialogue established, there remains the problem of interpretation: How did the dialogue proceed? Why were the questions being posed when they were being posed? What was being felt at the time? What was the significance of the response? How much of the dialogue should be presented directly and how much should be paraphrased? The Inquisition's secretaries were not allowed to comment on procedure or what they thought was the emotion

of the moment. Although they could note that a person was crying (because it was an observable action), they could not decide for the court
whether the person was crying out of sadness, fear, or relief. I do not know
for a fact if at a certain moment Sánchez "scoffed" or if Cortes "exploded"
or even why the inquisitor chose one line of questioning over another.
My role as a historian is to offer some interpretation of what occurred. At
the most basic level, I offer an interpretation of the transcript of Sánchez's
trial.

Sánchez was a natural-born storyteller, a good debater, and at times a
convincing liar. The inquisitors who dealt with his case indulged the wool
carder and allowed him on several occasions to speak at length, without
interruptions, in order to explain himself. These confessions, or mono-
logues, are highly unusual, both for the simple fact of their existence and
for their content, and I incorporate them virtually entire. They are full of
snatches of conversation, asides, and comments by Sánchez concerning
his emotional state and thought processes. The language is direct and
without artifice, yet intensely alive and personal. Like all Spaniards of his
time, educated or not, Sánchez spoke in phrases that were linked together
with an endless series of "and's." This practice would be tedious for the
modern English-speaking audience, so I have dropped many of the con-
nectives and rearranged the syntax to approximate the feel of modern
spoken English. I have tried to steer a moderate course between readability and literal accuracy. At all times I have respected Sánchez's own choice
of verb tenses and recollections of conversations.[6]

Finally, in my efforts to make sixteenth-century Cuenca as real to
readers as possible, I have resorted to a few other strategies that one normally does not find in a work of history. First, as Sánchez's trial unfolds
in this reconstruction, I have kept very close track of the calendar—the
days of the week, even the times of day, and the holidays—so that the
reader can experience the rhythm of an early modern work schedule and
feel the passage of time. Much to my own amazement, as I began to write
the first chapters of the book in the fall of 1995 I discovered that my
Thursday, October 19, had also been Sánchez's Thursday, October 19
(1553), and I was writing about the early days of his trial on virtually the
same days that the trial had taken place, 442 years before.

I have also incorporated a certain amount of "local color"—topographical and climatological observations that come from my experience of living in Cuenca in premodern housing and spending a fair amount of time walking the city's streets and the surrounding countryside. One of my informants, Elías, was a retired illiterate shepherd who had been born in a small village in the province a few years before the outbreak of the Spanish Civil War in 1936. During the spring of 1993, while living in Cuenca to do the research for this book, when the archive was closed I used to spend many hours conversing with Elias while we worked on restoring an abandoned garden. I learned that despite the vast differences in our education, upbringing, and life experience, his hopes for himself, resentments, and disappointments were as understandable to me as my own. This experience gives me some confidence that with effort, it is possible to understand Bartolomé Sánchez and his world as well.

1. The world of Bartolomé Sánchez

1
ⵍⵉⵎ

THE

BREAKDOWN

1

AT THE BEGINNING OF MASS ONE HOLY DAY IN MARCH 1552, THE villagers of Cardenete watched in amazement as Bartolomé Sánchez, tense and irritable, entered the parish church and walked to the front of the main altar. The fifty-one-year-old Sánchez carried a pilgrim's staff and a red bonnet, the latter decorated with the scallop shells of St. James. In the manner of a penitent, Sánchez also bore some saddlebags weighted down with five stones in expiation of Christ's five wounds. Further, he had wound a rope around his torso, and, most bizarrely to those who watched the unfolding scene, he limped along on just one shoe. Juan Caballero asked Sánchez why he went with one shoe on and the other off, and received the enigmatic reply that the world was turning topsy-turvy.[1]

Sánchez knelt before the altar to hear Mass, but at the elevation of the Host the pilgrim closed his eyes so he would not see the supposed miracle of Christ's presence there. This insult to the sacrament prompted several men to speak to Sánchez, who, still on his knees, rebuffed them: "Leave me alone—don't talk to me!" An incoherent torrent of invective came tumbling out: "Sátanas and Barrabas! Oh, cursèd Lucifer! St. Francis

2. Parish church of Cardenete. (Photograph by the author)

faith and St. Peter rock! Anyone here want to debate with me? I will not shut up!"[2] Miguel Caballero and some others took him outside the church, where Sánchez's cousin Bartolomé de Mora heard him declare that he had carried the pilgrim's staff all the way to Santiago de Compostela, five hundred miles away. He dared not contradict him.[3]

No one in Cardenete knew why Sánchez had donned the pilgrim's garb, or for that matter why he seemed so agitated. Before his blasphemous behavior in church, there had been a minor public incident or two, but nothing really to attract attention. Most people in the village knew only that since 1551 Sánchez had worked side by side with Juan García Masegoso carding wool for various neighbors, and to supplement his income he occasionally left with other men from the village to work as a migrant farm laborer in La Mancha, sometimes staying away for as long as three months. Once Sánchez had been a farmer himself, but he had not been able to make a living at it and had learned the craft of wool combing.[4] He was a good worker and a family man; if he was upset by his descent in the world, he kept his regrets to himself.

2

The village of Cardenete, where Sánchez had been born at the beginning of the century, was a settlement like so many others in New Castile: a clutch of whitewashed and red-tiled houses built around a central square, a parish church, and a castle on the hill. "Cardenete: míralo y vete," goes the refrain—"Cardenete: see it and get out." Set against the side of a small valley, the village guarded the western approaches to an area known as the Tierras de Moya, a rugged corner of New Castile wedged in between the kingdoms of Aragon and Valencia. Although settlement of the region dates back to prehistoric times, humankind's hold on the Tierras always seemed provisional. Too rocky for extensive farming, the Tierras de Moya were more of a place for passing through: first it was the Romans on their way from Córdoba to Zaragoza, then the Moors from Valencia to Toledo, and finally the Christians fighting their way south from Soria to Murcia. After the reconquest of the area by the Christians in 1183, Cardenete and thirty-one other villages were incorporated into a seigneurial territory with its seat at Moya, a hilltop fortress that dominated the area. At the time of Bartolomé's birth, the seigneury had only recently been elevated to the status of a marquisate, presided over by the royal favorites, Don Andrés de Cabrera and his wife, Doña Beatriz de Bobadilla.[5]

The fact of Sánchez's birth was unremarkable. More remarkable was that he survived to adulthood, for aside from the usual high infant mortality, plague and famine were on the prowl during those years, especially in 1507. As an adult, Bartolomé recalled that in addition to his grown brothers and sisters, he had "others who died on me while they were quite small."[6] Like his father and uncles before him, Bartolomé Sánchez was brought up to be a farmer (*labrador*). In rural New Castile, to be called a labrador meant that one had achieved a certain status and economic independence in life; Sánchez's father and uncles presumably all had access to some land and a few animals to work it. They were the lucky ones; as the century progressed, Sánchez's generation found it increasingly difficult to maintain the status of a labrador. Many, like Bartolomé, slipped into the great underclass of landless day laborers, called *jornaleros*, whose only asset was the sweat of their brow.

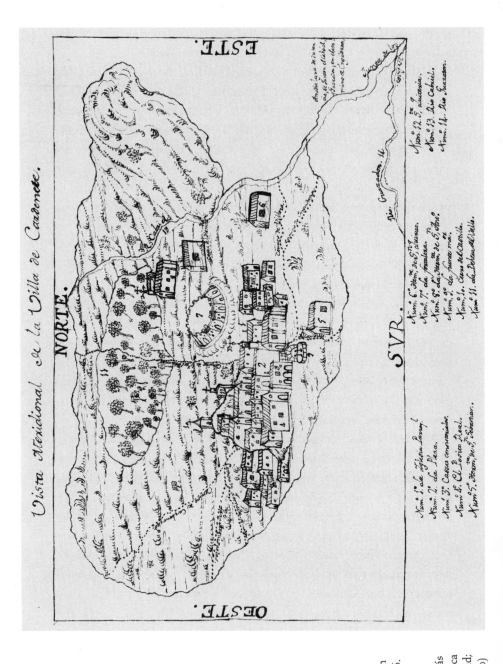

3. View of
Cardenete from
the south, 1786.
("Relaciones
Topográficas
enviadas a Tomás
López," Biblioteca
Nacional, Madrid;
ms. 7298, f. 230)

One reason for the growing impoverishment of rural families such as Sánchez's was the simple fact that there were too many people and not enough land. Plague or no, during the first half of the sixteenth century the population of New Castile was growing rapidly, finally replacing and then exceeding the demographic losses caused by the great Black Death of 1348–50. In the village of Cardenete, the natural increase of the population seems to have been augmented by some immigration from the Basque country and the mountains of nearby Cuenca.[7] Most of the village's residents were "Old" Christians; "old" because their ancestors had always been Christian and had never intermarried with converted Jews or Muslims, who were known as the "New" Christians or "converts" (conversos). All the same, even this fairly remote village harbored a community of converted Jews, some of whom had immigrated to Cardenete from the city of Cuenca and the kingdom of Valencia in the late fifteenth century. By 1528, immigration and natural growth had made Cardenete the largest village in the territory to which it belonged. With its 206 tax-paying households and two tax-exempt noble hidalgos, the village was wealthy enough to support two public notaries and a schoolmaster.[8]

From the authorities' point of view, a growing population was viewed as a good thing. More subjects represented taxable wealth, but for the village of Cardenete, the increased population was a burden. More families meant more people and animals to feed when the village lacked the land to support them. Although Cardenete's council lands were extensive, they comprised largely sterile rock and gravel, not at all the sort of soil needed for growing the cereals, vegetables, and pasture that made up the bulk of the villagers' and their animals' diet. In fact, so infertile was Cardenete's arable land that the best of it could be cropped only once every four years, and in some places, just once every twenty years.[9] Complicating matters, the inheritance laws of the time forced parents to divide their property equally among their children, so that each generation faced the dispersion of already insufficient landholdings. In poorer families such as Sánchez's, the result was that no child received enough land to support himself unless he married well or found a way to buy out the other heirs. With many other siblings surviving to adulthood, Bartolomé appears to have been one of those unfortunate ones who wound up with too little land.

The lack of adequate farmland in Cardenete was critical for the entire

4. The Vega de Yémeda, agricultural land leased by Cardenete.
(Photograph by the author)

village. While producing woolen cloth brought in extra income for many residents, it could not replace farming as a means of support. Around 1500, the village council, casting about for a way to increase the amount of arable land for its residents, entered into a long-term agreement with the lord of Víllora, who owned some fertile bottom land known as the Vega de Yémeda. In exchange for a yearly rent of 440 bushels of wheat, Cardenete acquired the land it needed plus a water mill. As the village council explained in a lawsuit in 1552, Cardenete "possesses sterile land, and cannot match cereal-producing lands as good as those [in Yémeda] . . . their principal sustenance and relief." Even better, the Vega de Yémeda was a scant league away, although just far enough to place it over the border into the jurisdiction of the city of Cuenca.[10] The acquisition of extra arable for the village, however, does not seem to have helped the extended Sánchez family. By 1553, three of Sánchez's uncles and three of his siblings had picked up and left the village. The favored destination was Villamalea, a settlement thirty miles to the south on the edge of the flat expanse of La Mancha, a parched plain where the climate matched the famous proverb's description of *nueve meses de invierno y tres de infierno* (nine months of winter and three of hell). Bartolomé, on the other hand, chose to stay in the village, where in 1532, at the relatively late age of thirty-one, he married Catalina Martínez, also from Cardenete. Her family had some land that she either brought to the marriage or later inherited, and with the little that Bartolomé had, for a while they made a go of farming. Meanwhile the children began to arrive. The couple's eldest child, a daughter, was born in 1537 or 1538, and by 1552 there were three more girls and a boy, Bartolomico.[11] Around 1550, when Sánchez was already an old man by society's standards, he was forced to abandon farming and began to work on the margins of the economy as a jornalero and wool carder. Is it any wonder that a few years later, Sánchez, as an elderly father of five young children with no sure means of support, suffered a public breakdown in the parish church?

3

Around the time of his breakdown, Sánchez's family had witnessed more strange behavior, but they were in the dark as to its cause. Sánchez had been beside himself with some unnamed fear. He stopped eating and they had to force-feed him. He did strange things, such as taking a clay jug, placing a lemon within it, blessing it, and declaring that it was God the Father's orb. At night he emptied the chamber pot in the street and said that the souls of the damned bathed and drowned in urine.[12] One day he appeared so disoriented that his cousin Bartolomé de Mora and two others tied Sánchez up with rope, but when Sánchez exclaimed, "You have me tied to the column just like the Jews did to Christ—which of you is to give me the first lash?" they untied him and took him to the parish church. At the doorway, Sánchez removed his left shoe before entering. Concerned by his cousin's behavior, Mora spent three nights with Sánchez, who was so agitated that it seemed his heart would leap right out of his body, and the poor man could not stay quiet—he kept on talking and repeating all of his prayers.

Mora became so worried that he took Sánchez to the village of Monteagudo, fifteen miles away, to see if Sánchez had some devil in his body that the priest there could recognize and exorcise. The priest saw the wool carder but could find no evidence of possession, and gave them some medicine for Bartolomé without telling them what it was.[13] A few days later, Mora returned to Monteagudo with Sánchez so that he could pray for relief at the shrine of Our Lady of the Candles. Sánchez stayed there the whole day without being able to speak, and if they spoke to him, he was unable to reply; all he did was sob. Later, when he came to and they asked him why he had been that way, he said that he had seen some men in yellow hose who were coming to kill him. Mora and his friends were unable to see any part of what Sánchez said he had seen, so they returned home. In fact, Mora was certain that Sánchez during this time was not in his right mind at all, and when Sánchez went back to Monteagudo a third time without telling anyone that he was going to see the priest again, they were sure he had done some mischief to himself and they went out to look for him.[14]

Although Sánchez seemed beside himself with fear and anxiety, so much so that Mora began to wonder if his cousin had gone mad, Sánchez still uttered no word of explanation for his actions. This silence was all the more surprising because the wool carder knew perfectly well what was the cause of his anxiety, but he had taken an oath not to say anything about it. Sánchez's travails had begun in 1550, around the time he gave up farming for himself. As he explained later, it happened this way:

> Around St. John's feast day in June,[15] I was coming back from reaping at the Vega de Yémeda, which is next to Cardenete, no more than a half-league away. The sun had set, but it wasn't night yet. Just as I was approaching a chapel that is called St. Sebastian's, there appeared in the air in the form of a luminous image the figures of two men and a woman. The woman appeared to me to be in between the two men, and above the woman there appeared to be a bird, which with the tip of one wing touched the other. When I saw this, I went down on my knees and prayed right there five Paternosters with five Hail Marys, and after that, three Paternosters with three Hail Marys, all on my knees, begging God that if this were a good thing, to tell me so, and if not, to take it away. While I was doing that, the thing that I saw disappeared, and it seemed to me that I felt consoled in my heart, and so I went home and I never mentioned it to anyone. I went around always wondering to myself what that could have been until Lent [1551] came. I went to confess with Martín de Almazán, the old priest of Cardenete, and to do that

I bought a book from Hernán Zomeño, which was a Roman rite book of hours in Spanish with its list of martyrs, and I would read in that book of hours. And where the hours for the Conception of Our Lady begin, I found on an illustrated page the figure that had appeared to me on the road coming back from reaping, and, confessing with Almazán, I showed him the illustration that was in the book of hours and I also told him that what had appeared to me on the road was the same as what was drawn in the book. The priest opened the book and saw that painted figure, and, having seen it and heard me, he told me, "I can neither censure this nor approve it because I can't understand it; how do I know what it is? Don't say anything to anyone." Shriven, I went home, but I could not rest until I knew from wise and learned people what that was. Any time that I saw some friar or learned person, I would kneel at his feet to confess and tell him everything, and show him the illustration from the book of hours. I did this with Fray Pizarro and Fray Sebastian, and I showed them the book of hours so that they could tell me what that figure might mean.[16]

Sometime after Lent in 1551, the old village priest died and things began to go badly between Sánchez and the new village priest, Bachiller Barca. No doubt on account of his poverty, Sánchez stopped paying his tithes. "One day," Sánchez remembered,

> after some excommunications had been announced in church, I told the village priest that the person who issued them and the one who read them aloud ought to be stoned, and the priest said to me, "See here, you have fallen under those excommunications," and I told him, "No, I don't," and he said, "What's gotten into you? You have got to ask me for those accounts" [i.e., to pay his tithes]. So I said to the priest that the Son of God did not come to win fortunes but souls, and those who excommunicated others for accumulating wealth were killing souls, and with that I said goodbye to him.[17]

Despite his run-ins with the local clergy, Sánchez continued to track down other priests for advice about his vision and the book of hours. Finally, late in 1551,

> there came to Cardenete to preach on St. Thomas's Day a friar from Carboneras. Since I was besides myself on account of the things I imagined that went beyond what the Holy Mother Church commands, I

A completas.   cxvij.
ston. Oracion. Todos tus san
ctos. zc.
¶Comiençancompletas.

Señor Dios de nfa salud
conuiertenos. E desuia ó
P iiij

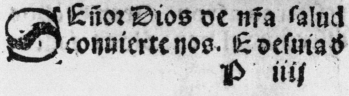

5. Woodcut of the Coronation of the Virgin in the *Horas de Nuestra Señora* (1565). (Biblioteca Nacional, Madrid; R 16814, f. cxvii–r)

6. Ruins of the Dominican convent in Carboneras.
(Photograph by the author)

went to confess with that friar. I told him the whole story and I showed him the figure from the book of hours. The friar told me that all that had been represented to me was the devil, and he did not want to absolve me. He told me to go with him to Carboneras to eat, and not to say anything to anyone; my life would be worthless if I did. With that I was left spinning.[18]

Sánchez waited until Lent of 1552 to go to the Dominican convent at Carboneras. This was a large foundation about twelve miles up the road from Sánchez's village. The friary served partly as a mausoleum for the first marquises of Moya and partly as a center for theological study. A friar from Carboneras certainly would have more spiritual credibility than Cardenete's village priest, with whom Sánchez was feuding, and if the friar said to come secretly or risk losing his life and soul, Sánchez had little choice but to go. Before leaving, the wool carder made some preparations.

I made a rope out of raw matweed and I wrapped it around my body at the waist. I gave it about five or six turns so I could go to the friar doing penance, although he had not ordered me to do any such thing. When

I was supposed to go there I had prepared five stones that weighed about twenty-five pounds and I put them inside some saddlebags so I could carry them as a penance to the monastery of Carboneras, where I had to go to talk to the friar so he could give me absolution. The night before I was supposed to go I had my rope tied around me and the rocks all ready, and so my wife couldn't see them, inside the saddlebags hidden underneath a threshing sled. I ordered my son, Bartolomico, to read from the book of hours some prayers that I had for devotion because I was so high and dizzy that I couldn't pray on my own. The boy was praying the Passion when I fell off the chair where I was sitting and began shouting and saying, "Get out, cursèd Lucifer, I did not give you permission to come in here!" all the while calling on God and the saints. When my wife and the boy saw the things I was saying, they went screaming their heads off to the neighbors, and lots of neighbors came, men and women, and a priest called Juan Gallego, and they asked me what on earth was so wrong with me that they were frightened. They picked me up and put me back on my chair, and I told them to go in peace to their homes, that I didn't know what it was or what had happened, and they all went home except the weaver Garci Pérez, who said he wanted to stay with me so that I would tell him what had happened. So he stayed and I went to bed and Garci Pérez sat beside me asking me what had that been and I told him I didn't know except that when I had confessed with the friar who preached on St. Thomas's Day, he had not wanted to give me absolution and I had to go to Carboneras. Garci Pérez told me I shouldn't go until he went to talk with the village priest.

The next morning Garci Pérez came by my house and told me not to leave because the priest had not gotten up yet. I said, "If he has to come, he better come quickly because I can't miss going to Carboneras to be absolved by the friar." Garci Pérez shut the front door from the outside so I couldn't leave. Once Pérez had gone I called a boy and he let me out. I got the stones from where they were, I put the saddlebags over my shoulder and take off for Carboneras. When I got pretty well outside of town, Garci Pérez caught up with me and took the saddlebags from me and wouldn't let me go. He made me go back until I talked with the priest, and took me home and brought the priest there. The priest said to me, "Come on, let's finish Mass at church and after Mass is over, we'll talk." So we went to church and the priest said Mass and I heard it, and afterward the priest told me, "Let's go out to the hillside by the tower that's next to the church." He asked me what was happening and where I was going, and I told him that I was going to Carboneras with that rope and rocks as a penance so that the friar would give me absolution. The priest told me I shouldn't worry, that he would absolve me of everything. He made me take off the rope and the rocks in front of him and told me to go home and work as I used to in order to feed my wife and children, and so I went home. All day long I was excited and spinning.[19]

"The priest said Mass and I heard it." That is all Sánchez had to say about the twenty minutes it took to say Mass the day of his public breakdown in church in March 1552. Apparently Sánchez had no recollection of his own behavior at the height of the breakdown, although he could remember all the events leading up to and following upon the outburst in the church. He seemed to be unaware of how his dress and actions (the penitent pilgrim's paraphernalia, the missing shoe, the shouting) had appeared to others. For their part, those of his neighbors who witnessed his bizarre behavior in church were entirely unaware of Sánchez's dilemma, that for two years he had gone without absolution because no cleric dared pronounce on the vision and book of hours, except for the Dominican who told him that it was all the devil's doing and that his life would be in danger if he spoke of it. Thus the village saw only a distraught man who for reasons unknown to them dressed like a pilgrim and disrupted services. In the end, Sánchez never did get to Carboneras; he confessed and received communion that Lenten season in Jorquera, a village several days' journey to the south, where Sánchez had relatives. This would be his last confession as an entirely faithful Catholic.

4

After the emotional and spiritual crisis in the spring of 1552, Sánchez attracted no further attention worth comment until the end of the year. During the Christmas holidays, the parish priest came to his house and confiscated the book of hours. Sánchez decided he wasn't going to get out of bed to go to Mass. "Since when did you stop going to Mass?" asked his wife in amazement, and she went off to get her relatives. Sánchez recalled,

When I heard the sound of the people who were coming, I got scared that they might do more to me. I got out of bed and picked up a staff to defend myself from them, so they would leave me at home and go away. They assaulted me and took away the staff. When they heard the things I said and saw the crazy things I did, they tied me to a post just in my nightshirt and bare feet, and left the entryway, closing the door from outside. Since nobody, not even my wife, wanted to untie me, I bite through the rope—it was just matweed—with my teeth, get free, and I throw myself at the door to knock it down to get out. The men were frightened—"Who let me out?"—and I told them, "God," so they made me dress and took me to Mass.[20]

Around Christmas in 1552, Sánchez's thoughts began to crystallize into an explanation for what was happening to him. He began to imagine things, as he put it, beyond what the Catholic Church allowed, and as Lent approached once more, he could no longer keep silent—he knew the truth about the Church and didn't care who heard it. Francisco Ruiz remembered in detail a long conversation he had with Sánchez in February 1553.

Sánchez told me that the cross ought to be burned, not worshiped [adorada], on account of the evil justice that had been carried out on it. The cross together with all the other images were idols. God did not enter into the Host when priests elevated it. In the Holy Trinity there were no more than the father, son, and mother, and the Holy Spirit had nothing to do with it. A fine thing it was to conceive the son in his mother and then leave her out! The promised Messiah had yet to come so that we could believe in him. And there was more. Sánchez was willing to bet that the body of St. Julian wasn't where it had been put in the city of Cuenca, because he had been there and it wasn't there. And the Veronica of Jaén which they say is the face of Our Lord—he had seen it but it wasn't anything but a bit of paper that is used to fool people, and he didn't care if the twelve councilmen of Jaén did swear that it was the Veronica.[21] The priests were all damned and excommunicated and the Pope was the devil and was damned and excommunicated. When I rebuked him, he said, "How dare they burn this book? Well, they're not going to!"[22] A few days later, I went back to Bartolomé Sánchez and I asked him if he had some book, or how else did he know the things he said. Sánchez said he didn't have a book; it was a divine grace he had. I asked him where did this divine grace come from, and he replied that one day, coming back from reaping in the Vega de Yémeda next to this village, near St. Sebastian's chapel, a very bright and beautiful figure had appeared to him and he had been very comforted on account of seeing it. The figure said nothing to him at all and a certain number of days later, on St. Matthew's Day, another figure appeared to him. It seemed to him that it was a cross with its crucifix, and it was lying on the ground. Sánchez told me that figure had comforted him like the first, and he would tell anybody who wanted to listen.[23]

Soon the whole village was talking about Sánchez's crazy ideas. A few individuals felt it was their duty to set him straight. So, when Sánchez went to ask Juan Caballero about some wheat he was selling, Caballero took advantage of the moment to take Sánchez aside. Sitting him down,

I told him I was frightened for him on account of the things people were saying he had said against our Holy Catholic faith. Bartolomé replied, "Why? Because I don't take the peace of God in church? That's the devil's peace because priests are damned and excommunicated!" I told him, "Shut up, you lost man, you're either crazy or a heretic! Don't you know that, however sinful a priest is, when he says those words that Our Lord Jesus Christ said at the Last Supper with His disciples, the bread turns into His precious flesh and the watered wine turns and converts into His precious blood? And that because the priest kisses that holy sacrament, on that account peace is given to the people and that is the peace of God?" Sánchez replied to this that it wasn't anything but the devil's peace because the priests were excommunicated and he didn't believe that Our Lord Jesus Christ had anything to do with that sacrament. I rebuked him and told him he was a bad Christian and a heretic, and he replied that there were other things deeper than this. I told him, "I guarantee you that they're going to burn you," and while I was correcting him and talking to him, he left my house.[24]

Juan Caballero couldn't let the matter rest, though, and a few days later he sought out the wool carder to see if he had changed his mind.

I found him combing wool in Widow López's house. I went up to talk to him where he was combing in the attic, and I said, "Are you in a better frame of mind than you were the other day?" He replied that the frame of mind he was in was fine and he would say so in front of anyone who wanted to listen. I told him, "I've seen them burn people who haven't said as many heresies as you have said and are saying now! A man of your age ought to be ashamed and to fear God to say what you say. May God bring you to a better understanding so that you won't be damned." Sánchez repeated that his opinion was fine and that there were deeper things yet. I asked him what were those things that he said were so deep and he replied that because Our Lord Jesus Christ had been innocent when he was placed on the cross, the crosses ought to be burned. I told him, "Shut up, you're a heretic!" Sánchez repeated that he knew even deeper things, and I replied, "How do you know that there are deeper things? You don't know even how to comb wool and you know that there are deeper things? It's the devil who talks to you!" Sánchez said that St. Peter had been murdered with a halberd and a dagger, and I said, "Did you see what you say? How can you prove that, because I'm older than you and I never heard that! How do you prove that?" He said, "By Holy Scripture," and I said to him, "I wish to God that you never knew how to read so that you wouldn't learn these heresies. Look, for the love of God, collect yourself and think something else so that you won't lose your soul!" Sánchez said he would say what he believed in front of anyone, and that when St. Peter was killed, they stole his gospel, and we are living under the same religion by which Our Lord Jesus Christ was killed.[25]

Juan Caballero's brother Miguel also tried to convert Sánchez, but he too was rebuffed. Sánchez told him his usual heresies and added for Miguel's sake, "You are the damned one and I am the saved because of the three religions that are under heaven, Christian, Moorish, and Jewish, the worst of all of these is the Christian one, the one that you have and uphold, and everything that the Pope says and does on earth is worthless, it's a joke and a lie, and the Messiah promised in law has yet to come." Since all the priests were damned, Sánchez added, no one should confess with them; instead they should go out to the countryside and confess to God in heaven.[26]

5

After Sánchez had spent some two months hereticizing, the village priest, Bachiller Barca, sent a denunciation to Inquisitor Pedro Cortes at the local tribunal of the Holy Office in the city of Cuenca. On Cortes's orders, the wool carder was arrested on Lazarus Monday (March 27, 1553) and held in the village jail while Barca began to take depositions from nine vil-lage men.[27] Sánchez had told many of them that he did not care who heard him; he would preach to anyone who would listen. This did not mean that he was oblivious of the danger he was courting by proclaiming his ideas to the world. He simply believed that a different fate was in store for him; the ordinary world's punishments no longer meant anything to him. While in jail, Sánchez told Miguel Caballero that the chains that bound him were nothing but roses and flowers. Sánchez reacted to the news that he would be taken to Cuenca by drawing a surprising biblical comparison, that they wished to take him as Christ had been carried off; they were just some Pharisees. When the village council and priest neglected to feed him and his family while he was in prison, Sánchez broke loose and escaped: if they weren't going to provide for him and take up a collection for his family, then he would go on his own to look for work to support them. He was entitled to that much.

Apparently no one was too concerned about Sánchez's escape, as it elicited no official reaction, and Sánchez did not go far. In October, In-quisitor Cortes finally sent to Bachiller Barca for Sánchez, who was found in the village. Barca wrote back that they were sending Sánchez to him in fetters, for better security. Barca also checked to see if Sánchez had any property that could be confiscated by the court to pay for its expenses. At home, he found a scene of pathetic poverty. Under oath Sánchez's wife, Catalina Martínez, told Barca that their entire savings consisted of eight reals (about one week's wages), one of which they owed to a tailor. Barca found no furniture in the house except for some broken-down chests and hutches. There was nothing more worth mentioning except for a heavy blanket and a mattress cover, which the family used to wrap around them-selves to sleep. Sánchez's wife, seeing her husband carted off in chains and their savings gone, asked if she could have her dowry returned to her, but was told it was all gone. Catalina Martínez was left without a penny to support five children, aged fifteen years to fourteen months, while Barca used seven of the eight reals to pay off the men who delivered Sánchez to Cuenca.[28] The prisoner arrived there after a four-day journey, with no more than the clothes on his back, and was handed over to the care of the warden of the Inquisition's secret prisons.

IN THE
SECRET PRISONS

1

THE PRISONS AND ROOMS OF THE HOLY OFFICE OF THE INQUISITION
were located on a dead-end street near the cathedral of Cuenca, an inelegant Gothic structure that dominated the stucco and stone buildings of the quarter. Sánchez's cell, which he shared with one other prisoner, contained several religious images, and had a window that looked out over the alley. The tribunal had not always occupied those quarters. In the early days after it was founded, from 1489 to 1521, the court covered a large and diverse geographical district in eastern New Castile in its pursuit of crypto-Jews. After 1521, the court settled definitively in the city of Cuenca, a prosperous town of some 12,000 inhabitants, whose main business was producing woolen textiles. The city and the tribunal's district, now defined as the bishoprics of Cuenca and Sigüenza and the priory of Uclés, kept the court reasonably busy with a variety of conversos, Moriscos (Muslims converted to Christianity), and other religious misfits.[1] At the time of Sánchez's arrest, two inquisitors served the court, Licentiate Pedro Cortes and Licentiate Don Enrique de la Cueva. In addition to the two judges there were a variety of wardens, ushers, secretaries,

Figure 7. The cathedral and Inquisition in Cuenca (1565). The Inquisition
was housed in the buildings to the left of the cathedral. (Drawing by Anton
van den Wyngaerd. Bildarchiv der Österreichische Nationalbibliothek,
Vienna; Cuenca [F],Vienna 31)

accountants, and lawyers, all on salary, as well as consulting theologians
and familiars who made their expertise and services available to the court
without charge. Pedro Cortes, who was on duty in Cuenca when Sánchez
was delivered to the Inquisition, had joined the court in 1535; before his
arrival in Cuenca he had served as an inquisitor in Córdoba. Don Enrique
de la Cueva, who joined the court in 1551, was on an extended tour of the
northern part of the large district covered by the Inquisition of Cuenca
and would not return to the city until the spring of 1554.[2]

Early in 1553, while Sánchez was haranguing his neighbors in Cardenete with his heretical notions, Licentiate Cortes wrote to his superiors
at the Royal Council of the Inquisition in Valladolid (popularly known as
the Suprema) requesting permission to retire from service. The inquisitor was at least sixty years old, was tired and ill, and longed to return to
his hometown. At the time Cortes requested his retirement, he was working at a steady rate to clear all of the court's business in time for the auto
de fe of February 19, and he probably hoped to leave Cuenca for good

when it was over. Shortly after the auto de fe, the Suprema turned down Cortes's petition, although the council did excuse him from the onerous obligation of the *visita*, which required a judge to go out on circuit in the district for several months at a time.[3] Having failed to receive the release from duty he so desired, for the next six months Licentiate Cortes behaved exactly as if he had retired. He tried no new cases—at least, no cases that involved living persons. To complement his colleague Cueva's prosecution of the communities of conversos in the towns of Sigüenza, Medinaceli, and Molina de Aragón, Cortes allowed the tribunal's prosecutor to go through old court records and initiate proceedings against many of the worthy dead of those communities who over the years had been accused of Judaizing. The prosecutor would put together seven or eight indictments at a time and present them to Cortes in one afternoon. Several weeks later, the court-appointed defense lawyer would present defenses for the group, and so on, until the cohort of deceased Judaizers had been marched through the tribunal and found guilty posthumously.[4] The process meant reams of paperwork for the court's secretaries but could not have been very tiring for the inquisitor, who may have felt that he was wrapping up the loose ends of twenty years of benchwork. Cortes took six weeks off from work in August and September, and returned to the job in late September.[5] Perhaps by then Cortes was feeling rested and ready to go back to his duties, or perhaps he was bored. Or maybe he was just curious. Whatever his reasons, one of the first things he did on his return to duty was to send for Bartolomé Sánchez, who arrived in Cuenca on Thursday, October 19, 1553.

2

On Friday morning Inquisitor Cortes ordered Sánchez brought to the courtroom. When the jailer delivered him to the room, Cortes looked up and ordered Sánchez to remove his hood and kneel before the courtroom's altar, where a crucifix and several statues and paintings of the saints were displayed. He asked the defendant to identify himself and say two Hail Marys to help clear his conscience and set him on the right road. From the villagers' depositions concerning Sánchez's beliefs that had been given in

Cardenete, Cortes probably guessed that his prisoner would be in no mood to kneel to statues, and he was right. The wool carder declared,

> My name is Bartolomé Sánchez, and I do not humble myself to idols, only to God the Father, His Son, and the Mother of God, who is God the Father's wife, all of whom are in heaven. I worship and believe in them, and in the Holy Spirit, which is present in all three and which makes the three, that is, father, son, and mother, one will, one desire, one love, and one cause.[6] The Son of God was incarnated in the virginal insides of Our Lady the Virgin Mary, and He became man by work of the Holy Spirit, not carnally like other men, but by order of God the Father, who sent His word to the Virgin Mary via the angel Gabriel, and thus the Virgin Mary conceived her son, or the son of God. I humble myself to these, who are in heaven, and in these I believe, and I do not kneel to idols on earth.[7]

Cortes explained to Sánchez the correct doctrine: that all men must worship the Trinity of God the Father, Son, and Holy Spirit in the first place, and venerate the Virgin Mary and the saints in the manner in which the Church commands. By venerating and praying to their images, one pays homage to what the saints signify, but it is not the same as worshiping idols made of stone, wood, or paint. Not to venerate the saints' images is a mortal sin. Sánchez ignored this correction and continued with the theme of the true nature of the Trinity. He challenged the inquisitor: "You tell me that God, who is three persons, Father, Son, and Holy Spirit and one true God, that God the Father had no more than one son incarnated in the womb of the Virgin Mary. From two persons, Father and Son, you cannot make three, unless you add the substance and love of the mother where He was conceived."[8]

Cortes began again. Patiently he repeated that the Trinity consisted of God the Father, Son, and Holy Spirit, and that God took human flesh when He chose to redeem mankind from sin. By doing this, Cortes explained, as both truly God and truly man, God could suffer on the cross to save us sinners, but the Virgin was not God, only a creature created by God. Cortes warned Sánchez that for Christians to believe anything else was heresy, a grave error, one that if not laid aside would lead them to hell. Sánchez's response was to try to change the subject by ending the interrogation. He pointed out that Cortes had been writing at length, and told the inquisitor that he did not have to say any more than what served God.

Cortes made another attempt to get Sánchez to cooperate with the court, at least to pay homage to the images on the altar. After a certain amount of talking,[9] he managed to persuade Sánchez to get down from his chair, but instead of kneeling toward the altar, Sánchez turned to the wall and declared that he would kneel to heaven. "I have no altar other than that of God the Father, Son, and Mother, and of the Holy Spirit, who is in all three, because holy is God the Father and true creator of heaven and earth, and holy is God His Son, and holy is the Virgin Mary, His Mother, wife of God, where the Trinity was contained. I have no more to say."[10] With that, he got to his feet and approached the bench. Cortes ordered him to place his hand on the crucifix to swear by it, but before the oath-taking could be completed, Sánchez removed his hand and repeated that he believed in God the Father, true creator of heaven and earth, but not in idols or images. Cortes, in a conciliatory gesture, agreed that one should not believe in idols, but that the purpose of the oath was to acknowledge God and to tell the truth. Sánchez repeated that he would say no more, and added that he had a headache. Still attempting to win over his prisoner, Cortes split Sánchez's prevarications in two. He told the wool carder that if he had a headache, he would be pleased to postpone the hearing. As for the oath-taking, the law required it, and it was needed so that the written record would be true and of use to men in doing justice. Sánchez repeated he was in no condition to reply and asked the inquisitor to order him back to his prison. Cortes complied, and so the first audience ended without Sánchez's making a single concession to the court.

Cortes was an experienced judge, yet within minutes he appeared to lose control of the hearing with this peasant. Was he indulging Sánchez? Normally, guilty prisoners tried to avoid answering questions, and many defendants, when first brought to the tribunal, had no idea why they were there, or pretended they did not. The inquisitor's opening gambit invariably was, "Do you know or suspect the reason why you are here?" Questioning would begin generally and gradually close in on the accusation, the ideal being that the defendant would eventually confess freely to having committed the act of heresy in question. Sánchez, far from hiding his thoughts, proclaimed them with a breathless intensity born of conviction for all the world to hear. For the moment, the aged inquisitor appeared content to follow Sánchez's lead and to work on his conversion.

3

The next morning, Saturday, October 21, as Sánchez entered the courtroom, Cortes silently pointed with his finger to the altar, indicating to Sánchez that he should kneel before the images.[11] Sánchez refused and crossed the room to kneel before a wall, saying defiantly, "I raise my eyes to God in heaven, who is my altar. I do not recognize any other altar that can save me except for God in heaven, the Virgin Mary, and her blessed son Jesus. These three are my altar, and I humble myself to them, because I do not humble myself to idols or figures, nor do I believe in or worship them."

Cortes began the hearing by asking Sánchez to explain to him what he meant by idols, but was stopped short by the peasant. He demanded, "Your Reverence is required by God to give me a lawyer to accompany me when I am with Your Reverence and to understand and know what I say." Cortes reassured his prisoner that everything he said would be written down faithfully; the court could be trusted by everyone unless there was a good reason not to trust it. Sánchez scoffed:

> Not everyone trusts what is said in this court, and before I declare what are idols and figures, I ask that a lawyer stay with Your Reverence to take down what I say so that I may be sure that what is written here [in court] and by him is all the same and that the trial transcript is not [only] in the hands of my adversary. When Your Reverence gives me counsel, I will declare what are the idols and figures, and make sure that my counsel is a layman, and not from the Church![12]

Surprisingly, the inquisitor took in stride this challenge to his authority and the credibility of the court. He tried again to reassure Sánchez that the court record would be accurate, and decided to explain to the wool carder why lay lawyers could not participate in the court's business.

> The material that is dealt with in this hearing, with you and with the others who are in these prisons, but especially in your hearing, is for

the Church to know, judge, and determine. . . . Laymen cannot participate in the knowledge of such things because the law so determines. But
to satisfy you, even though there is no reason for it, I will be happy to
call in a very qualified person to assist and be with you so that you may
comply with everything you ought to do before the two of us.[13]

Sánchez again insisted that the person be a layman; he would not speak in
front of an ecclesiastic. Once more Sánchez brought the hearing to a close
by declaring he had a headache and asking that his hearing be postponed
until Monday.

On Monday morning, Sánchez took the offensive. When Cortes called
for his prisoner, the wool carder strode into the courtroom, raised his head
skyward, blessed himself, and without glancing at the altar stepped up to
the bench and asked, "What do you want?"[14] Once again Cortes ignored
the challenge to his authority. Rather than lose another day by wrangling
with Sánchez over a point of doctrine, he began with a general appeal to
Sánchez's conscience, urging him to declare his transgressions against
God and to feel sorrow and repentance so that God might forgive him.

"To whom do I have to reveal and say these things?" Sánchez asked.
Did Cortes realize where this line of questioning would lead them?
Sánchez had been quite clear to everyone in Cardenete that he would not
confess to priests and that he thought that the Pope was damned. Nonetheless, Cortes began innocently enough:

You must state these things to Almighty God first, and secondly to His
vicars and priests, to whom His Majesty left His mandate, and He
wished for mankind to do this. Whatever touches on heresy or any sort
of unfaithfulness, which are cases reserved for the Pope, must be declared to this Holy Office, before its judges, whom Our Lord the Pope
has commissioned.

Sánchez bristled:

I will declare and confess these things to Almighty God, who is the one
who will save me, and not to any friar or abbot, because God knows the
circumstances of sin, and not the friar or abbot. I should reveal my
heart to the one who must save me, and not to someone who cannot
help me, just like when the good thief said, "Lord, when you are in
heaven, remember me." I'm not like the bad thief who saw the Son of

God hanging there and said ungratefully, not realizing that he was God, "You cannot save me; you can't even save yourself!"[15]

Cortes asked Sánchez what were the things that he would reveal to God but not to the friars, but before Sánchez would answer he asked the inquisitor to explain to him "the circumstances of mortal or venial sin, and of the heresies or infidelities that go against God's law." Cortes replied generally by saying:

The mortal and venial sins that are commonly committed by men are not for me at present to investigate or to know. What I want to know from you is anything heretical or unfaithful that you may have done, said, or seen committed by other persons against our Holy Catholic faith. As I am only a man, I cannot begin to know anything except by your statement or those of others. Once you make your declaration, I will explain the circumstances and all the remedies that are necessary for salvation and the discharge of your conscience.[16]

This was not good enough for Sánchez. "Since I asked Your Reverence to explain the circumstances of sin and you don't do it, I will explain them to you." But Sánchez forgot his promise as he warmed to his subject. Cortes wanted to know what were idols and why men should not worship them. Well, then, Sánchez would explain. The wool carder had thought a great deal about this matter, and here was someone who gave him unlimited attention and actually listened closely to what he had to say. He launched into a lengthy lesson.

4

When the Son of God came to earth sent to us by God the Father, He was sent to us in grace and it didn't cost us one thing. He came to give us the faith with which we could save ourselves. Now as it happens, we all are the children of God and descend from Him primarily and from Adam and Eve, so that being the children of the above, we form one lineage and we are all brothers. God was preaching His true evangelical word to our brothers, our forefathers, and because He rebuked them for the evil they did and for going against God's law, they slandered Him and said that He went against *their* law, because He went against their purpose. They said, "Look what blasphemies He says, look how He insults us!" Well, which would be the better law, the law that the Son of God gave or the way that they followed? They did not want to believe or worship Him like God and the true Lord, for if they had believed in Him, it was not just justice that they should kill the one who tells the truth. Instead, they would hold Him as God and Lord; it made sense then and now that if they had kept Him and followed and believed Him as it is today when people follow and keep a king and wait for him to call parliament and bring out his laws, then they wouldn't kill Him.[17]

But, since they didn't want to believe what He told them and they got upset by it, saying how a carpenter's son, a simple and poor man, reproached them for going against the law of God, our brothers, our forefathers, contracted to sell and buy Him. They sold the grace and they bought Him in exchange for thirty coins, that is, the Son of God and His Father and the very same Mother and Holy Spirit which is in all of them who should be honored and worshiped! So it came to pass that our brothers, our ancestors, brothers of the entire human race, killed Christ on that cross, not wishing to believe His evangelical law. They didn't want to believe in His Passion or in His law. Instead they got it all wrong, and they believe and worship the wood on which He was crucified. The right thing to do would have been to believe Him while he was alive, since He gave us faith and explained it, and not now to worship and honor the stick that is the cross, which is the devil's weapon that the visible devils used to defend themselves from Christ and kill Him. And since the devil was and is the enemy of God, thus they made that cross and stick with which they defended themselves from Christ in this human life, because they were offended by the law He gave them. Just like one man defends himself against another, his enemy, with his weapons, so the devil or the devils defended themselves with that cross which is held to be holy, whether it be wood or iron, and with that they killed Christ. And this cross and stick is what I mean by idol, and so I do not worship the crucifix, which is wood or iron; instead I worship Him who was crucified, He who was the Son of God.[18]

Cortes replied that if Sánchez really wished to understand what the Catholic faith taught, he would know that he should worship[19] the image of the cross and those of Mary and the saints for what they signify, either how Jesus on the cross triumphed over the devil and death and saved mankind, or how the saints overcame the devil and won God's kingdom and became intercessors on mankind's behalf.

Sánchez had thought about this as well. What were the consequences for mankind if Christ's mission of redemption had been frustrated on the cross? The question of salvation and the cross's place in it depended on whether or not God had meant the crucifixion to occur. Had this been God's wish, and Jesus had accepted His death, then indeed the cross was a symbol of Christ's triumph over the devil and of mankind's salvation. But Sánchez did not see things this way.

> Those men, who are devils who killed Christ, by force made Him suffer, and pushed Him into carrying the cross on His shoulders, and they killed Him on it. And so He said three times to His Father, "*Si possibile est*, let me not see or drink from this cup of bitterness." And He said, "Father does not wish that anyone kill the Just One." [20]

At that juncture, Sánchez seemed to stray from the point. He began to talk about an individual's responsibility to do God's will, that one can be saved only by one's own efforts, but one should not go against God's commandments. Then he seemed to switch topics, to the vengeance that God would send against those who killed Christ against His will. Sánchez waxed prophetic.

> God, as He is a just judge, cannot avoid doing just justice and God sends a judge, Elijah, who is prophesied to avenge Christ's death. [21] Because a sentence that Pilate handed down against the Son of God (which was the most outrageous that was ever given in the world), if that sentence, given without truth or justice, were to be excused, then every badly given sentence would be pardoned. And so Elijah is come and born, and he is coming to do battle and conquer the devil and Antichrist so that [they] won't come. He does not bring defensive weapons, crossbows or swords, or firepower or anyone to kill anybody, only the true faith of God with which he must defend himself.
>
> And this Elijah, together with the one they call the King of the Jews, and the Messiah promised in the Old Testament, and the Ruler who is mentioned in the Gospel of St. Matthew, where it says, "You Bethlehem, land of Judah, are not small, for out of you will come a ruler who will rule the people of Israel" [Matt. 2:6], these four are all one person, and he brings the word that God said, "Blessed will be he who does not see me and believes in me" [John 20:29], which St. John wrote, who said, "The light will come against the darkness, and the darkness will

not understand that light" [John 1:5]. St. Matthew says once more, "You Bethlehem, land of Judah, are not small, for out of you will come a ruler who will rule the people of Israel," and St. Luke concludes, "He will rule in the House of Jacob and of his kingdom there will be no end" [Luke 1:33], and concerning this speaks St. Mark the Evangelist, "That although they give this Ruler deadly things they will not harm him one whit" [Mark 16:17]. All these five words, which are, "Blessed are those who do not see me and believe," are confirmed by four evangelists, and all the evil there is in the world will be confounded, and these words will not fail to be fulfilled, because St. John said in another gospel, "They will see Him pierced through but they will not want of Him another scripture" [John 19:36–37].[22]

Cortes asked Sánchez how he understood that Elijah and the other names he gave could be all one person. Sánchez replied, "I say and understand it because I have and hold the four names in myself by the gift of the Holy Spirit and Elijah."

This enigmatic reply coupled with Sánchez's warning of vengeance due elicited no direct response from Cortes. Perhaps he did not know what to say at this point. He decided to return to firmer ground, the question of Christ's death on the cross. He told Sánchez that Christ had willingly accepted His suffering, death, and Passion. Since He was God, neither the devil nor the world could force Him to do anything He did not want, and what He wanted was to suffer in order to win pardon for mankind's sins. As for what Christ said on the cross to His Father, "Take from me this travail and cup of bitterness,"[23] He said that in order to set us an example, so that when we are afflicted with troubles, we will pray to God to remove them, or if we must suffer them, that they be in His service.

Sánchez would not accept this explanation for one minute. He countered:

> Christ did not want that or ever wish for it, nor did the Father send Him so that somebody could kill Him. In flight He sojourned in Egypt, and the thirty-odd days He spent in the desert without eating also was in flight, hiding out so that He wouldn't be killed. On what basis can they say that Jesus Christ accepted death or put Himself on that cross of His own free will? Judas of his own free will hanged himself and was damned, but by force they made the Son of God suffer that death and travails.[24]

Cortes replied that everything in the Church, the prophet Isaiah and other prophets, the evangelists and saints, testifies to the fact that Jesus Christ voluntarily accepted His Passion, and the faithful must believe this. As for the flight to Egypt and the fasting in the desert, He did these things because the time for His Passion had not yet arrived, and He endured the Passion, Cortes repeated, in order to set an example for men to accept similar suffering.

At this point Sánchez apparently had had enough of debate. He suggested that the inquisitor go to dinner and that he would have his answer ready at the next hearing. What Cortes said to this is not recorded, but the session was suspended until the next morning.

On Monday, Sánchez appeared to jump from point to point, one minute explaining why the cross was an idol that he could not worship, and the next moment warning Pedro Cortes that God was sending Elijah, who somehow was also Christ, to avenge Jesus' untimely murder on the cross. On Tuesday morning, when Cortes called for Sánchez, he entered the courtroom as before: raising his hands and looking skyward, blessing himself, and then going straight to the bench. Without any preliminaries, Sánchez launched into an accusation:

> May it please God in His infinite goodness to judge each according to his merits, and me the first, for I am the messenger. The messenger should not lie, and should declare the truth of what he is sent for. Once declared, it is just justice, having said the truth, that he be given permission to return to his home to work and put food on the table for himself, his wife, and children. Yesterday I asked Your Reverence to explain the circumstances of sin and you did not do it. I also told you that Elijah and the Messiah and the King of the Jews and the Ruler who will rule the people of Israel are come and born, and that these four are one person, and that everything I told you would be in God's service.

Here Sánchez finally came to the point, the secret of the gift of the four names that he carried inside him, and the meaning of Elijah's vengeance.

> The Son of God when He came to the world did not sentence anyone to mortal or eternal death. Those who killed Him because He told them the truth sentenced themselves to eternal death, because he who kills the one who speaks the truth condemns himself to eternal death. Well, I say that the Messiah is come and born, and I will point him out with

my finger and I will say where He is when it is necessary. If this is the truth and the Inquisition and its officials have killed and sentenced and burned countless people, holding for heresy and as heretics those who say that the Messiah will come, and since I have said and do say that he who kills the one who speaks the truth dies an eternal death, then the Inquisition has killed many in the manner I say. They have foully murdered those who have said and do say that the Messiah is not yet come, and I notify you from the feet of God—the summons I deliver is that before next All Saints' Day [Nov. 1] you will go with the dead whom you have murdered to God's Tribunal, and those whom you hold prisoner and in chains, you will release them. And if you do not do this, I protest the scandals, deaths, and damages that should arise from this, because the Messiah that the Inquisition believes in, who came about one thousand and five hundred years ago, that is He, and I confess that He came, and He is the Son of God incarnated in the Virgin Mary; but the *other* Messiah of whom I speak who is coming—the one who is the Elijah—he is the justice God sends on behalf of those whom the Inquisition has killed without cause, and this Elijah and Messiah, which are the four [*sic*] names that he bears, was born fifty-two years ago, more or less, and he is on the earth, and he is born and raised in the village of Cardenete.[25]

The court secretary, Ybaneta, recorded, "When asked to say who is this Elijah and Messiah that he says is born and brought up in the village of Cardenete, he said that he was, and that they don't have to believe him, but here I am, and neither did they believe the Son of God."

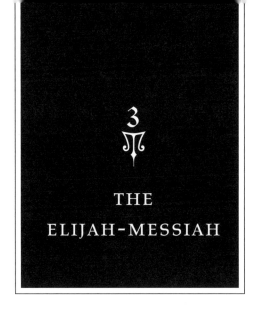

3

THE
ELIJAH-MESSIAH

1

MEN CLAIMING TO BE THE ELIJAH-MESSIAH DID NOT APPEAR EVERY day before the Inquisition, and one might have thought that Sánchez's outburst would prompt some reaction in the court. Yet Licentiate Cortes betrayed no surprise (at least for the court record) and proceeded methodically with the interview. He immediately set about learning the nature of Sánchez's conviction. Sánchez, however, would not be moved or trapped into committing himself further. In fact, after his bold challenge to the court, he seemed spent, for he answered all questions laconically and offered no new information. To the trap that Cortes laid, that the Messiah prophesied in the Old Testament would be the Son of God, the wool carder merely replied, "The Son of God was not believed or received as the Lord, so how is anyone going to believe me, a mortal man, sent by God's hand for justice's sake?" He refused to explain by what signs he bore God's commission.[1]

Realizing that Sánchez was not going to elaborate on his claim, Cortes dropped that line of questioning and went back to theology. Here, too, he met a wall of silence. Cortes reminded Sánchez that on the previous day he had promised to answer the inquisitor's questions concerning Christ's death on the cross, but Sánchez simply repeated that since no one had believed Christ, he did not expect anyone to believe him. Cortes tried lecturing Sánchez on the subject of confession with priests, and Sánchez merely replied that since the priests could not save themselves, how could they save him?

When Cortes asked Sánchez when was the last time he went to confession, however, the wool carder began to cooperate.

> A year ago last Lent [i.e., March 1552] I confessed in Villamalea, in the district of Jorquera, with Pablo Gallego, the assistant priest there, and since then I have not confessed, nor will I confess with any man, friar or abbot. Every hour I confess to God. Until a year ago last Lent . . . I was very firm [in my faith], but since then I have not [confessed] because God's will has moved me not to submit to friars or abbots, because in submitting myself to God and humbling myself to Him I have no need of any other.[2]

When Cortes tried to convince Sánchez of the necessity of confession to a priest, Sánchez refused to agree that auricular confession was part of the Christian faith. He argued that St. Peter and St. Alexis—that is, the very first Christians—did not seek out any friar to absolve them of sin, and of their own free will penanced themselves.[3] Back and forth Cortes and Sánchez sparred, until Sánchez, irritated at being asked when he last took communion (he thought he had answered that question by telling when he had last gone to confession), offered a new idea: "I take communion from God every day, but I have not received the Holy Sacrament of the altar because [when] the priest who is not in a state of grace says God's word and takes the Host, God does not come there like the priests say."[4] This dangerous idea had been around since the days of the Roman Empire. Had Sánchez thought of it on his own or had he heard echoes of the heresies proposed by the *alumbrados*, or Illuminati, who were active in La Mancha when he was a young man? The inquisitor had ready the standard reply, that it did not matter whether the priest was in a state of grace; when he said Mass and consecrated the Host, the bread and wine necessarily turned into the true flesh and blood of Christ. Sánchez, who must have been tired by this time, protested feebly, "Everything Your Reverence says to me is to give credit to your cause, and not mine, and I stand by what I have declared."[5] That was the signal to stop for the day. The court reporter read back the transcript to Sánchez for his approval, and with that, he was returned to his cell.

2

By now the inquisitor and the wool carder were settling into the semblance of a routine. Each morning the inquisitor called for his prisoner, who entered the courtroom, looked heavenward, blessed himself, and approached the bench without paying homage to the altar or images. At the end of each hearing, either Ybaneta or Cortes himself read back the transcript for Sánchez's approval. On Wednesday morning, as Sánchez entered the courtroom, he overheard Ybaneta recording his movements, so he added verbally for the secretary's benefit that he had no altar other than God, to whom he offered himself.[6] Six days into the trial, Inquisitor Cortes was beginning to show some feeling for Sánchez. On hearing Sánchez gratuitously insult the faith, he remarked that he regretted that the wool carder still insisted on his offensive speech and was refusing to yield to the inquisitor's words, on which his salvation depended. This comment led to an obligatory skirmish over the nature of images, Sánchez adding that since it was to God he principally owed respect, it was not necessary to worship sticks.

Pedro Cortes was not going to waste any more time on this topic—what he wanted was to find out more about Sánchez's understanding of the sacrament of the altar. He summed up their positions from the previous day, had the secretary read back the testimony to refresh Sánchez's memory, and asked Sánchez to explain what he really believed. Sánchez did not deny that Christ said what He did at the Last Supper or that the words He uttered then were efficacious: "When He said those words, they were His and He was in them, and they in Him, and He is divine and human." Nonetheless, Sánchez insisted, transubstantiation would not take place if the priest were not in a state of grace. Cortes pointed out that it was not by virtue of the priest that the Host and wine were converted into the true flesh and blood of Christ, but through God's power. Again he expressed feeling for his prisoner. "To believe anything else is wrong, and I say this to you because I take pity on your misguided belief and wish to restore you to the right one so that you may save your soul and not lose it."[7]

Sánchez was unmoved by the inquisitor's appeal and continued with his idea of the Eucharist. To defend their respective interpretations of what really happens at the consecration of the Host, the two men began debating the nature of God's power, each drawing on biblical example. Sánchez began:

> With His word God is sufficient to make out of the bread and wine the flesh and blood through His holy words, and no other human being is. It was just the same when He sent His word via the angel Gabriel to the Virgin St. Mary, and made in her the true God and man, something that no one, great or small, is able to do. Thus no one else is sufficient to make the true body and blood of God, only He is, and [here Sánchez tried to turn the tables on the inquisitor] whoever believes that someone else can do so without God, as I said, this is heresy.[8]

Cortes also argued from the position of God's omnipotence. He told the wool carder the story of Moses, who, without wanting to, worked miracles with the rod that God gave him. "Surely you have heard of this," said Cortes, as he summarized the stories of how Moses parted the waters of the Red Sea and got water from a stone, all through God's doing and not his own. Cortes then drew an analogy between the miracles performed by the unwilling Moses and unworthy Catholic priests:

> Thus [God] wished then and now that, although the priest may have in himself some unworthy thing that is harmful to his own soul, when he says Mass and the words of the consecration, by virtue of their action on the bread and wine they cease to be such and they turn into His true body and blood. To say anything else is wrong and I repeat this to you with the desire that you hear it and give up your error.[9]

Sánchez agreed that what the judge said about Moses was true, that God did give Moses that power. But he resisted the suggestion that the priests' words were the equivalent of Moses' rod, and would work regardless of the condition of the man who used them. In fact, Sánchez seemed inclined to do away with the Eucharist altogether. "God is the Holy Sacrament wherever He might be, and the host that the priests take is just a bit of kneaded flour, and no one is sufficient to make out of that host flesh and blood except God alone." [10] So then what is the Blessed Sacrament that is deposited at the altar? Sánchez replied, "The sacrament that Your Reverence means is nothing but a bit of kneaded flour, and the Blessed Sacrament is God who is in heaven."

This statement, so baldly heretical, so anti-Catholic, finally goaded Pedro Cortes into acting like the inquisitor he was. For the first time, he asked Sánchez to state where he had heard this idea, and if anyone had put him up to saying it. Sánchez swore that no one had, it was God's will, and by God's will he dared to say what he did. Cortes replied that it seemed to him that the devil had Sánchez in his power and was making him say what he did—"And you know what wicked company he makes of those whom he has in his power." Sánchez countered, "They said about Christ that He was possessed by the devil, and that He did what He did because of Beelzebub. Your Reverence tells me that what I say is the devil because you don't want to believe the truth, just as Christ wasn't believed when He was crucified. I don't keep company with the devil; I keep it with God, and I declare the truth and His just justice." Cortes insisted that what he said was the truth that Jesus Christ had said and wanted to be said to His creatures in His church. "What you say to the contrary is falsehood, and I tell you so in spite of your blasphemy because I want to bring you around to believe what you should, so you don't deceive yourself." [11]

Cortes's use of the word "church" diverted Sánchez's attention from their argument over who was in possession of the truth about the Eucharist. Basing his reasoning on Jesus' sermon in which He called the church the synagogue and temple of the Jews, the money changers, Sánchez began to reveal another element of his theology. "If the temple were God's, then He wouldn't throw the money changers out of it. . . . If it were the house of God, they wouldn't have sold Christ in it like they did. God is my temple, and not the stones and timbers that make the church that you take for God's temple." [12] Cortes told Sánchez that he mistaken; in the passage from Scripture that he cited, in reality Jesus had called the temple His Father's house, and He threw out the money changers because their illicit dealings were not compatible with His service. Sánchez did a disservice to God's house to attribute to the building the harm that was done inside it by evil men. To answer Cortes, Sánchez expanded on his thought: he meant house of God in the metaphorical sense of the house of His believers.

> God did not exclude anyone, and He wished everyone to believe in Him. He threw them out of the synagogue, which is the house of deceit, [but] if it had been the house of God He wouldn't have thrown them out from there. But since they didn't want to believe Him, they went back to following their own interests, although it saddened God to have thrown them out. To this day the synagogue has continued on with those who replaced it, those who are from the Church.[13]

As it was late in the day, Licentiate Cortes decided to stop the interview there and continue with the hearing the next morning.[14]

3

On Thursday morning, October 26, Sánchez entered the courtroom with more urgency than usual. As he approached the bench, he invoked God to judge each according to his merit, because, he said prophetically, the time was drawing near.

"What do you mean the time is drawing near?" asked Cortes.

Sánchez by no means had forgotten his warning to the court delivered only two days before. "'The time is drawing near' means that since Your Reverence and your associates were required and summoned to go to court before All Saints' Day [Nov. 1], the stated time is approaching and you haven't asked me one thing about it, so I want to remind you of it." He seemed surprised, even dismayed, that the inquisitor was not acting on his ultimatum, an ultimatum that he, as God's messenger Elijah, had delivered from the Lord Himself. Cortes, as before, ignored Sánchez's warning. He began where he had left off the day before, with the question of the Church. "Tell me," he asked Sánchez, "in what state of grace and friendship are you with clergymen and friars, and with other faithful Christian persons who uphold the Church of God and His house of prayer?"

Sánchez's favorite topic in his village had been his hatred for the ministers of the Catholic Church. Every single person who had testified against him remembered some part of his anticlerical invective. Sánchez

was more than willing to oblige the inquisitor on this subject. He began
with a blanket denunciation of the clergy.

> I am in bad relations with the entire clergy, with bishops and archbish-
> ops and the Pope and priests and friars wherever they are, because God
> is the Holy Mother Church, and I hold Him as such. I condemn them
> as outlawed and lawless and as damned and excommunicated, and as the
> biggest thieves in the world, and as changers of grace and as cheats.

The real reason for Sánchez's anger soon became apparent. He continued:

> The day a priest or friar [first] sings Mass, they promise chastity to God
> but they don't keep it. I pronounce them damned and excommunicated,
> because the day laymen take their marriage vows, [the priests] tell them
> that the curses and excommunication that God sent over the four cities
> [of Sodom and Gomorrah] will come over whoever brings evil and
> scandal between them. Well, these same priests break the said com-
> mandment by not remaining chaste, and for that reason I denounce
> them and hold them as damned and excommunicated just like the said
> clergy proclaim it when they marry people. And what I mean about
> thieves, I say it because I hold as the greater sin to have fornication with
> a woman than to steal a thousand ducats,[15] because when you steal
> a thousand ducats, in returning them you repay the person you stole
> them from, but when you fornicate with a woman, it is not possible
> with all the money in the world to make up for the harm that comes
> from doing that.[16]

Although Sánchez seemed most upset by the clergy's sexual philander-
ing, he also was outraged by their speculating in foodstuffs given to them
in payment of the tithe. "[The priests] freely take the tithes that working
people give to them in recognition of God, for it costs them nothing, and
then they sell them back for as much as they can get."

Cortes repeated to Sánchez that the worth of the sacraments and the
Church remained unaffected by the faults that might occur in some of the
clergy, and urged him once more to confess his error with true sorrow
and repentance so that God might see fit to pardon him. Sánchez, of
course, was unmoved by the appeal, so Cortes decided to reexamine another of the wool carder's heresies, his interpretation of the Trinity. This
exchange led to a restating of positions with the same result as before,
Sánchez maintaining that three persons cannot be made out of two,

unless the Virgin is added as well. True, Cortes admitted, all three persons of the Trinity were present in the womb of the Virgin Mary, but this
did not make her part of the Trinity; she remained purely a human creature, although one with very special attributes and prerogatives. "But,"
Sánchez replied, "the Son of God was also a human creature, born and
raised on earth just like His mother was. I won't take substance away from
where God put it. Each of us is speaking to his position, and I'll let God be
the judge of the truth of this question." [17] When Cortes began to explain
once more Christ's dual nature as God and human being, Sánchez again
appealed to God to be the judge of all the questions the inquisitor had put
to him.

Cortes returned to the question of where Sánchez had picked up his
heretical ideas. This offended the wool carder, who, as a self-taught man
of the lower classes, was well aware of the hierarchical nature of learning
and knowledge in his society. He protested, "I learned all this from no one
but God, by His divine command and order. Where did the apostles, evangelists, and prophets learn what they said? They didn't go to school at
Paris or Salamanca to learn!" [18] Cortes replied that all of these people
were instructed and taught by God and then their writings were approved
and verified by the Church, "but what you say goes beyond what was
written by them and determined. It is not from God and for that reason I
ask you to declare where you found out and learned it." Sánchez repeated
that God spoke through the apostles, and He was speaking through him.
"More like the devil does," replied Cortes, who pointed out to Sánchez
that everything he said went against what the saints said. With that,
Cortes closed the hearing for the day.

On October 27, Sánchez entered the courtroom as usual, saying this
time, "Lord, you with me and I with you." Cortes, now even more concerned for the future of his prisoner's soul, lectured Sánchez.

> If God were with you and you wished to be His son, you would not say
> or hold the evil words and propositions that it seems you do in offense
> to the Holy Trinity, confession, and the Eucharist, which are the faith
> that good Christians ought to believe, and the remedies and consolation
> to cure and pardon themselves when, after baptism, they may fall into
> mortal sin. Talking and holding forth as you do against them, you do
> not speak for God nor does God show you favor; instead the devil does,
> who makes you do it. Therefore, according to the name of Christ, which

you say you hold, you should be baptized in accordance with the commandment and law of God in His Holy Church. You ought to understand and look at what you do and say, submit to God and to what you're told you should believe, and not so deliberately wish to lose your body and soul.[19]

That morning Sánchez was in a more communicative mood. He chose to respond to the inquisitor in kind, and gave his own lecture to the court.

The words of God are good wherever they are said, and that is what I say. Keeping the word of God with me, and God in me, by His will I don't plan on losing my soul or body, because my work is not to kill or rob; that's the devil's job. That's what is done in this so-called Holy Office of the Inquisition,[20] where you have killed and taken the property of countless numbers who have not prejudiced or harmed you in any way. When God came to the world and they told Him blasphemies, He didn't kill or rob anyone—why in the Inquisition do you make yourselves better judges than God? The Inquisition should look at the way it ought to go, because that's what the Elijah and Messiah are sent by God and coming for, to account for those senseless murders you have committed. With good reason God, and I in His name, will damn you people of the Inquisition to hellfire for murdering and taking people's property in this fashion.

What Your Reverence says to me about baptism, by holding what God said, "Blessed is he who does not see Me yet believes in Me," I am baptized with these words and the other four I named which I believe, Elijah and the Messiah, as I said, and with the faith I have declared, and not with the salted water of the Church, which God called in His sermon synagogue. Because Holy Scripture says that if men were to have as much faith as a mustard seed, a hill would move from one part to another, and that faith without works is dead, and in another place it says that faith alone saves—you from the Church, what faith do you give us?—since with what you tell us, you don't have and can't even achieve as much as one mustard seed![21]

The inquisitor could not let this attack on the good name of the Holy Office go unanswered. He explained to Sánchez why it was necessary to put heretics to death as well as to confiscate their property.

If you were to say good words that were from God, no one would contradict you. The bad words that you say and the opinion you have against the holy sacraments are not for God but against Him. . . . If in the Inquisition some are condemned, it is for holding and believing the things that you say and similar others. By condemning [these people] and taking their property, better service is done to God than by allowing them to stay and live in the world to offend and harm others with [those things]. You know how a sheep, sick with some contagious disease, does harm to the entire flock where she is, but by killing her the rest of the herd is saved. For this reason, God ordered that the grape vine[22] that does not give fruit and is infected, or is capable of infecting others, should be cut off and thrown into the fire. If God, made man, while on earth did not kill anyone, He will kill them for their sins on the day He sees fit to judge them.[23]

Cortes told Sánchez again that he misunderstood the authorities he cited, and that anyone who truly believed in the Catholic faith would believe just the opposite of what Sánchez held. As for vengeance, he told the wool carder, let God take care of that.

Sánchez dismissed Cortes's warning by repeating that everything the inquisitor told him was to support his own case, and not the wool carder's. He had not finished yet with his attack on the sacrament of baptism, and he returned to it. Over the course of the week, it becoming clear that Sánchez had arrived at an understanding of Christianity that was stripped of all intermediaries, rituals, and symbols. He had no use for priests, churches, crucifixes, or sacraments to bind his faith in God. Only His word was true. Sánchez spoke passionately of a baptism in faith that replaced the empty ceremonies of the Church.

As far as the sacrament of baptism goes, I don't hold myself or my children as baptized, having been baptized with the water and salt and other ceremonies that are performed in church during a baptism. . . . I don't find fault in the words of God that are spoken during the baptism. On the contrary, they are good, holy, and true wherever they may be and are said. But the water and salt and that thing they call the chrism, and the other ceremonies that are done in the baptism at the synagogue, I maintain that they won't save me, only faith and the word of God will . . . each according to his merit.[24]

Cortes pointed out to Sánchez the apparent contradiction in his argument. If the wool carder accepted the words of God that are said during a baptism, he would know that the ceremony was ordered by God for the benefit of His faithful. At this point Cortes began to show some frustration with what he considered Sánchez's continual twisting of doctrine. He told his prisoner that beyond committing the sin of infidelity and heresy, he so contradicted himself that sane persons would flee from him. Sánchez declined to answer to that, so the inquisitor drew the hearing to an official end.[25] Yet on this day Cortes would not allow Sánchez to return to his cell without trying to make some connection with him. They lingered on in the courtroom. The judge could not understand how anyone could be quite so perverse, and wanted to know from Sánchez, off the record, why he confused everything so thoroughly.

Sánchez replied, "I say it because I am destroying the Church." With the calm conviction of a man who held God's favor, Sánchez explained to Cortes that God had given him the authority to undo the Church. He saw his situation as exactly parallel to Jesus', who undid the temple by throwing out those who desecrated His Father's house. "Right now everything is the temple of the Jews just like when God said so." There was no reply to this analogy, and the two men parted company.

4

Cortes did not call for his prisoner over the weekend, so Sánchez had two days by himself to think about his predicament. Time was running short; the promised day of judgment, November 1, was nearly upon them, and yet the inquisitor still did nothing while Sánchez remained locked in his cell. His sense of urgency mounted; on Monday morning, back in court, he declared, "Lord Jesus Christ, Your justice now is presented; I beseech Your Lofty Majesty to send Your judgment to bring it forth." He continued, "God sends His last judgment to kill the dead. The dead are those who are blinded and embedded in mortal sin, and those who are thus blinded and embedded in mortal sin are the Inquisition and all its associates."[26] Sánchez went on to repeat his warning, first delivered on October 24, that the Inquisition would soon pay for the murders it had committed. This time, Sánchez's provocative words drew from Pedro Cortes an eloquent, although brutal, reply about the nature of the institution he served. He abandoned the rustic metaphors drawn from Scripture that he perhaps had thought would resonate in the peasant's mind, and spoke with all the authority of language he had at his disposal.

> Our Lord Jesus Christ, seeing that the souls He created withdraw from the guild of His Church and acquire pestiferous opinions that are harmful to their persons and those of whoever hear and follow them, and taking pity on His Holy Church and desiring to return and reduce these persons to it, has ordered and instituted the Holy Inquisition to do this with all good charity and love for those who freely wish to return, and, so that they can no longer hurt or offend anyone, to expel from the gathering and communion of the Church those who, hardened in their evil purpose, do not want to return. This is true justice. . . . To go about and persist in saying the silly things that you do and to be so obstinate in your errors and evil opinions pains me to the bottom of my soul as a Christian.[27]

Sánchez did not appear to hear even one word of Cortes's lecture. He seemed possessed by his own thoughts, and having assumed his role as God's messenger, was unable to stray from the sequence of ideas that formed the basis of his conviction. This time, as he went through the message, he filled in the last elements of his eschatological vision.

> The Son of God . . . came to save the whole world and they didn't want to believe Him and they killed Him. If they had not killed Him, no one would be damned, but since they did kill Him, no one was saved except for the apostles and those who came after whom He saw fit to enlighten. To avenge that death and injustice that was done to Him on the cross, He said "Heli, Heli, lama zabatani [sic]: Come Elijah, come Elijah to avenge my death for they've killed me." [28] God, as just justice, did not come to kill anyone, and you people from the Inquisition, doing your justice, kill those who have not offended you. If they have offended you, explain it to me.[29]

Sánchez's theology was now completely revealed. The odd comparisons to Christ that he made in Cardenete stemmed from the fact that Sánchez already had begun to think of himself as a second Messiah nearly a year before his arrest by the Inquisition. Only under the pressure of his trial did he give voice to his ideas in their entirety. In brief, God sent His only Son, Jesus, to save mankind, but our forefathers rejected Christ and killed Him against His will, before He could complete His mission of salvation. As a result, except for the saints, no one since then had been saved. But Christ seemed to give His commission to Elijah to avenge His murder, and this Elijah, as proved by the New Testament, was a second Messiah who would complete the process of salvation. The Elijah-Messiah took human form in Sánchez, who, as Christ had done before him, preached the Word so that mankind might be saved, but the Inquisition and the Church, the latter-day Pharisees and priests of the temple, were conspiring to do away with him just as the original Pharisees had managed to murder the first Christ. All of salvation rested on Sánchez's shoulders. Would he, like Christ, be powerless to prevent his own murder? Would mankind miss its chance for salvation a second time?

Pedro Cortes had more mundane things to worry about: a prisoner who was completely uncooperative, who seemed hell-bent on his own destruction. He told Sánchez that the Inquisition punished only those who looked for trouble by deviating from the Church's teachings, but Sánchez, consumed by his thoughts, continued to repeat what was in essence his credo, interjecting at one point, "If I believe all this, where can Your Reverence infer that I've sinned?" and ending with "I have nothing more to say." Cortes replied at length that everything Sánchez believed was in error, and to persist in his beliefs was only to increase his guilt. He warned Sánchez not to cite Scripture because he did not understand it, and appealed once more to him to recognize his errors and weaknesses. Sánchez, thoroughly dug into his position, repeated his stock answer, that everything the inquisitor told him was to support his own position, and God would be the judge of these questions.

Cortes gave up trying to convert Sánchez and went back to questioning him more on his unorthodox ideas, and encountered resistance here as well. Finally, Cortes wanted to hear Sánchez once more on the question of the messenger. "In the hearing that was held with you on October 23, you said that you were the messenger. . . . Declare from whom you are a messenger and the truth that you say you must declare."

"I told you, I am God's messenger, and everything I've said to you has been the truth, and as such I say it. Your Reverence and the others can believe what you want."[30]

Cortes began to ask Sánchez to explain again what he meant by the second Messiah, Elijah, but as he was summing up what the wool carder

had said, he interrupted himself. The whole notion was just too sacrilegious and incredible to think about. He exploded:

> You're lying! It is an enormous perversion and lewd thing for a man
> like you, without any learning or prudence, or even with it, to speak
> and say such things! There never was or was hoped for more than one
> Messiah, and that one came, who is Jesus Christ Our Lord, as you have
> been told, and Elijah is not dead, instead it is said that he and Enoch are
> deposited in Paradise on earth to do for His Divine Majesty whatever
> service He should command them. . . . For you, a sinner and man of
> such base material, to venture and dare to say in such a tribunal as this
> such things and the other ones you've said before, beyond their being
> heretical and reprobate, they are sheer craziness and nonsense, which
> this tribunal ought not even to consider, let alone deal with! Because I
> am zealous to reclaim you and separate you from your errors and idio-
> cies, I indulge you and I tell you what you hear. If you put [these er-
> rors] behind you, have the remorse you should, collect yourself and
> confess it all as badly said, held, and believed, and if you amend your
> life from here on out, His Divine Majesty will see fit to forgive you.[31]

Sánchez merely replied to this outburst, "Tomorrow I'll answer your
questions since right now it's time for dinner." The inquisitor immediately agreed.

The next morning as Sánchez approached the bench, he announced,
"Lord Jesus Christ, the case is closed. I beg Your Majesty to send Your
judgment for sentencing." Whose trial did the wool carder think was
closed? The Inquisition's or his own? Sánchez did not elaborate, and
Cortes did not ask. Cortes, who had recovered his composure somewhat,
told Sánchez that it deeply grieved him to see him so deliberately put his
soul in such danger, and that he should try to keep the articles of faith and
the Church's sacraments.[32]

Sánchez objected that far from abandoning God's articles of faith, he
followed them all, and, confusing the Fourteen Articles of Faith with the
Ten Commandments, which Cortes had not mentioned, he began to list
all of the commandments that he had obeyed. Here his statements betrayed the haphazardness of his theological self-education. He said, "The
article and commandment that God left in which He ordered, 'Thou shalt
not kill or steal,' you won't find that I ever broke it, and the other that He

ordered, 'Thou shalt not fornicate with another's woman,' even less will you find fault with me after I got married. These two commandments are the mortal ones, and keeping these along with the others God left, and bringing His faith, God will save me. Where can you find sin in me?" Clearly, in Sánchez's understanding, the only sins that were "mortal" were the ones that in criminal law happened to be punishable by death.[33]

Cortes did not bother to correct Sánchez, and listed the various sacraments of the Church that he had denied: baptism, auricular confession, communion, as well as the articles of faith he also denied: the doctrine of the Trinity, the Crucifixion, the Messiah Himself. . . . Still hoping to convert Sánchez, the inquisitor cited the passages from Scripture that proved the divine institution of each of these things. He marveled, "Correcting you with love and charity has had so little impact on you, I cannot help but say to you, 'Look, hell is drawing near if you don't confess your sins and do penance, taking faith in God.'"[34]

Sánchez, unmoved by Cortes's knowledge of Scripture, suggested that all the lawyers in Cuenca come to examine *his* scripture. Cortes (pitying him?) answered that that would only lead to upset and confusion for Sánchez, and advised him that the better solution would be confession. Sánchez objected, "It is not my wish that everything I've said and declared in this trial since the day it began be covered up. Instead, let the whole world know, and if I'm wrong, I'll suffer the consequences."[35] Cortes tried to reassure him: "But your error does not have to harm you," if only Sánchez would recognize his sins; but the wool carder would hear nothing of it.

Cortes knew when to move laterally in an interview, and as he had done several times before, he dropped the current line of questioning to return to an unanswered question from a previous day. Cortes did not like the fact that Sánchez, when he explained why he would not worship idols, particularly the cross, had drawn the conclusion that *all* men were responsible for Christ's murder through their common descent from Adam and Eve. Cortes told Sánchez that it was the Jews who insulted and killed Christ, but they were not our brothers because "among Christians no one can be called brothers except those who are baptized and keep God's law."

Sánchez replied with a radical idea: "I call them brothers because they come from one line, which is the first father, but now I won't have them for brothers because they killed Jesus Christ."[36] He refused to lay blame on the Jewish people for the murder. "Anyone who kills someone else I take for a devil, not a Moor, Jew, or Christian."

The two quickly reached an impasse, and the inquisitor could not draw a response from Sánchez on any of several subjects, until he returned to Sánchez's anticlerical views. As might be expected, here he elicited a response. Cortes tried to persuade Sánchez to feel better about the clergy, "who pass sleepless nights in order to indoctrinate us and save our souls, and the Pope, who grants us pardons, jubilees, and remissions of sins." The subject of indulgences had never come up before, and Sánchez made sure that the court knew that he thought they were worthless and he had wasted his money on them. The money raised by the sale of indulgences was used to build churches (synagogues), and worst of all, to wage war against the Moors. And that, he declared, "is against my religion, because the Moors also believe in God, like the Jews and Christians. They all believe in God and they are killed because they don't want to believe in or worship idols, which I've called images, nor do they want to humble themselves or have a church, since God called it the synagogue."[37]

Cortes explained to Sánchez that the Muslims' and Jews' belief in God went only so far as their saying it in so many words, but in every other respect they did not believe in God as the Church orders; without receiving baptism and believing in the Articles of Faith, they could not be saved. This did not seem fair to Sánchez. He said, "They shouldn't kill someone who believes in and worships God; instead they should indoctrinate him. But the Church doesn't do anything except kill them and take their property from them." True, replied Cortes, if the Jews and Moors wanted to receive indoctrination, the Church would not kill them or take their property, but they did not wish to do so, and so were responsible for their own deaths.[38]

Sánchez had had enough; he called for a halt in the interview. Perhaps exhausted by the strain of the week's hearings, he did not even want to have the transcript of the day's proceedings read back to him. He admitted, "There is no need to read to me what is written down in this [hearing] because it's been read back to me many times and for now there is nothing in it to correct."[39] Without further comment on either side, he was returned to his cell to wait for the promised day of judgment.

4

LESSONS LEARNED
AT HOME

WHILE SÁNCHEZ WAITS FOR GOD'S JUDGMENT, WE MAY PAUSE TO
wonder how it was that a wool carder could preach, quote from Scripture,
and issue a summons laced with legal concepts and terminology. It seems
almost miraculous. Yet there was Sánchez, who did all these things and
more, confidently accusing his superiors of murder and proposing to bring
them to justice. How could he do it? Just as important, how dare he do it?

Lessons learned at home tend to make the deepest impression, so let us
begin there, in Cardenete, when Bartolomé was still a youth. Despite its
small size, Cardenete was not an idyllic, homogeneous village of the sort
depicted in the literature of the time.[1] The fact that the marquises of
Moya and a small number of converted Jews chose to reside there brought
the conflicts of the outside world directly to the village. What happened
in Cardenete involving these individuals very likely laid the foundation
for Bartolomé's future attitudes about social justice and religious prejudice. Sánchez condemned the religious persecution of the conversos, refused to recognize the division of society according to an individual's

religious ancestry, and questioned the authority of the aristocracy and the Church.

1

By the late fifteenth century, having fled persecution in the larger cities, conversos were to be found in towns and villages all over Spain, including Cardenete.[2] Of its two hundred families, several were Jewish in origin. If Bartolomé Sánchez's family had a few converso ancestors, as some villagers seemed to think, they kept out of the Inquisition's way, as no one bearing any of the family names was tried by the court. Others in Cardenete were not so successful at eluding the tribunal; about twenty-five men and women were tried by the court between 1490 and 1560, as well as many more from neighboring villages and the town of Moya.[3] In 1514–15, when Bartolomé was thirteen or fourteen, the tribunal worked methodically on the accusations against one family in the village— Alonso Montero, his wife, Angelina, and their children. The family had settled in Cardenete sometime in the 1480s; Alonso was from the city of Cuenca and Angelina was from Chelves, across the border in Valencia. Both had been tried for Judaizing in 1489: Angelina admitted to observing the Sabbath and fasts, and to putting on a clean shirt on Saturdays; Alonso had cursed the Virgin. At the time they were given light sentences, but in 1514 the Inquisition reopened their cases (although both were long dead) and also prosecuted two of the children, now adults, even though there was no fresh evidence against any of them. Whatever the reality of the situation (the Montero family may well have been sincere converts), in this second trial, Alonso and Angelina were posthumously declared apostate heretics and condemned to death. The long arm of the Inquisition reached for its victims beyond the grave, or more accurately into it, for such a sentence required the disinterment and burning of the couple's remains so there could be no resurrection at the end of time: the Inquisition's justice, like God's, was meant to be eternal. The sentence also required the confiscation of the couple's property from their heirs, and the public display, also until the end of time, of Alonso's and Angelina's sanbenitos in the parish church. The two sons opted to plead guilty to having observed the Sabbath as children while they lived with their mother. For this crime they were imprisoned and their property was confiscated.[4] In the Monteros' treatment Bartolomé observed the Inquisition's single-minded, savage pursuit of the descendants of Spain's Jewish minority. Many people in the region believed, as Sánchez did, that the Inquisition was only really interested in such persons' property and that religion had nothing to do with it. Statements to that effect were prosecuted vigorously by the court.

2

If the conversos were Cardenete's most notorious residents, the marquises of Moya were its most distinguished. In the 1470s, the dynasty's founder, Don Andrés de Cabrera, maneuvered his family from obscure Jewish origins in the city of Cuenca to a position of wealth and honor high in the government of King Ferdinand and Queen Isabella. In 1480 the couple were given as their reward the seigneury of Moya, which was elevated to the status of a marquisate. Around the time that Bartolomé Sánchez was born in Cardenete, the marquises began to take some interest in the village. Perhaps they found the official seat at Moya too isolated and forbidding. Cardenete possessed an ancient tower, and was only two days' journey from the city of Cuenca, where Andrés de Cabrera had been born, and just that much closer to the royal court and the marquis's more important holdings in Segovia. A new parish church was built; it was fitted with a special entrance and side chapel where Don Andrés and his wife, Doña Teresa, could enter and hear Mass in relative privacy.[5] The marquises began to maintain in the village a noble residence, which was appointed handsomely with tapestries, gold and silver, and other luxurious items.[6] Halfway between Cardenete and Cuenca, on the edge of the marquisate's frontier, the marquises built a Dominican convent in Carboneras. They could rest in the convent on their journeys to Cuenca and Segovia, and after death their bodies would find permanent repose among the friars.

The Cabrera family's residence in the village undoubtedly brought wealth and sophistication to Cardenete; in the early part of the century, the community was prosperous enough to support two notaries and a schoolmaster. But the Cabreras also brought controversy and ultimately violence, intrigue, and litigation on a grand scale. The crux of the matter was that many people believed that the marquisate did not legitimately belong to the Cabreras. The inhabitants of Moya and Cardenete never accepted the Cabreras as their rightful lords; they had documentary proof that over one hundred years ago, in 1390, their ancestors had bought the territory's freedom from the widow of Don Juan de Albornoz, the deceased lord. Complicating matters, another noble family, the marquises of Villena, claimed that their ancestor Juan Pacheco had been promised the seigneury by King John II back in 1440. In short, the true status of the area was so murky that Queen Isabella came to doubt that she possessed the right to alienate the lands from the royal patrimony. In her testament of 1504 she ordered an investigation into the matter and promised to give Cabrera equivalent lands and privileges in Granada if the original donation proved to have been illegal.[7]

Matters finally came to a head in the summer of 1520, when the cities of Castile, dissatisfied with way the new monarch, Charles V, was treating them, rose up in a general rebellion known as the Comunero Revolt. What began as a constitutional and national crisis soon touched off antiseigneurial rebellions all over the kingdom. In September rebels in the marquisate of Moya forged contacts with Comuneros in the city of Cuenca, the national junta in Tordesillas, and rebels in the kingdom of Valencia, which lay right across the border of the seigneury.[8] In their search for allies, the Comuneros of Moya were not concerned with the details of who should be king of Castile and under what conditions; their quarrel was more basic—they wanted freedom from seigneurial rule. In late September, when Bartolomé Sánchez was about nineteen years old, the people of Moya and Cardenete rose against the marquis and successfully expelled him, first from Cardenete and then from the territory. The marquis, Juan Fernández de Cabrera, found the treason of his subjects in Cardenete particularly offensive, as he explained in a letter to royal officials:

> My vassals talked amongst themselves and made a league and compact against me. One night they rose up against me and they all rebelled except the village of Cardenete, where I and my wife were at the time. (For thirty days I had been ill in bed with the quartans.) When this happened, I sent for some of the inhabitants of the place, who in the name of the entire village took an oath of fidelity to me. The next morning they said that more than 3,000 men were coming against me, and once

8. Carboneras, the scene of action during the Comunero Revolt.
(Photograph by the author)

I got safe in the countryside with some of my retainers, I thought that
my vassals would show me some obeisance, but they, filled with the dis-
loyalty and treason they bore me, were determined to move against me
in Cardenete. At great risk and danger to myself I was able to get the
marquise and one of my daughters out of there and I took them to my
fortress at Víllora, because the residents of Cardenete, once they saw
the people, began to riot. Some with others went to my house and they
sacked everything that I and the marquise, my wife, had in it. They carried off all the silver, tapestries, things of gold and everything else we
had in that place and in our storeroom, and likewise they sacked the
houses of many of my retainers.[9]

During the rebellion in Moya, which lasted from late September 1520
to late March 1521, the conflict surged back and forth, as first the marquis was chased out of the region, then reinstated, forced out a second
time, and finally restored to power for good.[10] In the process, two of the
marquis's nephews were captured and executed, the convent in Carboneras was sacked and the town burned, and royal and noble forces fought
pitched battles against the Comuneros, who were reinforced by their

9. The unfinished fortress in Cardenete. Legal action by the crown
halted its construction. (Photograph by the author)

Castilian and Valencian allies. During the siege of Moya (late January
1521) the marquis was trapped without sufficient supplies and starved
into submission. According to the terms of the surrender, the marquis
agreed to return the seigneury to the crown and pardon his vassals.[11] It
was a great victory, but it did not last long. The rebels' success provoked
an all-out response from the royal forces and their noble allies. In a matter of months the rebellion was suppressed, some 800 sentences were
handed down against the rebels, and the marquis resumed control of the
territory. Regarding the agreement made in January, he had no intention
of keeping his word, forced from him at sword point.[12] Instead, he turned
his attention to punishing Cardenete for its treasonous conduct.

Before the year was out, Cabrera began the construction of a modern
fortification on a hill overlooking Cardenete. Rather than hire the men
needed for this costly work, Cabrera exercised what he imagined were
his seigneurial rights: he compelled the men of Cardenete to work on the
castle and forced the villagers to contribute money for the project. The
construction was completely illegal, since a noble needed a special license
from the crown to build a castle, and eventually the matter came to the
attention of royal officials in 1523.[13]

At the same time, Cabrera began to squeeze the villagers for compensation for his losses, which he calculated came to 24,000 ducats, a huge sum that exceeded the annual income of all but the very highest nobility and prelates.[14] To think that the two hundred families of Cardenete could begin to pay off this fortune was insane, but Cabrera would try, using two strategies: direct appropriation of assets and manipulation of his seigneurial rights. The marquis levied reparations on the village, which he said were in payment for what had been stolen from him during the revolt; he also singled out individuals and fined them for their participation in the revolt. He confiscated the village's water mills and then required the villagers to take their grain to those mills, charging for the service two bushels of grain from every twenty milled. The village found its common pasturelands confiscated as well. The marquis then forced the village to enclose the lands to make hayfields for certain individuals he wished to reward.[15] Altogether, it was more than the village could bear.

During the summer of 1524, several former Comunero leaders in the village plotted an uprising against the marquis, set for St. Bartholomew's Day (Aug. 24), 1524. Joining them were several men from Moya and an inquisitor in Cuenca, himself a former Comunero from Toledo. At the last moment the plot was betrayed, and the conspirators fled to Cuenca to take refuge in Inquisitor Juan Martínez de Mariana's house.[16] The inquisitor was unable to protect them, and before long eight refugees from Cardenete were arrested and imprisoned in Valladolid, where the government was in residence. In the prison in Valladolid, the men of Cardenete's conversion from the tactics of rebellion to those of litigation and intrigue began. The imprisoned villagers first decided to sue the marquis for damages for abuse of his seigneurial privileges. They won this case in front of the royal council in less than a month. Finding themselves successful in court and supported by a sympathetic member of the royal council, a year later Cardenete's representative decided to sue for the return of the entire marquisate to royal jurisdiction. To give the plaintiffs an advantage over the marquis, the sympathetic royal councilor kept news of the pending lawsuit secret; it was only by accident that the marquis's accountant found out what was afoot.[17]

The people of Cardenete's success at legal warfare sent the marquis's agents scrambling. They tried several stratagems to upset the various cases, including intimidating and suborning witnesses, even kidnapping villagers on their way to Moya and throwing them into the castle's dungeon. The rebels were not above bending the law, either, and submitted forged documents and on one occasion beat up the marquis's supporters in the village. For three years both parties sent one appeal or motion after another to the royal council. Both sides were so desperate to win their case that on separate occasions their representatives at the royal court managed to intercept Charles V on his way to or from Mass and present appeals to his personal justice in hurried, impassioned statements.[18] In 1528, with a royal investigation into the status of the marquisate already begun, the marquis settled out of court with most of the villagers, and both the chief judge in charge of the case and Cardenete's representative died, thus effectively putting an end to it.

From his vantage point in Cardenete, Bartolomé Sánchez doubtless formed some opinions about the nature of seigneurial rule and the legal process. He observed that the marquis of Moya and his officials were arbitrary, ruthless, and sometimes violent, and that poor people like himself could never expect anything good from the nobility. As an able-bodied man, he probably was forced to work on the marquis's construction project and certainly knew others who were. His family could ill afford the marquis's demands for compensation for his destroyed and stolen property; perhaps it was these demands that forced some of Bartolomé's relatives to emigrate. Very likely the Martín Sánchez charged with taking part in beating the marquis's men was Bartolomé's father or brother (both were named Martín), and eventually Bartolomé married a woman from a Comunero family in the village.[19]

In contrast to the marquis's brutal tactics, the distant king and his government held out the promise of justice and the rule of law. For four years Cardenete buzzed with news of the progress of its lawsuits and its imprisoned men. Royal judges appeared in the village with writs and summonses, demanding to interview witnesses and inspect documents. Cardenete's victories over the marquis were explicitly based on rights and laws confirmed by the parliaments of Castile and applied by the Council of Castile to their case. Bartolomé could see for himself exactly what could be accomplished by a good lawyer in a just cause, but he also knew that the legal process could be tainted and judges and courts could not be automatically trusted. Thirty years later, standing before Inquisitor

Cortes, the wool carder remembered these lessons and demanded his own lawyer.[20]

3

In the first few days of his trial, Sánchez exhibited not only some familiarity with legal procedure and terminology but also considerable religious knowledge, which, according to him, he had learned in order to discover the meaning of his vision. As he explained, "I could not rest until I knew from wise and learned people what that [vision] was. Any time that I saw some friar or learned person, I would kneel at his feet to confess and tell him everything."[21] In his search for an explanation, Sánchez was not limited to the priests and friars in the immediate vicinity of his village; his work as a migrant laborer took him around New Castile. Without any training, he leaped feet first into a complex religious world, where millenarian traditions met with heterodox ideas, all swirling just beneath the surface of outward conformity. Lacking any formal education, Sánchez uncritically absorbed the facts and attitudes that came his way, many of which were less than completely orthodox. Dissident ideas were not difficult to come by in Sánchez's world; in the early 1550s, censorship of books was in its infancy and the Inquisition had not completely silenced the several generations of Spaniards alive in Sánchez's day who, like Sánchez himself, had grown up under more heterodox conditions.

First, there was Bartolomé's book of hours, which was meant to inspire him to piety, not heresy. We know that it was in Spanish, illustrated, and cheap enough for Bartolomé's neighbor Hernán Zomeño to sell it to him at a price that even an underemployed wool carder could afford.[22] Sánchez never explained how he had learned to read; probably his parents paid the village schoolmaster to give him a few lessons, at least enough to enable him to sound out a text when it interested him. Literacy was an unusual enough achievement for a man of his age and social rank that Juan Caballero, whose social standing in the village was considerably higher than Bartolomé's, blamed the wool carder's heresies on his ability to read. Caballero was overstating the case, repeating conservative misgivings about the growth of literacy among the lower classes; in actual fact, Bartolomé never mentioned owning any other publication and nothing in his speech echoes a printed text other than the book of hours and the Bible, much of which he would have heard quoted in sermons.[23]

Books of hours once had been exclusively the property of wealthy bourgeois and noble families, but in the sixteenth century, thanks to the printing industry, such books were among the most common and affordable in the marketplace. They were practical items as well as devotional texts: along with the several psalms and extracts of the Passion according to the four evangelists, many included a list of saints' days, a movable calendar for determining future holy days, prayers of the catechism, and prayers for special occasions. All this, plus illustrations, in a book that easily fitted in one's hand or sleeve and cost less than a day's wages. At midcentury the Toledan printer Juan de Ayala had produced multiple editions of just such a book, one of which eventually found its way into Bartolomé Sánchez's hands.[24]

Bartolomé bought the book to use while preparing for annual confession. Apparently he did not flip through its pages first to look at the illustrations, but read through it until he came across a woodcut at the beginning of the hours for the Conception of Our Lady. He did not realize that his vision had been an exact representation of the coronation of the Virgin as queen of heaven, a common iconographic theme that appears in almost every surviving book of hours and in many paintings and prints as well.[25] Instead, Bartolomé read the vision/print as a representation of the true Trinity: God the Father, the Son, and the Mother, united in purpose by the Holy Spirit. The idea was not as farfetched as it sounds. In the late fifteenth century the cult of the Virgin had reached such a pitch of popularity that artists regularly depicted the pseudo doctrine of the Quaternity: the Virgin flanked by God the Father and Son, surmounted by the Holy Spirit. It was the coronation, but more than the coronation, for in this interpretation, the Virgin became co-equal to God while the Holy Spirit served to unite the three persons into one godhead. This misperception of the Virgin's place in heaven continued to circulate into the late sixteenth century.[26] The miraculous appearance of the Quaternity in Sánchez's book of hours was confirmation that the vision he had received nine months earlier was genuinely a gift from God. But what did God want from him? At that point, the book of hours, itself largely made up of the Word of God, became part of the answer. Bartolomé spent so much time studying the book that he could quote parts of it by heart to the court.[27]

4

At the same time, the wool carder began to question friars and "learned persons," and as he did so, the certainties that had held in place his belief as a Catholic began to collapse, for Bartolomé's informants seem to have given him far from orthodox information. We cannot know what sort of person in Sánchez's estimation would count as learned. Given his own lack of education, he may have been impressed by anyone who could read fluently and owned a few books. If that were the case, then the range of persons with whom Sánchez could have conversed was almost limitless. Between the growth of literacy and easy access to devotional books, there existed a whole class of people who, without having studied Latin, taken orders, or attended the university, regarded themselves as religiously adept. Some were avid readers of Desiderio Erasmus's works before they were banned; others were well-to-do descendants of Jews, and still others simply liked to read and speculate about religion. In the 1520s and 1530s, a group of lay men and women, most them of converso descent and from the area between Guadalajara and Toledo, became involved in a new religious movement known as *alumbradismo*. The alumbrados, known elsewhere as Illuminati, emphasized meditation and criticized external, ritualized signs of faith and some key aspects of doctrine.[28] Sánchez was no mystic, but several of his ideas are contained almost verbatim in some of the points included in the 1525 Edict of Faith condemning the alumbrados prepared by the Inquisition of Toledo.

4. God enters more completely in the soul of man than He does in the host. . . . The host is just a bit of dough and man is in His semblance.
16. One should avoid doing reverence to the images of Our Lord and Our Lady because they are sticks of wood.
18. A certain person while preaching said that the cross should not be worshiped, saying that it was a piece of wood and that they should worship Jesus Christ crucified.
27. For what are excommunions, fasts, and abstinences since they are just hindrances and the soul ought to be free?
28. There is no need for indulgences.[29]

It is extremely unlikely that Sánchez both heard the edict and would remember it after twenty-five years, but the fact that he could repeat several of its points shows that before 1560 the Inquisition was not very successful at suppressing various heterodox ideas circulating among the population.

At some point in his wanderings Sánchez seems to have spoken with people who had some familiarity with Protestant ideas. As happened with his apparent knowledge of alumbradismo, Sánchez could quote some of the key Protestant phrases and yet not subscribe to Protestantism. For example, like a good Protestant Sánchez stated his desire to confess only to God, and maintained that he would be saved not by the ceremonies of the Church but only by faith and the word of God. But then Bartolomé stated clearly that he believed he would be saved only by his own efforts, and on another occasion he stated that each person should be judged according to his works, not by his religious background. So far removed was Sánchez from direct contact with Protestants (who did occasionally turn up in Cuenca, often as migrant workers from Huguenot areas near the Pyrenees)[30] that in the one direct reference he made to "Lutherans" he repeated the common belief that they were nothing more than robbers and murderers. He did not seem to realize that his position on the authority of the Pope, good works, the Eucharist, and the requirement of confession turned him into a Protestant.

5

In addition to "learned people" Sánchez consulted with friars. "Friars" also comprises a very large category of people, but given Sánchez's residence in eastern La Mancha, he was sure to run into members of three orders in particular: the Dominicans, whose closest convent was at Carboneras, a day's walk to the north of Cardenete; the Carmelites, who maintained a house in Requena, two days' walk in the direction of Valencia; and the Franciscans, who were ubiquitous in La Mancha, with a house in Iniesta, two days' walk to the southwest, as well as others in Belmonte, Valverde, and San Clemente. All three orders preached in their houses and sent out brothers to evangelize in the surrounding communities. In their sermons Bartolomé found his best source of information as well as a model for self-expression.[31]

During the first few interrogations with Inquisitor Cortes, Sánchez delivered a polished sermon on the nature of the cross and several partially developed others on themes related to Elijah. Having heard a lifetime's worth of sermons, the wool carder intuitively knew what religious oratory ought to sound like. Such discourse could take one of two general approaches, narrative or argumentative. Sánchez's sermon concerning the cross takes the narrative form, as he reveals his theme, that the cross is the devil's weapon, through the unfolding story of how Christ came to earth and was murdered against His will. The sermon's theme is confirmed at the conclusion of the narration. In the course of the narrative, the wool carder introduces a secondary theme, mankind's collective responsibility for Christ's murder. Sánchez is at pains to emphasize that guilt for Christ's murder transcends the Jews, for "we are all the children of God . . . and form one lineage." Thus the consequences of that murder affect not merely the Jews but all people. In a proper sermon, complicated rules governed the subdivision of the hour-long oration into easily distinguished subthemes. Sánchez divided his short sermon into two parts, joined in tension by the promise of what could have been (the possibility of freely given grace) and what actually happened (mankind's perverse rejection of salvation). In choosing his form of expression for this discourse Sánchez remained literally historical (*dilatatio*) but on other occasions, like the preachers, he could lapse into allegorical, tropological, or even anagogical language. Finally, to enliven his historical presentation and vary its cadence and color, the wool carder used the devices of invented dialogue and various explanatory asides. Altogether, the sermon is so well crafted that Sánchez must have thought it through, perhaps even practiced it somewhere, before his arrest.[32] Inquisitor Cortes was not interested in Sánchez's rhetorical skills, but he certainly took notice of them, because on several occasions he felt compelled to deliver short homilies of his own to match Bartolomé's.

6

More important than elocution and rhetoric was what Sánchez could have learned from the sermons and religious discussions he heard. Each religious order had its own theological outlook, which left a distinctive imprint on its members' religious teaching and activities. The Dominicans, whose founder, Domingo de Guzmán, was from noble stock, prided themselves on their orthodoxy and university credentials. Royal confessors tended to be Dominicans. St. Vincent Ferrer (1350–1419) led the Christian attack on Spain's Jewish population and spent the last years of his life preaching the coming of the Apocalypse.[33] His sermons were still being read in the sixteenth century. Given Sánchez's sympathy for the Jews and conversos, his links to the antiseigneurial Comuneros, and the absence of apocalyptic references in his statements, it is unlikely that much of what Sánchez heard in Dominican sermons found its way into his thinking.

The Franciscans, on the other hand, had a tradition of forging close contacts with the poor and were known for their radical ideas concerning the social order, education, and the end of time. The spiritual Franciscan from Valencia, Francesc Eiximenis (c. 1340–c. 1409), wrote works on the life of Christ, millennial prophecies, and politics that were infused with criticism of the existing order. In his *Dotzè del Crestià,* published in Valencia in 1484, he predicted, "From here on out there will be no more kings, dukes, counts, nobles, or great lords; instead, from here to the end of the world popular justice will rule in all the land, and the whole world will be divided into communes."[34] Such ideas continued to be repeated well into the sixteenth century. In 1545, Fr. Luis de Maluenda published in Spanish a book on the impending arrival of the Antichrist, in which he railed against the injustices committed against the poor by the rich and by prelates who neglected their flocks. In the prologue he cautioned, "The dangerous thieves are the rich and powerful people of leisure, who are robbers by royal command and papal bull; the poor, robbed and dispossessed, complain of their luxury." Eleven copies of his book were for sale in Toledo in 1556.[35]

Working closely with the poor and dispossessed, the Franciscans took the position that simple folk could attain more insight into religious matters than the wealthy and educated. In fact, they distrusted the learned and preferred the humble, following the advice of the Valencian Arnold of Villanova, who wrote that Jesus "revealed to St. Peter and St. John, who were ignoramuses, what he did not reveal to the Pharisees and rabbis."[36] This attitude guided the observant Franciscan cardinal Francisco Jiménez de Cisneros (1436–1517), who listened raptly to the revelations of unlettered female mystics and seers, and caused many works of mysticism to be translated into Castilian for common people to read. It led directly to the moral authority of the alumbrados, who believed that their lack of education privileged their religious insight.[37] In a society in which knowledge of Latin and a university degree were normally required before one could discuss, write, or preach about religious matters, the Franciscans' position raised the ire of the Dominicans, who promoted the scholasticism of their spiritual father, St. Thomas Aquinas.

Some factions among the Franciscans were also responsible for spreading notions about the arrival of an egalitarian millennium. This prophetic tradition went back to Joachim of Fiore, whose theory of carefully elaborated stages of history culminating in a perfect age found many prominent followers in late medieval Catalonia and Valencia.[38] The chaotic political situation in Spain from 1519 to 1522 allowed these obsessions to take full form, most spectacularly in the figure of El Encubierto, the Hidden One, who led a true millenarian movement in the mountains of southwest Valencia in 1522. Apparently modeling himself on the prophecies to be found in Johan d'Alamany's *Coming of the Antichrist*, published in Valencia during the Germanías Revolt (the *germanías* were guilds in Valencia), the Hidden One also spoke in his sermons of the unfolding of history in stages leading to perfection and promised social justice for the poor. His followers believed that El Encubierto was invulnerable to harm and would lead them to an earthly paradise in Jerusalem. The Hidden One was assassinated before he could cause too much damage, but legends and imitators surfaced from time to time, attesting to the powerful attraction that millennial prophecies held for Valencian artisans and peasants.[39]

El Encubierto's bad end and the cessation of hostilities in Valencia and Castile did not dampen interest in millennial prophecy and apocalyptic scenarios. According to the astrological predictions, the year 1524 was supposed to be a calamitous one, with destructive rains flooding crops and cities all over Europe. Franciscans living in the ducal town of Escalona (which would soon share the same lord as Moya) expected the year to bring about a radical transformation of the Church. In a sermon delivered in February to the people of Escalona, Fr. Ocaña laid out his millennial vision. He told them that the time to go to Jerusalem had arrived, for all the prophecies written about the Son of Man would be fulfilled.[40] They were the most blessed people in the world and the leaders of the Church would be "thrown out like pigs." Ocaña explained that their marquis, together with Charles V, would defeat Francis I and depose the Pope. Then the true reform of the Church would begin. One of their number, Fr. Santander, would become the Angelic Pope of prophecy, and the illiterate visionary Francisca Hernández would rewrite the Scriptures.[41]

In the Franciscans' radical socio-religious program Bartolomé Sánchez would have found confirmation for his own social prejudices. The Spain of his youth was saturated with millennial prophecies, which were brought to fever pitch during the Comunero and Germanías revolts. At some point between his vision in 1550 and his arrest in October 1553, Sánchez made the connection between the vision, the millenarian tradition, and the figure of Elijah. In short, he decided that he was a second savior, who would be a combination of Elijah and the Messiah.

7

For Spaniards and all other Europeans in the sixteenth century, the figure of the prophet Elijah was pregnant with various meanings. Sánchez would have encountered references to Elijah everywhere, beginning at home in the sermons given by the third religious order in his region. The Carmelites traced their spiritual allegiance back to Elijah, whom they saw as the founder of their order on Mount Carmel. In the Old Testament, Elijah signified belief in monotheism, was the destroyer of idol worshipers, and prefigured the coming of the Messiah. In the New Testament, Jesus called John the Baptist another Elijah, and some thought that Jesus called on Elijah from the cross to avenge his murder. In the apocalyptic literature, Elijah, along with Enoch, would fight the Antichrist and usher in the Second Coming. Elijah and Enoch were the only persons in the Bible who did not die; instead, God swept Elijah up in a chariot of fire and transported him to heaven to await the end of the world. The spiritual Franciscans, following the prophecies of Joachim of Fiore, believed that Elijah would inaugurate the Third (and final) Age of the Holy Spirit. Elijah, in short, was a revolutionary prophet no matter to which tradition one subscribed. His name one did not invoke lightly. El Encubierto claimed that he had been brought to Valencia by the prophets Elijah and Enoch, and in Anabaptist Münster, where in 1534 people believed that the new Jerusalem would not be long in coming, one of the leaders, Melchior Hoffmann, styled himself as Elijah.

In choosing to identify with Elijah, Sánchez thus was tapping into a complex and volatile nucleus of eschatological meanings, some Christian and others Jewish. Having eliminated Jesus Christ from the scene by calling him a failed messiah, the wool carder needed to create a plausible alternative messianic figure with whom to associate himself. For Christians, Elijah generally was associated with the Parousia, but in Sánchez's scheme of things, the *first* coming had been frustrated, so that Elijah was left with his original meaning, as the precursor of the Jewish Messiah, defender of monotheism and destroyer of idols. If this in fact was Sánchez's intention, he was not the first Spaniard to become so convinced. Around 1500, conversos in Andalusia believed a woman in Herrera del Duque when she prophesied that Elijah would rescue them and take them to the Promised Land. News of the prophetess spread as far north as Alcázar de Consuegra in La Mancha, where in 1519 an old conversa woman remembered the story.[42] Perhaps Sánchez's conversations with "learned people" included some crypto-Jews, from whom he learned that the Messiah had yet to come, and Elijah was his precursor. To add legitimacy to his appropriation of Elijah's identity, Sánchez quoted extensively from the New Testament passages that predicted the coming of the Messiah.

Was Bartolomé Sánchez in fact a converso, as some in Cardenete suggested?[43] Not self-consciously, though he clearly sympathized with their sufferings. The more likely possibility is that many of Sánchez's informants were crypto-Jews or sympathizers who confirmed that Jesus could not be the Messiah (adding fuel to Sánchez's own delusion) and showed the dissatisfied wool carder an alternative to Catholic practice: to worship God in heaven by turning toward the wall or going out to a field; to confess to God alone; to view Christian images as idols; and to place one's faith in righteous works and God. Sánchez's well-developed sense of justice led him to rebel against the persecution of the religious minority and to insist on seeing the Jews (and Moors as well) as his brothers. This sort of ecumenism was not unique to Sánchez. Christopher Columbus wrote in his religious diary, "I believe that the Holy Spirit works among Christians, Jews and Moslems, and among men of every faith, not merely among the learned, but also among the uneducated," and the Italian miller

Domenico Scandella was similarly broadminded in his acceptance of Islam.[44] Given the eclecticism of Sánchez's sources and his idiosyncratic interpretation of theology, all we can say for certain is that once Bartolomé Sánchez decided that he was the Elijah-Messiah, the Catholic Church became his enemy; and if its ministers did not free him, they would soon be obliterated by God, who was the Just Judge. Or so he hoped.

5

TRIAL
MOTIONS

*El día de los finados, andan los
muertos por los tejados.*

—Spanish proverb

1

SÁNCHEZ WOKE TO THE SOUND OF CHURCH BELLS. NOT THE JOYOUS pealing that accompanied marriages and news of military victories, but the solemn tolling for the dead. The metallic voices of Cuenca's many churches joined into one long lament of mourning. Close at hand, the cathedral and St. Martin's parish church combined forces; across the canyon the Dominicans' bells rang out, while the rest of the city merged into an indistinct ringing sound. November 1, All Saints' Day, had come and gone, chased out by All Souls' Day, a time when Castilians' thoughts turned toward their dead and the wintry parts of their own souls. Somewhere a cat scampered over the roof, the tiles shifted, and a child, clutching her sweetened holy day biscuit, was reminded of the proverb that on this day the dead walk the roofs. Around the city, inside all the churches, requiem masses echoed through the chantries, while widows and daughters left small wax tablets, cups of wine, and bread over the places where their dead were entombed. Listening to the bells toll, Sánchez perhaps thought about the souls of the damned, who he once said bathed and drowned in urine—a fate no doubt reserved for the inquisitors, who had failed to release their prisoners on November 1. Or perhaps he speculated that God would send their spirits into animals, or maybe He would just let their disembodied souls wander forever through the air.[1]

Whatever Sánchez thought that day in his prison cell, the plain reality was that God did not visit His judgment on the Inquisition on November 1, as the wool carder had predicted He would. Instead, when court reconvened on Friday, November 3, it was clear even to Sánchez that his situation had not changed. Moreover, the gears of inquisitorial justice were beginning to grind faster. Cortes had a trial to conduct, and although he still worked on Sánchez's conversion and allowed the wool carder to hold forth in his usual style, the mood of the court had changed. Soon Sánchez would have to pick a lawyer for his defense and the prosecution would issue its formal accusation. There was no doubt in anyone's mind that Sánchez would be on trial for his life.

At first Sánchez could not quite accept God's failure to intervene. As he had done for the past few hearings, on Friday, when he entered the courtroom and approached the bench, while standing in front of his earthly judge, he directed a prayer to his heavenly one asking for His verdict. On Saturday he prayed again to Jesus: "I am awaiting your decision." But on Monday, Sánchez abandoned his supplications for a judgment—he had come to the realization that the balance had tipped against him, and, if he were to come out of his trial unharmed, he would need special attention from God. Invoking the persons of the true Trinity, he now prayed:

> Lord God the Father, Thou art the bread. Lord God the Son, Thou art the wine. Holy Virgin Mary, Thou art the flesh. Lord, by Thy most holy Trinity, do not let me fall. And if I should fall, Thou shalt raise me up. Lord, teach me Thy wisdom, reveal to me Thy goodness. Let all see in me the marvels of Thy most holy splendor so that in Thy name I may overcome and vanquish this burden that Thou hast given me with the Antichrist and the devil.[2]

Cortes asked what he meant by the burden that God had given him, and Sánchez replied, "This trial." So not only was Sánchez God's special messenger, but now he saw that God was testing him to see if he would be a worthy bearer of His Word. After all, just like Jesus, God's chosen ones must often suffer persecution at the hands of unbelievers.

Meanwhile, Cortes began to take a more decisive role in the trial. On November 3, after Sánchez proved more intractable than ever, the inquisitor decided it was time to move the case to its next stage. He arranged for the respected canon Dr. Alonso Ramírez de Vergara to participate in the process.[3] That afternoon he recalled Sánchez to his courtroom and explained to him that since it appeared that Sánchez had nothing further to say and he had refused to swear to tell the truth at the beginning of the trial, he had invited Dr. Vergara to accompany Sánchez while they confirmed the accuracy of the trial transcript. Left unsaid: this was a necessary preparation before the lawyers presented their opening arguments. Sánchez was persuaded to swear an oath over a missal, and then for the remainder of that afternoon and through the next morning's hearing they set about reading back the transcript to him, inviting him to correct any passage that did not represent what he had said. Sánchez confirmed that it was all accurate; then Dr. Vergara spent some time privately with the prisoner to see if he could convince Sánchez of his errors. At the price of his own tears, he managed to weaken the wool carder's resolve, but as soon as the trial resumed, Sánchez returned to his heresies.[4] After a few words of discussion about the cross (the devil's weapon), he was returned to his cell.

Cortes was determined to move the trial along; later that day, he conducted a rare Saturday-afternoon hearing. As soon as the jailer delivered the prisoner, with Vergara in attendance and without any preliminaries, Cortes asked Sánchez directly if he ever had communicated any of the heretical things discussed in his trial to anyone else, and if so, to give their names. Sánchez replied,

> First, I don't think these things offend our Lord God or His Holy Catholic faith. I have spoken of them wherever I've gone to work, as much in Cardenete as in other places. If I saw many people, [I told] many; if I saw few, few. This coming Christmas it will be more or less three years since I began, although I was not so convinced as I am now since Lent of this year.[5]

Cortes asked Sánchez to explain one more time the doctrine of the Trinity, and after he received the same reply as before, he began the formal interrogation of his prisoner by asking Sánchez to give his name, age, occupation, personal history, religious ancestry, and genealogy. Sánchez complied, balking only at revealing his religious ancestry. "I don't have to say what is my ancestry, whether it is Christian, Jewish, or Moorish, as Your Reverences told me in conversation—God knows what it is by my works." [6] Nonetheless, he did provide verbally a complete genealogy, which told the court that his family were farmers (labradores), some of whom lived in Cardenete and others of whom had migrated to Villamalea, to the south. Although his parents were deceased, two of his father's six brothers and sisters were still alive. His own generation was not so fortunate in health: except for one brother ("who earns his living with an ox train wherever he may be found"), all of his many siblings were dead, including a half-witted brother who had been a swineherd. At age thirty-two or thirty-three Bartolomé had married Catalina Martínez, a local weaver's daughter, and had always lived in Cardenete, although he left often to look for temporary work in Cartagena, Murcia, Toledo, Granada, and "many other places." In twenty years of marriage Sánchez had fathered five living children, the youngest of whom was only fourteen months old. [7]

Having ascertained Sánchez's identity and history in an earthly social sense, Cortes now wanted to know more about his credentials as a Christian. "Have any of your relatives been condemned, reconciled, or penanced by this Holy Office?" No, Sánchez swore, not that he knew. "Cross and bless yourself, and say the prayers of the Church." Sánchez refused to cross himself, and try as he might, Licentiate Cortes could not persuade Sánchez to comply, so they proceeded on to the prayers of the catechism.

Sánchez reproduced the Hail Mary with reasonable accuracy. Only the last line of the prayer, which invokes Mary to pray for us sinners, was wrong. Sánchez prayed, "Holy Mother of God, please pray for me and for the entire people of Israel, forever and ever. Amen." If Cortes thought that this was an innocent mistake, that perhaps Sánchez had gotten confused, the next prayer banished such a charitable notion from his mind. Sánchez's Paternoster was a sacrilegious reworking of the words that

Jesus Himself gave to His people. In the revised prayer, Sánchez put himself at the center of God's design for His people. The people of Israel are not Jews, but all those who suffer injustice and long for redemption.

> My Father, who art in heaven, hallowed be Thy name. Thy kingdom come in me. Thy will be done in me; just as it is done in heaven, let it be done in me on earth. Give me this day my daily bread, to me and the entire people of Israel, and to whomever else Thou pleasest. And deliver me from temptation forever and ever. Amen.[8]

It was customary at the end of the first official interrogation of the prisoner to issue the first of three formal warnings, each the same. Cortes told Sánchez that if he confessed completely with true contrition, the court would treat him with whatever leniency the law provided. This way, Sánchez could avoid a formal accusation and trial with third parties (which would certainly end in a guilty verdict, Cortes did not need to add). Sánchez replied, "As I told you, while I was going about working I told it to many people. I don't remember anything else, and I'm not sorry for what I've said. I have nothing more to say."[9]

On Monday, November 6, the day Sánchez began to change the tenor of his prayers to God, Cortes gave the wool carder his second warning. Canon Vergara spoke privately to the prisoner, who afterward told the court that he would pray to God for inspiration and would inform Dr. Vergara of his decision at the next hearing. Several days went by before Inquisitor Cortes called again for Sánchez. Sánchez entered as usual, praying this time:

> Lord, Thou said, "Place thyself at my right hand and I shall make of thy enemies a footstool." So, Lord, please do Thou this for me, because I have placed the Most Holy Trinity in Thee, Lord God and thy Son and His Mother, in whom I must believe and worship, and Thou wilt save me according to my works.[10]

Licentiate Cortes did not condescend to respond to this prayer and went straight to the point. He apologized for having been occupied by other business over the past few days, but pointed out to Sánchez that he was supposed to have contacted the inquisitor when he was ready with his decision, and he had not done so. At any rate, he and Dr. Vergara were now ready to hear what he had decided. Sánchez, in fact, had come to a decision. Tacitly acknowledging that Vergara had won his confidence, he authorized the canon to oversee the truthfulness of the trial transcript. He selected for his defense lawyer Licentiate Moya, a layman whom he had never met, because he had heard that he was a man of conscience. Had Sánchez not listened to a word of what Cortes had told him two weeks before? A layman was unacceptable to the court. But Moya was unacceptable for other reasons as well. Cortes explained: "Licentiate Moya has studied canon law, and this material cannot be dealt with so casually by just any lawyer: instead [it needs to be dealt with] by those who principally have worked with and studied theology and the things that touch on God's law."[11] He went on, trying to persuade Sánchez to accept Dr. Vergara as his counsel. There were many good reasons: Vergara was a theologian; he offered his services out of his sense of Christian duty; he was impartial; and he would tell Sánchez everything he needed to know to save his soul. Cortes warned his prisoner, "You're making a mistake. It's possible that at some moment you will be sorry that your counsel does not have the qualities necessary to deal with such things." Sánchez replied that he had made his decision about what they should do, and if they didn't want to do it, then let His Reverence work his will and God would work His. Cortes replied that he was motivated only by his desire to administer justice and to do right by the prisoner and his own conscience. He had brought in Dr. Vergara for the same reasons, he told Sánchez, "so that you won't go straight to hell like some ignoramus!"[12] Sánchez was unimpressed, so he was returned to his cell without further comment.

November 11 was Sánchez's last opportunity to ask the court for leniency: to confess all, repent and accept that he was wrong, that God had never chosen him as His messenger, and that priests and inquisitors were his friends and advocates, not the enemies of mankind. Sánchez paused at the courtroom door and looked upward . . . and then approached the bench as usual. Applying the words of the Magnificat to himself, he asked God to render revolutionary justice:

> My Lord, Thou didst say that him that Thou held, Thou wouldst make a fortress of his might. So Lord, please make a fortress of my might, and please overthrow the proud with the will of my heart, and cast down the powerful from their seat, and raise up the humble, and the

hungry, fill them with goods, and the rich, leave them empty so that we, the people of Israel, who are the lay people, may receive God, our Saviour. I have nothing more to say.[13]

Cortes told Sánchez that when he abandoned the pride that he abhorred in others, then God would grant him the fortress in his heart that he asked for. If he followed the Church's sacraments, then he could count himself one of the people of Israel and receive his reward in the next world. Sánchez, however, was still thinking about the crimes committed by the Inquisition. He replied, "Christians have to serve God, and they must not be Lutherans or robbers, or killers of those who have done them no harm. I say it on account of the deaths and confiscations of property that the Inquisition has done to many."[14] Sánchez could not have realized the irony of the situation — in his mind the Inquisition was no better than its sworn enemies, the heretical Protestants. The wool carder, however, appeared to know nothing about the religious rebels in the north except that they were lawless criminals.

Cortes made one last appeal to Sánchez's reason, telling him his vain ideas had so filled his head that no advice seemed able to shake them out of it. He spent several minutes urging the wool carder to give up his notions and to repent with all humility. Angrily Sánchez exclaimed:

> You talk to me about humility and repentance?! God knows my heart and to Him I humble myself, and I've done the penance to Him that I've wanted to give to Him. I do not humble myself to the devil or the Antichrist! The devil is Your Reverence and your associates who kill and take away the property from those who have not done you evil or harm. . . . The Antichrist is the religion that those from the Church give to the people whom they indoctrinate. The people from the Church who killed God were the pontiffs and those who are descended from them through the synagogue. They killed His apostles because they said and preached the evangelical law. It comes down to this: the Inquisition has killed those whom it has because they say that this Elijah and Messiah has yet to come, as I have said and declared, and for this reason you want to kill me, because everything I've said in this trial is the truth![15]

With a heavy heart, Cortes delivered the court's final warning. "It pains me that instead of understanding and correcting [your beliefs], you always go from bad to worse. Therefore, as a Christian and on account of the position I hold, I warn you—remembering God, Who created you, Who redeemed you with His Holy Passion, and Who must judge you as His creature—understand what you have been told and correct your life with true repentance so that God will be pleased to pardon you."

Sánchez replied that God was his judge, not Jews who killed Christ. This was the signal for the prosecution, represented by Diego de Tapia, to enter the courtroom and deliver its accusation. "Very Reverend Sirs," began Tapia. Tapia, who normally was the warden of secret prisons, was substituting for the court's official prosecutor, Licentiate González, who had accompanied Inquisitor de la Cueva on his tour of the north. He charged Sánchez with eight counts of heresy, using Sánchez's own words on the subjects of idols, Christ's Passion, confession, communion, baptism, indulgences, the nature of the Trinity, and the Church's authority. Tapia made no attempt to associate the accused's ideas with any heretical sect, although the prosecution often did so in order to increase the gravity of the offenses. Inasmuch as any one of the heresies mentioned was sufficient to burn the prisoner, perhaps Tapia did not feel the need to do any further work on the case. He concluded the charges by asking for the maximum penalty, release to the secular authorities; in other words, death.[16]

Despite the overwhelming evidence against Sánchez, the formalities of the law had to be observed, and the accused was given an opportunity to respond to the charges under oath. The wool carder accepted all of the charges as true, except the third, which dealt with confession. He did not deny it, but wanted to make a slight correction to the accuracy of the text, saying that he may have misspoken while giving his statement. At that point, Inquisitor Cortes ordered that Sánchez be given a copy of the indictment so that he and his lawyer, whoever that would be, could respond to it at the end of three days.

"I don't want a copy or any other lawyer except God, who directs me," said Sánchez. But, just to have someone to communicate to him what needed to be said, Sánchez agreed to accept the advice of one of the court-appointed lawyers, whoever was least busy. And, taking his copy of the accusation with him, Sánchez was returned to his cell.

2

From this point on, Sánchez did everything in his power to bring his trial to a rapid conclusion, while Cortes, responsible for bringing him to justice, dragged his feet. The wool carder saw no point in defending himself; he had nothing to be sorry for, and if he was right, God would save him. On Monday morning, November 13, when Cortes called him in to meet his lawyers, the inquisitor asked if he brought the copy of the indictment with him. Bartolomé replied, "I burned the copy because I already said that I didn't want it and it was unnecessary." No matter, Cortes told Ybaneta to read back the court transcript to the lawyers Brizeño and Aguilera, who tried to get Sánchez to think about some sort of defense. Sánchez brushed them aside, saying, "I have nothing to add to or inform my defense for you sirs; God is my advocate and the one who must save me." Brizeño and Aguilera made one feeble attempt to persuade Sánchez to listen to their advice, but lacking Cortes's patience, they quickly washed their hands of Sánchez. They told him, "Believe us and do what we advise, and if you don't, you have no one to blame but yourself." In good lawyerly fashion, they then said they wanted it known for the record that Sánchez had refused their help so that his fate wouldn't weigh on their consciences.[17]

Cortes began stretching out the intervals between meetings with Sánchez and the lawyers in order to give the prisoner ample time to think over his situation and to slow the inexorable march toward the guilty verdict. He could not give up hope that his prisoner somehow would come to his senses before it was too late. When Sánchez refused again to defend himself on November 15, Cortes granted another extension until Friday, and when on Friday Sánchez refused for a third time, Cortes granted yet another extension until Monday, November 20. Meanwhile, both Tapia and Sánchez argued with the judge to allow them to get on with the trial. Sánchez took the position that no defense was possible because, even if he wanted to do so, he could not take back anything he had said: he had preached his ideas all over the mountains of Cuenca and through southern Spain.[18]

On Monday, Cortes finally had to allow the prosecution to present the testimony of the witnesses from Cardenete. Before such a presentation, however, normally the witnesses would be asked to ratify their depositions. The depositions, then, would have to be sent back to Cardenete. But Sánchez said there was no need for that, he accepted the depositions as genuine and would not contest their validity. The testimony from Sánchez's nine neighbors was read back to him, and he confirmed it as all true. He added for the benefit of the court, "The souls of those who die, men and women, are in the bodies of animals. Others go through the air wherever God pleases until I give God's sentence, which is the same as what Elijah, who is me, asks for against evil and whoever has gone against God's law and the truth, and whoever has persecuted it." [19] Cortes gave Sánchez two days to prepare a defense against the witnesses' testimony and tried to give him a copy of their depositions.[20] Sánchez refused it, and having learned his lesson, this time Cortes did not insist that he take it.

At the end of the two days, Sánchez still had not changed his mind, despite the urgings of Licentiate Aguilera, who had stayed on as Sánchez's defense lawyer. Again Sánchez and Tapia requested a conclusion to the trial, but Cortes merely said that he heard the two parties and was prepared to come to a decision . . . but no decision came. Finally, five days later, on November 27, the warden Tapia came to Cortes's afternoon session to say that Sánchez was asking for an interview with the inquisitor. Cortes gave the order to bring him.

"The warden told me you wanted to speak with me. What do you want?" asked Cortes.

"It's true," said Sánchez, "I asked for an audience because I want to say that since the proceedings are over and the deadlines have expired, Your Reverences should do your will with me, so that God will do His." [21]

Cortes told Sánchez he was mistaken that there was some kind of deadline to the things that touched on God's service and men's consciences. Cortes was not going to be rushed through this trial; nor was he going to be forced into handing down a death sentence if he could help it. In layman's terms, he explained to Sánchez the difference between ignorance and heresy.

As I have told you many times, if you want to understand your errors and heretical propositions . . . and recognize them as badly said and as such you confess to them with true repentance, then, as you've been told, God will forgive you for everything. But if you insist on saying and repeating them more, the damage to you grows worse." [22]

Sánchez replied, "God knows if I have offended Him, and concerning the reprimands that you make to me, I ask God for His final judgment against me if I do not tell the truth, or against Your Reverence and your associates."

Faced with such defiance, Cortes began to think that it just did not make sense that a peasant, as he had said before, "a man of base material," could be this persistent or misguided. He told Sánchez, "Some despicable teacher has put you up to these stupid things. I warn you to testify to it, and give up talking about [your ideas], and repent for what you have said, as you should." [23]

"I never will be sorry for having said the word of God, nor will I ever go against it. On the contrary, I should increase it."

Cortes, in a moment of exasperation, told Sánchez either the devil had control of him or he was crazy, but then, regaining his composure, he returned to the idea that someone had to be responsible for this obstinate peasant's behavior. "As I told you before, because you are a man of such little learning and not well read, and you are so stubborn in your speech, some person or persons have put you up to this, or you read it in some book. I charge you to tell the truth about everything and not to hide anything, so that your book can be seen or your teacher or teachers can be examined. When their words are understood, then we'll see who is right!" [24]

Sánchez replied, "I don't have any teacher who may have indoctrinated me or a book in which I may have read it. It's God's divine science and on account of that I dare to say it."

Cortes thought he had a lead here. Divine science was the first subject covered in Thomas Aquinas's *Summa Theologiae* and therefore the concept was known to any beginning student of theology; Sánchez's use of the term seemed to betray a knowledge of things that he pretended not to have. He challenged Sánchez to explain what divine science was— "Where have you read that and why do you dare to say what you've declared?" The wool carder probably had heard the words on the lips of preachers when they spoke of understanding God, so Cortes's challenge was only an invitation to Sánchez to say, yet again, that God was his authorization. "Although Your Reverence says He is not, I say yes, He is, and so we're opposed." Cortes explained to the wool carder what the authority of God really was, ancient writings confirmed by holy doctors of the Church and the Roman pontiffs. Sánchez countered, "God's authority is the greatest authority I can have to say what I say." Clearly, Cortes was losing this argument, and when Sánchez said he had nothing more to say, the inquisitor ordered him back to his cell.

Cortes may have lost the latest battle with the lowly and uneducated wool carder, but the inquisitor seemed determined not to lose the war: he was going to convert Sánchez and save his soul. He had another idea: he knew that Sánchez seemed to respond to Dr. Vergara's ministrations. In fact, only the day before, on Sunday, the inquisitor had seen Vergara and had asked the canon to come by the tribunal to talk to Sánchez, either in private or with him present, whatever seemed best to him. On Tuesday afternoon, the venerable canon appeared at Cortes's courtroom, ready to do as the inquisitor had asked. Sánchez was brought up from his prison, and Cortes retired to his chambers while Vergara remained to speak with Sánchez. Ybaneta stayed behind in order to witness the conversation but wrote only a general summary of its content. Vergara spoke to Sánchez at length about his situation and salvation, and seemed to make an impact on the recalcitrant peasant. Sánchez asked the canon to give him until the following afternoon to pray to God and think over what the canon had told him. There was hope yet that Sánchez would convert.[25]

The next afternoon, Dr. Vergara returned to the Inquisition's rooms and told Cortes that he had come to learn of Sánchez's decision. Cortes vacated the courtroom, and Sánchez was brought in, with Ybaneta attending as before. The canon gave him another talk, and at the end of it asked him what he had decided. Sánchez replied, "I have thought about it last night and today, and I have entrusted it all to God, and He tells me, since He is my lawyer, not to do any of the things that you, Sir Doctor, have told me. So I don't plan on going back on anything that I have said."[26]

Vergara made one last attempt, giving many reasons why Sánchez should return to God's service and save his soul, but it was useless; the wool carder would not listen. He was polite; he avoided arguing, but he was very firm: he would not take back one word, and so the interview ended.

3

The next day was a holiday, St. Andrew's Day, but when the court reconvened on December 1, Cortes did not call again for Sánchez. For the better part of six weeks he had devoted himself exclusively to the wool carder's case. Whatever he thought about the trial, one thing was clear: while he had dedicated himself to it, the other business of the court had mounted up. Cortes turned back to his paperwork. There were more cases of dead Judaizers to be dealt with, plus a number of live prisoners, sent to the court by Cortes's colleague Licentiate de la Cueva, who continued his tour of the northern part of the tribunal's district. With the exception of one Frenchman accused of Protestantism, the seven or eight prisoners were charged with Judaizing.[27] While the lone Huguenot was a novelty, Cortes regarded his converso prisoners with heightened suspicion. First, the principles of Roman law, which guided the judge's deliberations, assumed guilt, not innocence, on the part of the arrested person, and the court rarely began proceedings without sufficient evidence of wrongdoing to convict. Few cases ended in acquittal. Nor could Cortes ignore the work of three generations of inquisitors before him. Doubtless he knew that the Catholic Monarchs of blessed memory, Ferdinand and Isabella, had brought the Holy Office to Spain in 1478 in order to put an end to, from their point of view, a very particular and loathsome brand of heresy: Judaizing. The Inquisition maintained that Jewish converts, while enjoying the privileges and freedoms that Christianity confers on its followers, secretly followed the law of Moses, and these descendants of the murderers of Christ turned into a mockery everything the Redeemer gave to mankind by the price of His blood. From time to time, Cortes's colleagues had tried cases of Judaizers who had deliberately profaned Christian symbols. Cortes had heard of cases of Judaizers who even sacrificed Christian children in their despicable rituals.[28] And here they were, eighty years later, and they were still having to deal with these people.[29]

For these reasons, Cortes could not regard the new prisoners without thinking of the inheritance of the past, which the unfortunate men carried in their very blood. Legally, through no fault of their own, the descendants of converts were excluded from the country's highest professions and honors, and if a converso were arrested by the Inquisition, his Jewish ancestry automatically compounded the assumption of guilt. For the Inquisition there could be no room for leniency or understanding: conversos arrested for Judaizing knew the price of their apostasy, which they practiced at their own peril. Thus when Licentiate Cortes met with the other voting members of his tribunal to review the new prisoners' cases, he agreed to the judicial use of torture in order to obtain confessions. The confessions would reveal the extent of the men's conspiracy to defraud the faith, but would also pave the way for their reconciliation with Christian society.

Over the next few weeks, Cortes worked continuously on the cases that Cueva had sent him, voting to torture this person and then conducting the interrogation, sentencing that one to a posthumous death penalty, interviewing prisoners . . . and completely neglecting Bartolomé Sánchez, who waited impatiently in his cell for a resolution of his case. On Sunday, December 10, Sánchez finally took matters into his own hands. He attacked what he called "the idols" in his cell, smashing into pieces the wooden crosses and stuffing the paper images of the saints out the window of the latrine, where they fell to the street below.[30] Had his cellmates not stopped him, he would have set fire to the broken bits of the crosses as well. If he was hoping that this sacrilege would draw a response from Cortes, he was disappointed. Cortes continued working through his dockets and did not call for his iconoclast prisoner until the following Friday, December 15.

What could Cortes say? He reminded Sánchez that he had explained the doctrine concerning images to him many times, and he had to conclude that the devil had Sánchez in his thrall. He asked Sánchez if he had ever seen anyone destroy images before, or if anyone had told him to do it. Sánchez said no, nobody. Cortes replied somewhat testily:

> If you haven't seen any Christian person do it, then what reason impels you to do and say it, since you know that many Christians are very good Catholics, servants of God, and very learned, and they honor and venerate images? You are such a depraved and ignorant man—what

reason can you have to invent and do what you do all on your own, and for wanting to show that you are such a bad Christian, and to want to lose your life and soul?[31]

Sánchez replied that God moved him to do so. He added, "Give me the city for my prison for eighteen days and I'll show you more lively reasons if you're not happy with the one I just gave you." Cortes suggested to him that if his authority did come from God, he would find it easier to demonstrate in the Holy Office than out on the street, where he would be likely to be upset.[32] With a surfeit of warnings, Cortes sent Sánchez back to his prison. On second thought, the next day he decided the time had come to punish Sánchez not only for the sacrilege, which was bad enough, but also for his continued contempt for the court and its officials. He ordered the warden Tapia to remove Sánchez from his cell and place him in the stocks until further notice. And there he remained for a week, until the inquisitor, on his rounds of the prison, went to see him. With some words about hoping that God had put some understanding into Sánchez, he ordered his release. The wool carder had the good sense to thank him, and promised that from that day forward he would not insult any more crosses or images. It was the day before Christmas Eve, 1553.[33]

4

For the next two months, Pedro Cortes forgot about Sánchez, at least in his official capacity as Sánchez's judge. There were no more interviews, no recorded discussions with other members of the tribunal about the wool carder's fate. Cortes continued to work on his other cases and probably went on his weekly rounds of the prisons. He also took a few weeks off in January, one of the coldest months of the year in Cuenca. If it snowed that month, the city's steep streets turned into treacherous pathways. Men and beasts would lose their footing on the slippery stones; once in the late sixteenth century a truly unlucky man slid off into one of the canyons that girded the city.[34] The elderly judge, who suffered from unnamed infirmities, could not risk navigating the icy streets and would have stayed in his rooms, trying to keep warm. By January, the stone and stucco buildings of Cuenca had finally lost all of the heat they had absorbed during the summer, and the temperature in the unheated rooms hovered around

40 degrees. Like any well-to-do individual, Cortes would have owned a brass brazier to burn charcoal in his rooms, but there were no stoves, few fireplaces, and little glass on the windows. Not far away from Cortes's rooms, Sánchez spent the time in the cold prison pacing back and forth in his cell.[35]

Cortes's lack of attention to Sánchez's case was not due to inexperience. In his long career, the judge had tried men of many conditions and many heretics. Aided by the secretary Ybaneta, only a few years earlier Cortes had conducted a case that bore some similarity to Sánchez's. In 1549 Luis de San Pablo, a failed friar and hermit, declared before several witnesses and a notary that he was the Great Messiah promised in law (i.e., the Bible), and that he was simultaneously Jesus Christ, St. Mary, and the Living Sacrament. He denied the existence of angels, demons, hell, purgatory, and sin. For six years he had heard a voice that told him he was God, and that he was obliged to conquer the sun from sunrise to sundown each day and to eat realgar with all of his meals.[36] The good voice was his guardian angel, but he was also assailed by a bad voice, which he took to be the devil, who urged him to hang himself. Although he was God, Luis also was convinced that he was the heretic Fray (Martin) Luther.

When brought to the Inquisition of Cuenca, Luis confirmed the entire story and filled in the details. Unable to prevent himself from saying his heresies, he had spent most of the last few years being whipped from town to town all over the Iberian Peninsula. If he was to be believed, Luis had made something of a tour of the various tribunals of the Inquisition, having been arrested and whipped by the inquisitions of Valladolid, Toledo, Murcia, Barcelona, Zaragoza, Seville, Llerena, and Evora in Portugal. Released from Evora, he had gone to Calahorra, and from there directly to Cuenca. Cortes interviewed the repentant hermit several times, and privately came to the decision that although at the moment the man appeared to be rational, he could not be held accountable for his actions. Even while he admonished Luis to try harder to control himself and went through the motions of his trial, Cortes wrote to the Supreme Council for permission to commit Luis to one or the other of two insane asylums, and eventually was able to place the hermit in Toledo's house of innocents.[37]

That had been five years ago. Now Cortes was faced with a man who claimed he was the Elijah-Messiah. From the moment the inquisitor had first learned about Sánchez from Bachiller Barca's letter to the tribunal, he had suspected that something might be wrong with the wool carder. If so, the judge would need to proceed very carefully. Although Nicolau Eimeric's manual of inquisitorial practice urged the judge to be skeptical of prisoners who appeared to be mentally ill, contemporary jurists and theologians were quite clear about how to treat the insane. To be guilty, even of heresy, the accused had to have criminal intent: he had to understand that what he planned to do was wrong and then deliberately set out to break the law in spite of that knowledge.[38] If Sánchez actually were insane, no court in Spain would find him guilty of any crime, whether it was heresy or something else. Therefore, among the questions Cortes originally had sent to Cardenete for the witnesses, several probed for evidence of mental illness. The witnesses had been asked if Sánchez presented any signs of physical illness, if he appeared to be in his right mind or out of it, or if he had committed any acts that could be taken as evidence of insanity. The nine witnesses had been unanimous in their opinion that Sánchez was healthy, even though his outburst of shouting in the parish church had seemed rather strange to most of them. Their testimony had forced Cortes to order Sánchez's arrest, since, except for the cousin Mora's deposition, the witnesses said nothing to indicate that the wool carder had ever lost control over himself, much less that he was insane.

On February 14, 1554, Licentiate Pedro Cortes summoned the wool carder for the first time since December 23. As before, Sánchez entered the courtroom and without kneeling before the altar blessed himself while standing. This time Cortes refused to indulge the wool carder. He told him to give up the old habit and follow the way of God and the Church, which was, upon seeing an altar with figures of Christ and the saints, to kneel and cross and bless oneself while repeating one's prayers. Anything less would be taken as a sign of unrepentance. Sánchez was not intimidated, and replied, as usual, that he would not kneel to idols.[39]

Cortes made an attempt to be conciliatory. He told Sánchez that Lent had begun and it was time to think of his sins and confess them to a priest. Sánchez replied, "This holy time that you call Lent I take to be the time of the devils because during this time the Jews insulted Christ and crucified Him. I don't say this about the days that God Himself established."

"Stop changing the subject and pay attention to what you're told. Work on those things so that your conscience profits as you've been told."

Sánchez replied that he would say whatever God sent him to say. Cortes countered that what God orders is that every Christian confess during Lent. No, Sánchez shot back, "What God orders is not to kill or rob or separate couples whom He joins together in marriage, like Your Reverence and your associates, the Inquisitions, do . . . bringing [spouses] to this Valley of Josephat, which is this courtroom."

Cortes told Sánchez for the second time to answer to what he was told, to prepare for confession. Sánchez replied, "I've already confessed and communed with God, and I've offered my soul and body to Him. He has received me, and I have no need for another confessor." Cortes spent a few more minutes with the unrepentant wool carder, asking him twice more to confess like a good Christian, but Sánchez insisted he had nothing to be sorry for. This was enough to convince Cortes that, despite what Sánchez's neighbors had said about the wool carder, it was time to determine his mental competence. He dismissed Sánchez, and two days later Ybaneta interviewed various people who had come in contact with the wool carder since he arrived in Cuenca, and then drew up a "Report on the Comprehension and Judgment of This Prisoner."[40]

The first person to be interviewed was Diego de Tapia, warden of the secret prisons. After swearing to tell the truth, Tapia answered as follows.

Question: How long have you known Bartolomé Sánchez, and have you dealt with him and conversed and communicated with him many times?

Answer: I have known Bartolomé Sánchez by sight and conversation since he was brought a prisoner to these prisons. Ordinarily every day since he became a prisoner I have seen, talked, and communicated with him two or three times a day, and some days more, providing him with his ration for his meals and whatever else is needed. Many days I have been with him in the cell for long periods of time, chatting with him.

Question: During the time since you have held Bartolomé Sánchez prisoner in these jails, have you seen him by deed, word, or anything else to be deprived of his senses or understanding like a man who is defective or lacking in [reason]?

Answer: What I have seen and felt about Bartolomé Sánchez since he has been in these prisons, talking to him about his affairs at present, is that he is in his right mind and understanding and I have not seen him do or say anything that might make me judge him as insane. Certainly, I think that when he holds forth against our Holy Catholic faith he is just a pure villain, because when he doesn't talk about his case, I have always seen him be very sensible and of sound reason in everything that is done with him. I take him to be a [sane person], and I have never seen him, nor has his cellmate, Luis Vélez from Almazán, do anything badly.

The next person to be interviewed was Juan Gómez de Villanueva, the tribunal's doorman and superintendent. He had little to say, other than to assert that Sánchez was perfectly sane like other people, and that if Sánchez had committed any act of insanity, he certainly would have heard about it.

The last person to give testimony was Luis Vélez, Sánchez's cellmate. Vélez said he had known Sánchez since last St. Lucas's Day, the day Sánchez was brought to Cuenca.

Question: During the time since Bartolomé Sánchez has been your companion, have you seen him by deed or word to be deprived of his senses or understanding?
Answer: In all the time I have known him, in his words and deeds I have not seen Bartolomé Sánchez out of his senses or understanding; instead he is like a man of good reason and understanding. He does nothing but eat and sleep and walk to and fro. We have continuously been good friends.

Ybaneta's report confirmed what the villagers in Cardenete had already said, and what Cortes had seen for himself during Sánchez's trial: Sánchez appeared to be perfectly rational, except when he got onto the topic of religion, and then he was just a very obstinate man with some very offensive heretical opinions. Apparently he never mentioned to anyone that he was the Elijah-Messiah. Off the subject of religion, Sánchez paid attention, was a good worker, and behaved like any other man. However, Cortes was not ready to give up quite yet—one month later he decided to ask for testimony from an expert witness, Dr. Luis de Esquivel, a physician in the city. Perhaps the doctor would find the evidence of disease or loss of mental function that casual observers could not detect. Esquivel examined Sánchez and talked to him at length about his work, life, and trial. At the end of his examination, Esquivel reported that he judged Sánchez to be a sane man, that there was nothing about him by which he could be judged to be crazy, and as a result there was no basis for a legal defense on the grounds of insanity.[41] It was beginning to look as if Cortes and Sánchez were running out of options.

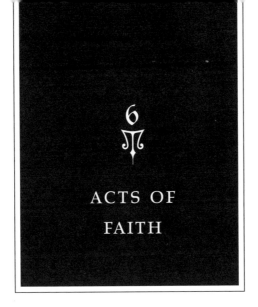

ACTS OF
FAITH

1

THE FORTY DAYS OF LENT WERE BUSY ONES FOR CORTES, CAUGHT UP as he was in the work of the tribunal. Luis Vélez, Sánchez's cellmate, was tortured a few days after he deposed for the court concerning Sánchez's sanity.[1] The inquisitor, though, chose to ignore the wool carder, who remained undisturbed in his prison. Finally the month of April came to Cuenca. Sánchez's prison had not yet lost its chill, but through the cell's one window, milder air, redolent of spring, began to take an edge off the damp. In the valleys below the city, the winter wheat was greening in the fields, while on the terraces around the city, almond and quince trees flowered in private gardens. Soon groups of women would go out to search the warming hillsides for wild asparagus, nettles, and other greens. Sánchez had been in prison for almost six months. Several times he had asked Cortes to let him return home to feed his young family. In Cardenete, his wife's land lay neglected. Who would dig the earth for this year's kitchen garden? How had his wife and children, the youngest of whom was only twenty months old, managed through the winter?

On April 2, the day after Easter Sunday, Cortes held his first interview

93

with Sánchez in more than six weeks. He wanted to know if the wool carder had fulfilled the precept of annual confession and communion at Eastertide.[2] Sánchez told him that he had already confessed and taken communion with God, and it was not necessary to confess with the devil. "Explain to me," said Cortes, "how you understand you have confessed and communed with God." Sánchez replied, "He who is on good terms with God has no need to reveal his sins to the devil, and he who tells the truth [as he had done in his trial] has no need to look on it as a sin or to feel sorry for it." Cortes could see that five months in prison had done nothing to temper Sánchez's views, but he had no desire to argue with or interrogate Sánchez; on this day, as a priest he merely wanted to know if all of the tribunal's prisoners, including Sánchez, had done their Easter duty. Cortes appealed twice more to Sánchez's conscience and even brought in the image of Bartolomé's wife and children as an inducement, all to no avail. Sánchez said that they were just breaking their heads and he would not take back what he had said.[3]

Cortes's colleague Licentiate Don Enrique de la Cueva had returned to Cuenca for Easter and for the auto de fe that would be held later that month. Cueva was curious to learn about Sánchez's case at firsthand, so on April 11 Sánchez was brought to the afternoon session of the court to meet the inquisitor. Introductions were made. Cortes explained to Sánchez that Inquisitor Don Enrique desired to inform himself about the wool carder's case, and, doubtless thinking of his many run-ins with Sánchez, warned Bartolomé to behave and to respond respectfully to Cueva's questions. Cueva went over Sánchez's case with him, discussed, as Ybaneta put it, some of "the unusual things pertaining to Sánchez's person," and then dismissed him.[4]

The date of the auto de fe was set for Sunday, April 29. If the court failed to persuade Sánchez to recant in the remaining two weeks, the wool carder would be the only live person at the auto to receive a death sentence. Judging by the pattern of convictions in the tribunal, Cortes and the others had no qualms about handing out death sentences to deceased Judaizers, or even to living ones if they deserved it, but it was unprecedented in Cuenca to burn an Old Christian, a member of the majority population, for heresy. In Cortes's twenty years with the tribunal, it had never happened. In fact, only one person from the bishopric of Cuenca, a converso, had been killed in all that time; all the rest had been from the converso communities in the northern part of the tribunal's district, which were so far away that they actually belonged to another bishopric.[5] Given the situation, Cortes's anxiety over Sánchez's conversion was understandable. Ordinary people, simple country folk without any real religious education or any Jewish or Muslim ancestry, were not supposed to become heretics and reject everything that society held dear. It just didn't make sense. On April 16 the tribunal held another interview with Sánchez for the purpose of convincing him to recant, and yet another on April 23.

The audience of April 23 was different from others held with Sánchez. Licentiate Cortes did not attend, nor did Sánchez's own defense lawyer; instead, Don Enrique de la Cueva directed the hearing. Present also were Dr. Alonso Ramírez de Vergara, who as the bishop's representative had an official as well as a personal interest in Sánchez's case, and an entirely new participant in the proceedings, Fray Juan de Aguilera, the guardian of the city's Franciscan convent. Their only interest was to persuade Bartolomé to confess. With just six days left before the auto de fe, the wool carder seemed to relent the slightest bit. He considered the possibility that he might be wrong about God's protection. Sánchez told the court, "If Your Reverences sentence me to burn, you put down as much wood as you want, and you set it on fire and throw me in it, I am certain that God will rescue me and I won't be burned. If I should be burned, then I would ask for mercy."[6] The next morning, Licentiate de la Cueva decided to clear up one last point of law for the satisfaction of the court. In the interests of justice, the court needed to confirm Sánchez's religious ancestry, which he had always refused to reveal to the court. There were rumors in the village that Sánchez was descended from Jews on his father's side, but they were unsubstantiated, so vague that not even a name or specific degree of relationship was offered. Cueva asked Sánchez to declare for the court's satisfaction the true nature of his background.

"I have nothing more to say," said Sánchez, "except to add that I hold myself to be from the caste of the very first parents, Adam and Eve. According to one's works each should be held as a Christian, Jew, or Moor."[7]

Unlike the inquisitor and many of his social superiors, Sánchez was not willing to judge a man by his blood. Each became what his works made him.

Cueva, like Cortes before him, fell into the trap of debating with Sánchez. In this instance, he felt the need to defend the social order to the peasant.

> As you say, everyone who is born, by birth is descended from the very first parents [Adam and Eve]. But then, in going forth in the world there arose divisions among the descendants with respect to the provinces they inhabited because of the religions they professed. Thus, some were called Moors, others Jews, others gentiles, and ourselves Christians, some of whom were called Old Christians because among their ancestors there never was a Jew or Moor, and others New Christians or "confesos" because their ancestors originally were Jews or Moors.[8]

As Cueva continued, he betrayed the illogic of the Inquisition's prejudice against persons of mixed religious backgrounds. He concluded, "Although it's true that as far as God is concerned an Old Christian is he who performs the works of one, in the end there is a distinction between persons." In other words, in the end blood would tell.[9]

Sánchez refused to be convinced, and Cueva began arguing with the wool carder, offering him many more reasons and warnings. Finally Sánchez admitted that according to Cueva's reasoning, he could be called Old Christian because all of his ancestors had lived and died according to the Christian faith. He added that he too had lived according to that faith for forty years, from the time he was old enough to understand it until two years ago, when God enlightened him.[10] The law he now followed was the religion revealed to him by God, which he had declared in his trial. Cueva's secretary recorded, as Ybaneta had done before him, that although the inquisitor strove mightily to separate Sánchez from his errors, his efforts were to no purpose, and the unrepentant wool carder was sent back to his cell.

Time now was truly running out for Sánchez. On Thursday, April 26, Cortes and Cueva held a last interview with their prisoner. They began by reminding him that many wise and religious persons had warned him to understand his errors and give up his blindness. Hoping that someday he would recognize his errors and be saved, they had waited for him to come to them to confess. Since he seemed to have omitted to do this, they were reminding him that this was his last chance to ask for forgiveness before his body and soul were lost to hell forever.

Sánchez replied that nothing he had said was in error. "Since I owe you nothing for you to persecute me so, I don't hold you to be my judges, only God, Who knows if I have offended Him by what I have said and is the one Who must punish me."[11]

The inquisitors repeated that if what Sánchez said were not heresy, they would not say to him what they did. But since what he said was against everything he had promised with his baptism—that is, with his acceptance of the Christian faith—it was their duty as his ministers to attempt to warn him as often as they could. But now time had run out, and they did not want to see him go directly to hell with his eyes wide open. "This is the last time you'll be told."

Ever the one to get in the last word, Sánchez retorted, "About what you say I promised with my baptism, it was not I who promised it, but my godparents, and I take God to be my father. If my godparents were deceived, then they also deceived me, but God has cleared up this deception, and He has given me safe-conduct to dare to say it to the whole world."

Not for the first time, the inquisitors suggested to Sánchez that the devil had control over him. There was no other explanation for such obstinacy. "Don't pay any attention to your imaginings or to the evil inspirations that the devil has given you to say what you do. Believe the opposite as you are told; there is no other road to heaven except to give up what you have said, and in repentance confess it to us." Sánchez stood firm and repeated that he would not take back one word of what he had said and they shouldn't waste any more time on it; they could work their will and God would work His. For the last time Cortes and Cueva warned Sánchez, "Your reward will be hell if you don't return to God's law," and then dismissed him.[12]

2

The auto de fe of April 29, 1554, was not a large one: only eight prisoners appeared for sentencing in person while ten individuals were condemned posthumously. For this reason, the ceremony may well have been conducted inside Cuenca's cathedral without the extravagant pomp and hordes of spectators that usually attended such events.[13] Nonetheless, even a small auto de fe was a solemn event that required the presence of the highest religious and civil authorities. Dr. Vergara represented the bishop, who was traveling with Prince Philip, the future king of Spain, and two other canons stood as witnesses for the cathedral chapter. The marquis of Cañete, Don Diego Hurtado de Mendoza, who was one of the most powerful men in all of Spain, and two city councilors bore witness for the secular authorities. All of the Inquisition's officials, including the city's familiars (lay officers of the Inquisition who apprehended and imprisoned the accused), and many of the city's prominent citizens, priests, and friars turned out for the ceremony.[14]

The night before, according to custom, the Inquisition's distinctive green cross probably was paraded through the city streets, accompanied by the men of the religious brotherhood of St. Peter Martyr, dedicated to upholding the honor of the Holy Office. On Sunday morning the eight prisoners, all men, were marched the short distance from the Inquisition's quarters to the entrance of the cathedral. If all went according to custom, each wore a yellow sanbenito and carried a green candle. Because Sánchez was to be punished as an unrepentant heretic, his sanbenito and special cone-shaped hat were decorated with the red flames of hell. Once inside the cathedral's gloomy interior, the men took their places on wooden scaffolding erected for the occasion. The light from their candles and the torches carried by many of the spectators punctuated the dim interior. The cavernous space soon filled with a smoky pall that smelled vaguely of incense, but more intensely of burning tallow and beeswax, the press of unwashed bodies, and, from underneath the flagstones, a hint of decomposing flesh.

The auto de fe comprised three parts: the traditional sermon, the publication of sentences, and a Mass. After the sermon was delivered, the inquisitors read aloud the sentences of the other seven men, who had accepted the offer of reconciliation with the faith. Next, the ten deceased Judaizers were condemned to eternal infamy. Finally, the tribunal turned to Sánchez. The wool carder's case was so unusual and abhorrent and his punishment so extreme that the inquisitors had prepared in advance a thoroughgoing public description of Sánchez's heresies and trial, which took a full twenty-five minutes to read aloud. The document began in the usual way, naming the parties in the criminal case and proceeding to the prosecution's indictment, now proved as true. Sánchez heard his own words read back to the horrified and scandalized crowd. His insults to the cross, to the Pope and the Inquisition, his defiant braggadocio that he had been so careful to confirm, word by word, to the court, now reverberated through the temple, the synagogue of his enemies and persecutors. But they had censored him! Where was news of the Elijah-Messiah? Where was the proof that he was the messenger sent by God to punish the Inquisition? The Pharisees and priests of the temple had trampled it all underfoot, just as they would soon burn him and destroy all memory of his mission.

Sánchez heard the final sentence being read out:

> We declare the said Bartolomé Sánchez to have been and to be a heretic and apostate, and on this account, to have fallen under and incurred the sentence of major excommunication . . . we release him to the secular arm of justice according to and in the manner voted by us . . . we declare all of his property confiscated . . . and we declare his children, grandchildren, and descendants via the male line for two generations, and via the female line for one generation, to be deprived of all and any benefices, dignities, and offices, be they religious or secular . . . they are ineligible and incapable of holding any other office and of bearing weapons, riding on horseback . . .

On and on the sentence went, all, as the document stressed, according to the laws and uses of the realm and the Holy Office. He and his family were crushed.[15]

When Mass was concluded and the final notes of the Te Deum faded, the crowd headed down the streets to reassemble on the parade ground at the edge of the city, where Sánchez's execution would be carried out by the government authorities.[16] Sánchez, now stripped to the waist with his hands bound and a rope hung around his neck, was mounted backward on a donkey for the humiliating procession through the city. Through the narrow main square and then down still narrower, twisting streets the procession made its way, the donkey carefully negotiating the stony track that at times cut through the living rock on which the city was built. Finally clear of the Valencia gate, they entered open ground and quickly

10. The Campo de San Francisco, Cuenca (1565). The Church of San
Francisco is in the center. (Drawing by Anton van den Wyngaerd.
Bildarchiv der Österreichische Nationalbibliothek,
Vienna; Cuenca [F], Vienna 2)

arrived at the Campo de San Francisco, where the lieutenant governor
prepared to receive his prisoner. Some six months before, Sánchez had
passed along these streets on his way to the secret prisons. Then he had
been certain that he held God's favor. The Virgin had visited him only
weeks before; the words of Scripture were clear in his head—there could
be no doubt then that he was the messenger and God would hold him safe
in His power. But now? Did Bartolomé dare to look at the stake and the
faggots of wood, the soldiers holding back the excited crowd, the smol-
dering brand held in the executioner's hand? He lost his nerve and cried,
"Mercy! I confess! I want to convert to our Holy Catholic Faith!"[17]

Willing hands reached out to lower Sánchez from the donkey, and he
was rushed into the Franciscan convent that stood next to the parade
ground. While he was seated on a chair in the Chapel of the Name of
Jesus, the convent's guardian, Dr. Vergara, the lieutenant governor,
and many others, including the public notary who was recording the
entire event, squeezed into the space to witness the heretic's conversion.
Sánchez announced:

Everything I said and was accused of in my trial by which I was condemned is public error, and the opposite of it is the truth. I hold and believe and confess as a good and faithful Christian everything that the Holy Mother Church believes, holds, and confesses. For my crimes and sins I beg for mercy from God and for penitence from the very magnificent and reverend Lords Inquisitors. I am ready and prepared for the penance that the Lords Inquisitors may impose upon me.

Eager hands brought a cross, and as a sign of his conversion, Sánchez adored it, kissed it, and touched it to his eyes, and said in Latin, "Adoramus te Christi et benedicimus tibi." He then turned to the lieutenant governor and asked him, since he had converted and begged for mercy, to suspend the execution and return him to the Lords Inquisitors so that they could penance him. He asked the assembled party to witness his conversion and, finally, turning to Dr. Vergara, he asked the canon to sign his confession for him, since he could not write.[18] The public conversion of the heretic completed, two constables took Sánchez back up the hill to the secret prisons, where Diego de Tapia waited to receive him.

3

Inquisitors Pedro Cortes and Don Enrique may not have been too surprised to see Sánchez again. They never really had wanted to burn Sánchez, but as long as he remained unrepentant and no one was willing to swear that he was insane, there was no way out of their obligation to uphold the law. Finally Dr. Vergara, who of all of them seemed to understand Sánchez the best, had found a way out. He had suggested at a meeting of the tribunal on April 16 that they sentence the wool carder to death with the proviso that they would wait for his confession up to the moment he was tied to the stake. Licentiate Aguilera, Sánchez's own defense lawyer, had first recommended that they burn the heretic alive. But the other members of the tribunal, worried about the unusual aspects of Sánchez's case and their own consciences, immediately and unanimously voted for Vergara's idea.[19] The walls of the Holy Office were not impervious to leaks, and on April 23 Sánchez seemed to tell Vergara, Cueva, and the guardian of the convent where he ultimately would confess that he had heard the tribunal's offer: "I am certain that God will rescue me and I won't be burned. *If I should be burned*, then I would ask for mercy." On the Campo de San Francisco, the staged conversion had gone off without a hitch. The people were edified and uplifted by the public humiliation and then the miraculous conversion of the heartless heretic. For his part, Sánchez had delivered his lines flawlessly and had escaped execution. The question was, would he really convert to the faith?

On May 2, Wednesday, Cortes called for his prisoner to find out. As Sánchez entered the courtroom, he knelt before the altar, blessed and crossed himself, and then, beating his breast in a sign of contrition, recited correctly in succession the Our Father, Hail Mary, Creed, Salve Regina, and other prayers. Approaching the bench, he finally said, "I ask God for penance and pardon for my sins."

Testing Sánchez's understanding of the situation, Cortes asked him why he was returned to the Inquisition's prisons after the auto de fe, and received a general answer from the penitent.

> I finally understood the error I was in and in which the devil kept me fooled. Like a crazy man and a person who was not in his right mind [*persona que no estaba en su juicio*] I've said to Your Reverences what is written down in my trial. I am sorry for all of it, and I beg to God for mercy. Attend not to my cursings but to your great mercy and give me the penance you want because I'm ready to carry it out.

Sánchez's answer got Cortes's attention. The inquisitor asked him to explain what he meant by the error he was in.

> The error is the vision of light that I mentioned I saw in the fields next to my village near St. Sebastian's chapel when I was coming back from reaping. I saw it on high, and on seeing it, I entrusted myself to God and I took guidance from it and asked God to reveal to me what might be in His holy service and so I wouldn't lose my soul. That's why I've fallen into those errors.[20]

Sánchez was not the first person to blame his misadventures on a visionary experience. To deal with such cases, theologians had developed a means of distinguishing between good and bad visions, which Cortes began to test on the wool carder. He told him that if the light had been sent by God, it would have enlightened him and not led him to say heresies against God, especially if Sánchez really had entrusted himself to God, as he claimed. "Therefore," he continued, "I charge and warn you to tell the whole truth and nothing but the truth, without any shadings or excuses, about everything you have held in your heart that has moved you to say [what you have], and to have the great stubbornness about it that you have."

Sánchez protested, "But I'm not twisting anything; I'm telling you the whole truth, and there's nothing more about it for me to tell you."

Cortes explained his thinking a little more, thus giving Sánchez a hint of what to say. "Often when the devil wants to fool men, he creates their inspirations by showing signs of the angel of light; but when men, with pure hearts, commend themselves to God as you said you did, His Divine Majesty does not allow them to be deceived as you were. . . . Your error has come to you from some other place, and for your salvation it is necessary to declare it openly."

Sánchez resisted the suggestion and denied that his errors came from any human teacher. Instead, he insisted that the vision had come from his imagination, and that became the source of his insanity and loss of his right mind. Cortes rejected this explanation. He told Sánchez:

> Sane men of good understanding and good Christians as you said you were before this all happened aren't fooled and confused into giving up what they believe and confess to be good when a similar light and imagining comes to them as you say. . . . In God there isn't the capacity to say and bruit about evil in His own offense and against His holy sacraments and the things of His church, as you have done and said.[21]

Sánchez could offer nothing further in this direction, so Cortes asked him to explain in particular what it was that he wished to be pardoned for. The wool carder must have been waiting for this question, because he had prepared a lengthy answer. Systematically, he took back every heretical proposition he had ever expressed to Cortes, with one important exception, the assertion that he had been God's messenger and the Elijah-Messiah, which he omitted entirely. He finished by asking again for pardon, telling Cortes, "Don't pay attention to my insults or the stones that I threw at you," and promising to tell him more if he remembered anything else.[22]

Cortes quite graciously invited the wool carder to feel free to request a hearing with him whenever he wished, and Sánchez answered, "I am happy to do it. Because I have a short memory, Your Reverences may know something I've left out; you have only to point it out to me, and I will take it back." Now totally compliant, Sánchez took an oath to swear to tell the truth in the usual way, by the cross, and the transcript of the morning's hearing was read back to him for his approval.

Cortes did not have to wait long to see if Sánchez would volunteer more information. Two days later the wool carder requested an interview with the inquisitor. Sánchez knelt before the altar and, weeping copiously, recited several prayers. He approached the bench, kissed the cross that was on it, and then told Cortes he had spent a miserable night, racked by a cough and aches and pains in his body. He still wanted Cortes to understand that everything that had happened to him was the fault of the vision.

> I lied in everything that I've said in my trial, in saying that I was Elijah and that I brought the word of God, and in the authorities I quoted from SS. John, Matthew, Luke, and Mark. I lied when I said that God ordered me to say it under the guise of that bright thing I've mentioned. It did not tell me, nor did it order me, nor did it say anything, contrary to what I said [before]. Since the time I saw that vision, I was high and agitated, and so with that agitation by the vision, I have said and sustained everything that I've said in this trial.[23]

Asked to clarify what he meant, Sánchez said, "The exaltation was born in me and came from my imagining of the bright thing that I mentioned, because since then I went around looking for Catholic persons, ecclesiastics, friars, abbots, and preachers."[24]

Cortes wasn't going to accept these excuses. First he told Sánchez that the religious persons whom he mentioned having sought out never found him to be possessed. Rather they had suggested to him that he entrust himself to God and arrange for some masses to be said. As for the insanity defense, he told Sánchez,

> The witnesses who deposed in this trial do not consider you to have said the things you did like a man out of his mind [*un honbre enajenado*]. Not even in saying the things in this courtroom has such an alienation appeared, so what I ask you and what you have to do for the discharge of your conscience . . . is that you fully and plainly confess the truth.

Sánchez was at a loss for words. He replied, "God is my witness, there is nothing left in my heart to confess." Cortes could see that Sánchez was not feeling well, so he dismissed the wool carder with hopes for his rapid recovery, and reminded him of his standing offer to hear his confession at any time. Sánchez agreed, but as he went out the door, he could not resist adding, "On account of my imagination and insanity I burned the crosses and I threw the images in my cell out the window."

Over the weekend Cortes's routine was interrupted by a sensational crime. On Sunday, two familiars of the Inquisition murdered a man right on the cathedral steps as he came out from vespers. The two familiars, who were kinsmen, barricaded themselves inside the bell tower and claimed the Inquisition's protection. A large crowd of clerics and townspeople gathered inside the church to see what would happen next. Finally the authorities decided to send for Inquisitor Cortes, who, as the head of Cuenca's tribunal, was responsible for the two familiars. The messengers arrived at his quarters at 8:00 P.M., but by that hour the judge had already retired for the evening and his servants refused to wake him. In the morning Cortes ordered the familiars transferred to the Inquisition's jail, but the lieutenant governor claimed jurisdiction and arrested everyone who got in his way, including Secretary Ybaneta, who had been sent with the commission to transfer the familiars.[25] For the rest of the month, much of Cortes's time was occupied in sorting out the conflicting claims to jurisdiction over the individuals caught up in the case. It was especially important for the Inquisition to stand up for its privileges; part of the court's authority rested on the image of its superior rights. If its officials could be arrested and pushed around by other authorities, the Holy Office's appearance of superiority would be shaken. So inquisitors routinely quarreled with Cuenca's other authorities over any point involving the tribunal's prestige and rights to jurisdiction. Housing, seating in the cathedral, rank order in processions, disciplining of officials, jurisdiction over certain religious crimes . . . the scope of the turf to be defended was endless.

Cortes, who for the second time had just requested permission to retire, must have been sick of it all. The inquisitor had written to the Supreme Council on April 28 that because of his advanced age and infirmities he was now having difficulty carrying out his duties in the courtroom. The Suprema, however, was reluctant to let the valued judge step down from the bench, and, begging poverty, offered him on May 12 a retirement settlement of just half his salary. If it was not enough, they suggested, he could petition the king for a supplement.[26] Fifty thousand maravedís! Many parish priests in Cuenca earned two or three times as much. Cortes probably didn't know whether to laugh or to cry at the offer. But, conscientious man that he was, he kept on working while he intensified his letter campaign to his superiors, and part of this work required him to deal with Sánchez.

The wool carder had taken to heart the inquisitor's invitation to request a hearing whenever he felt ready to confess anything further. On the Monday after the murder, probably oblivious of the inquisitor's various problems, Sánchez sent word that he wished to see the judge. This time Sánchez stood before Cortes and simply wept. He pulled a handkerchief out of some pocket somewhere and began wiping the tears from his eyes.[27]

"Why are you crying?" asked Inquisitor Cortes.

Sánchez recited a litany of reasons.

Because I offended Our Lord God and abandoned His commandments, and because I didn't believe Your Reverences when you told me so many things about it, and other learned sirs when they explained the truth to me. Because what I said was nonsense and craziness, and since I didn't want to believe you, I with my little knowledge and madness told you that I was sent from God and that I dared to say it on His command. Neither God or any other person ever ordered me to say it nor did they tell me anything. It was the imagining and the insanity that I had that made me do it, and Your Reverences, as judges of the case, sentenced me justly for my stubbornness.[28]

Sánchez's tears did not convince Cortes. Without using the precise theological terms, he explained to the wool carder the difference between contrition, in which men feel sorrow, atone for their sins with true repentance, and mend their ways, and self-serving attrition, in which men confess for earthly reasons or out of unhappiness. Sánchez's repentance seemed of the latter type. With some sympathy, he advised Sánchez to dry his tears and focus on contrition. He told Bartolomé:

Separate yourself from that [crying] and throw it away. Serving God with work, He will give you the reward and consolation that you desire.

As much as it is possible, we wish to console you and treat you with the benevolence and works that are permitted to us. So we charge you that since God does not wish more from hearts and betterment of works than this, don't get so upset, because when you do so it diminishes your person and is ill done. I charge you as a sane man to look at and take stock of your soul.

After reminding Sánchez again to take advantage of the opportunity to confess, Cortes returned to the question that was foremost on his mind. "From your manner of speech, talk, and the stubbornness in the things that you've spoken of in this trial, there never appeared or was represented in you any insanity or imaginings [*imaginación*]. On the contrary, one would have presumed that you took [your ideas] from somewhere, or that some person or persons put you up to it." [29] Sánchez in turn once more insisted that no one, human or divine, spoke to him orally or through a book. Instead, because of his imaginings or insanity, he did not know what he was saying, and he asked again for pardon from the Virgin and her Son, and for penance from the inquisitors. Cortes listened without comment and then sent Sánchez back to his cell.

The wool carder spent a few more days in prison, turning Cortes's advice over in his mind. On Friday, May 11, he appeared once more in Cortes's courtroom, this time without any of the histrionics that characterized previous meetings. He announced that he had remembered more things that he wished to recant, and began directly to list them. He kept to his story: on account of his imagination and insanity, he had not known what he was saying at the time. Such was his zeal to recant, he began to list things he had said that he knew were not part of the trial record, but he wanted to do penance for them as well. Cortes explained to him once more the doctrine of contrition, told the wool carder that he did not believe that his confession was genuine, and sent him back to his cell.[30]

Sánchez no longer knew what to do. He requested no further audiences for ten days, until May 21. When Tapia brought him to the courtroom, Cortes asked him what he wanted. Sánchez made a pathetic, rambling appeal to the inquisitor.

The first reason I wanted an audience was to appeal to Your Reverences that by Our Lord God's Passion you see fit to remove me from the solitude, darkness, and captivity in which I am held. Or, if I am not worthy of that, then kill me or do to me what you most want, because to win [forgiveness] I don't have anyone else to plead for me except the Holy Trinity, God's Passion, and the Virgin St. Mary. . . . My wife and children are poor and on account of my sin they should not have a motive to go and steal or do other evil sins.[31]

Thoroughly desperate now to win the inquisitor's forgiveness, Sánchez continued his appeal for mercy by declaring his intention to retract things that he had never been accused of saying, such as that there was a certain seven-headed serpent that swallowed children who were fifteen years old and above, and others it killed but did not eat.[32] And, he remembered, he had said that Lent was the devil's time, for which he now was sorry.

Cortes responded by lecturing Sánchez again on the subject of true contrition. "Recognize your weakness and sins . . . and amend you life with good works and words with which you can recover the credit you lost . . . abhor and flee from illusions and imaginings sent by the devil, and God will give you the constancy of good firmness to do so, and will see fit to pardon you for the past." The inquisitor heard the desperation in Sánchez's plea, and explained to him that they were holding him in prison in order to indoctrinate him and to figure out what was best for his case, but they did have an obligation to do this as rapidly as possible. The best way to help his wife and children would be to take all of this to heart, and confess whatever remained to be said. Sánchez protested that he had nothing left to say. "God knows how burned my heart is and how broken are my insides for having offended Him by breaking His commandments." He concluded by affirming his desire to repent and uphold the Holy Catholic Church.[33]

This time the tribunal was inclined to believe the penitent, and on June 7 it voted to admit Sánchez to reconciliation with the Church. The terms, however, were harsh. They condemned him first to abjure his errors publicly while wearing a sanbenito. The rest of the sentence dictated that he was to wear his sanbenito, the mark of his shame, over his clothes for the rest of his life. He was given the city of Cuenca as his perpetual and irremissible prison. On every Sunday and holy day he was required to attend Mass at the cathedral and listen to the sermon delivered there, and on Saturdays he had to go on a short pilgrimage to Our Lady of the Bridge, just outside the city walls, where he was to pray five times the

Our Father with the Hail Mary, Creed, and Salve Regina. If that were not enough, Sánchez was further ordered to confess and commune three times a year, at Christmas, Easter, and Corpus Christi. Finally, as the law required, he was declared ineligible for all public offices and honors, a punishment that was lost on the destitute wool carder.[34]

The sentence and public reconciliation were carried out the next day on the steps of the cathedral. As had happened at the auto de fe, a summary of Sánchez's crimes and reconciliation was read aloud to the curious crowd, and after a brief meeting with Inquisitor Cortes, whose purpose was to swear Sánchez to secrecy concerning everything that had happened to him inside the Inquisition, the wool carder was released to begin a new life.

7

DÉJÀ VU

1

WE HAVE NO INFORMATION ABOUT BARTOLOMÉ SÁNCHEZ FOR THE next fifteen months. He was released from the secret prisons a pauper and probably first had to beg to support himself. Christian charity was a fine ideal, but Castilians at this time were divided over whether able-bodied men and strangers (as opposed to a city's widows, orphans, and handi-capped) were worthy of their charity.[1] Then again, who would want to give alms to a reconciled heretic whose sanbenito announced his crime to the world? So begging was not easy. Eventually Bartolomé got hold of some cards for working wool, and we can imagine him tramping around the city, plying his trade as best he could. The city's economy was based largely on the manufacture of woolen textiles, and there was work to be had. So let us leave Bartolomé with his cards and combs for the time be-ing, for that is boring work, and follow Licentiate Pedro Cortes.

Late in May 1554, while Cortes was still handling the fallout from the murder on the cathedral steps, the vicar general of the diocese asked the inquisitor to take over a witchcraft case that had come to the ecclesiastical courts. (Witchcraft properly fell under the Inquisition's jurisdiction in

Castile.) The people of Pareja and Sacedón were convinced that Ana la Roa, her sister Mari la Parra, and their deceased mother all were or had been witches (*brujas* or *xorguinas*). According to her neighbors, Ana was a poor widow who took advantage of her evil reputation to frighten them into giving her food. And if they refused? Forty residents of Pareja testified that infants had mysteriously died, apparently smothered to death, shortly after their mothers had been in some dispute with La Roa. Juan Sánchez recounted how one night a dark form had entered his bedchamber, where he and his wife were sleeping with their infant child between them. His wife had fallen into such a deep slumber that he was unable to wake her. As he sat up in bed, the mysterious figure killed the light and tried to snatch away the child. Juan resisted, a fight ensued, and when he woke in the morning he discovered that he was covered with welts and bruises, and he was unable to get out of bed for three days. After examining the evidence, Inquisitor Cortes ruled that although there were many plaintiffs, and without doubt they had suffered, he could not prosecute Ana because no one in fact could swear to having seen her actually commit any of the crimes they attributed to her. Following the Inquisition's rules of evidence and policy, which advised extreme caution in such cases, Cortes refused to try the woman and sent the case back to the diocesan officials, who, as events would show, did not subscribe to the same standards of jurisprudence.[2]

The vicar general, Licentiate Brizeño, quickly yielded to community pressure to have something done about the witches of Pareja. Brizeño invited the public to testify about any incidents of witchcraft in the area, and forty more "witnesses" delivered evidence. Ana and her sister vehemently denied all of the accusations, and when the vicar general decided to torture the women to obtain confessions from them, the sisters' defense lawyer protested in vain that not a single one of the eighty witnesses had testified that they had actually seen Ana or her sister Mari commit any crime. Without the requirement of at least one eyewitness, the lawyer pointed out, the vicar general lacked the legal basis for resorting to torture,[3] but Brizeño forged ahead anyway. The ensuing scenes were a travesty. Whereas the Inquisition's rules of procedure required the judges to decide in advance which method of torture would be used and how severely (the idea being that the information obtained was worth only a

certain amount of torture), Brizeño, in his desperation to obtain a confession, employed in succession three forms of torture on Mari la Parra,
who screamed all the while that she was innocent. When that effort failed,
Mari, whom some witnesses had described as "simple," was tricked into
confessing with promises of freedom. Her jailers told her what to say—
that she and her sister had celebrated secret conventicles with other
women, where they met the devil in the form of a handsome nobleman,
who whisked them off to a distant field. There they applied ointments to
their bodies, feasted, danced, kissed the devil's ass, and copulated with
him. After they had renounced their faith, he forced them to fly to the
homes of their victims and murder the infants in question. Never mind
that the whole story was a page copied right out of some witch hunter's
manual that poor Mari could not even recall correctly (she confused "Sa-
tanás" with "Barrabas"); Mari was allowed to see her sister so that she
too would confess the same story and the vicar general would have his
success. Fortunately for the sisters, eventually the Suprema stepped in
and ordered Cuenca's tribunal of the Inquisition to take the case back. The
court quickly found the sisters innocent of witchcraft but punished them
for their false confessions, which had caused other women to be arrested
as well.[4]

After washing his hands of the supposed witches and finishing with
Sánchez, Inquisitor Cortes took the months of June and July off, most
certainly on account of illness.[5] Don Enrique de la Cueva had returned to
Molina de Aragón soon after the auto de fe on April 29, so that no work
was done in the tribunal during the months while Cortes was ill. Cortes
recovered enough to return to work in late July, but did not embark on
any lengthy trials or important new business. Around that time a letter
from the Supreme Council promised him that he could retire as soon as
Cueva returned to Cuenca.[6] This hope was quickly dashed. Don Enrique,
it turned out, was a corrupt judge who employed a violent young servant,
and the Suprema began to receive complaints and appeals from aggrieved
parties in the towns where he had conducted trials and his servant had
committed crimes. Sometime later in the summer, Cueva was recalled to
Valladolid and placed under arrest, and in December, after an investigation, was stripped of his judgeship in Cuenca and permanently barred
from holding any position in the Holy Office.[7]

While all of this was going on, in November yet another letter from the Suprema brought Pedro Cortes both good news and bad. The good news was that the grand inquisitor, Archbishop Valdés, had approved his request for retirement and granted him a yearly pension of 60,000 maravedis (about 105 ducats). The bad news was that with Cueva's arrest, if Cortes retired immediately, the Inquisition of Cuenca would be left without an inquisitor. Although the Suprema could not order Cortes to remain at work, the council appealed to his conscience to delay his departure until he had trained his newly appointed replacement, Dr. Riego, an untested canon from the cathedral of Sigüenza.[8] Cortes complied, and wound up staying in Cuenca through another winter, working primarily on just two cases, neither as involved as Sánchez's. Sometime after June 1, 1555, Licentiate Cortes died without having enjoyed his well-earned retirement.[9] Bartolomé Sánchez certainly would have heard of Pedro Cortes's death and may even have witnessed his funeral procession, since at the time he was living in the Inquisition's quarters near the cathedral. What he thought at that juncture, though, has not come down to us.

2

Cuenca was a small city, one where it was possible for all the adults to know one another by sight or reputation. Sánchez was known around town for his crime and by his brown cape, sanbenito, hat, and gray hair. Eventually fresh reports about Sánchez's offensive behavior came to the Inquisition in the fall of 1555. A man who lived in the upper story of a house next to one of the city gates related that one afternoon he was leaning out of his window and saw Sánchez come through the gate. Sánchez was probably returning from his required weekly pilgrimage to Our Lady of the Bridge, which was just outside the Puerta de Huete, where the witness lived. According to the witness, the old man, as Sánchez was described, turned around to look at a statue of Our Lady that guarded the city gate. The witness, Juan de las Heras, said that he saw Sánchez remove his bonnet, and, hiding his hand underneath his cape in such a way that only his fingers were visible, make a gesture at the Virgin by placing his thumb between his index and middle fingers. The old man looked around to see if anyone were watching him, and then, emboldened, extended his

11. Our Lady of the Bridge and the Puerta de Huete, Cuenca (1565).
The city wall and gate are the crenallated structure to the right of the
bridge. (Drawing by Anton van den Wyngaerd. Bildarchiv der
Österreichische Nationalbibliothek, Vienna; Cuenca [F], Vienna 2)

arm fully and made the gesture again, this time hiding his hand under his bonnet. Heras did not need to explain the significance of what he claimed to have seen: Sánchez was making the sign of the fig to ward off the evil eye directed at him by the Virgin. If true, it was a most horrific insult to the Mother of God. Scandalized, Heras called his wife over to the window and told her what he had seen. The two of them began to spy on the wool carder, and over the course of several weeks, they said, they saw Sánchez insult the Virgin each time he went through the gate. Then, after a certain amount of time, Sánchez abruptly stopped the behavior, and instead began to go through the gate without doffing his hat or looking at the statue at all. That attitude was nearly as insulting as the first.[10]

By coincidence, Sánchez happened to work for a couple who lived on a lower floor of the house where Juan de las Heras and his wife lived. Around this time, he stopped by to claim his payment of one real for some worsted he had combed, and his employers found him to be a very Christian man. But as soon as he left, the upstairs neighbors, who had observed Sánchez enter the house, rushed down to tell them the truth, and turned the couple against the wool carder. Juan de las Heras and his wife were not content with that, however. They spread the story around to their friends and finally denounced Sánchez to a minor official in the Inquisition, who relayed the information to the new inquisitors. They were too busy reviving the moribund tribunal to pay much attention to such petty stuff. They told the witnesses to come back later to give their depositions, and forgot about the story. When Sánchez was asked months later about the whole episode, he explained that he had heard that people were saying that he was giving the fig to the Virgin, and to avoid accusations, he had stopped removing his hat or even looking at the statue when he went through the city gate, even though he knew he would be criticized for not showing the Virgin proper respect.[11]

As Lent approached in 1556, Sánchez began to chafe under the weight of his penance and the vow of secrecy, which prevented him from talking about what had happened to him while he had been held in prison by the Inquisition. One day during Carnival, Sánchez was at a tavern in the hamlet of Palomera, six miles outside of Cuenca. No doubt everyone had been drinking heavily, and as Carnival was a time for criticizing the high and mighty, Sánchez got drawn into the spirit of the holidays. He began to brag that no one had said worse things about the friars and abbots than he had while he had been a prisoner in the Inquisition. And then he repeated, virtually word for word, all the evil things about priests he had said to Licentiate Cortes just over two years before.[12]

Nothing came of the conversation at the time, and Sánchez later confessed during Easter with Mateo Sánchez in the cathedral, and reconfirmed his penance. But as he took communion, something snapped inside him. As he explained about a week later to the inquisitors,

> After I took communion, I was seized by such torment and unhappiness that I was beside myself. With that misery I spent the days of Easter thinking and looking at what was going to become of me and what could that [unhappiness] be. In my misery I decided I would go with my combs to the village of Villar de Saz de Arcas to see if I could find work there because a young man had told me that there could be work in the village once the holidays were over.
>
> So the last day of Easter in the morning I got up, picked up my combs, and left for the village. Once I was outside of the city and got to the road that turns off to Arcas, which is one-eighth of a league away, I was overcome by another thought and more anguish. I would not go to the village of Villar de Saz; instead I would go home to my village of Cardenete. And then another thought came to me while I was standing there, that once I got to Cardenete I would burn my penitential habit in the village plaza. So, with this thought and fighting with myself, saying to myself that if I did it even the children would stone me because I was going against the inquisitors' orders, I decided to go. I arrived in Cardenete on Wednesday afternoon and I went straight to my house, and I stayed in it that night with my wife and children. Thursday morning my wife told me to go turn the earth in a garden plot that belonged to her, because it had not been dug the entire time I was in Cuenca, and that she would bring my lunch there.
>
> So I took my mattock and I went there by myself, and my wife and children came for lunch and some women came to visit me as well. When I finished digging the garden, I left for home, where my wife and children had already arrived. When I got to the house, my wife told me that the stew wasn't ready yet and I should wait a little while to eat. I waited and we ate late.[13] After dinner, I took my cape with my habit on top as I used to wear it, and I left the village by the road to Cuenca. There, with the anguish and unhappiness that I felt, the thought

returned to me that I would take some kindling by the road and go back to the village and burn my habit in the plaza. Struggling with myself and seeing the evil I wanted to do, conjecturing with myself which was the worse sin, to burn a bit of cloth or a Christian, and fighting with myself that that wasn't cloth but penance and it was disobedience and went against Their Reverences' orders, and not being able to overcome this thought and the unhappiness I had, I picked up by the road some vine cuttings from some vineyards and some rosemary from underneath an elderberry.

I went straight to the plaza, where I took out from my purse my flint and tinder, which I always carry with me, and I lit a flame with it. When the cuttings and rosemary started to burn, I took off my penitential habit from my shoulders and I threw it in the fire, and stood aside. At this point there arrived a neighbor who is called Madrid (I think he's a weaver and he lives off gambling) and Madrid took the habit out of the fire and he handed it over to me, saying to me, "Oh, evil man, what have you done? The aldermen will arrest you!" I said to him, "Don't you play the inquisitor," or "Let no one make himself into the inquisitor since you aren't," and I threw the habit back into the fire so it would burn. That done, I went by a street up by the fortress and then I went home.[14]

Several men besides Madrid had witnessed Sánchez's act of defiance, and they ran for the alderman to arrest the wool carder. They put him in chains and shackles and took him prisoner to the alderman's house. While he was there, a group of men gathered out of curiosity to see the heretic and talk about what he had said in the past. One of them said to Sánchez, "What, you don't believe in the cross?" Sánchez had to respond to this challenge, so he told the man, "Neither a stick nor a piece of iron is going to save me; only God will, who was crucified, and I have to believe and worship Him, and not some stick or iron. You go embrace a stick or some iron made into a cross and I'll embrace God, and we'll see who gets saved the best." The others protested that those things were images that they had to worship, and Sánchez retorted, "God did not make a stick or piece of iron in His image, but man, and for that reason man ought to be honored; a stick or piece of iron, whatever way it is made into a cross or crucifix, is just a stick or piece of iron." The men continued to argue with Sánchez, so he asked them, "If someone killed your father or mother with a sword or stick, would you hold and worship as a relic that weapon which was used for the murder?" One of the men replied, "Surely not," but one of the others remained doubtful and didn't answer. Sánchez pressed home his point.

> Now, you've confessed to me that you would not hold as a relic or worship the sword or stick with which your father or brother was murdered. Now suppose someone says to you some words that bother you. You tell him, "Don't say that to me or else I'll start an argument with you," but that person starts to say it again to injure and anger you more. For his revenge the injured person takes some weapons and kills the other with them. Well, in just this way the Son of God talked and preached to those visible devils, giving them the faith with which they would save themselves. Which would be better, [the law] that he gave them or the one they had? (The visible devils I hold are those who crucified Christ.) The visible devils answered Christ, arguing with Him, "We don't want to believe what you tell us, or for you to believe it either." God said to them, "Bow down to me and follow me because I come to save you," but they didn't want to humble themselves or believe Him. They made a cross to defend themselves from those words and doctrine that Christ gave them, and they crucified Him on it; with that cross and on that cross they killed Him, and so with just truth one can say that the cross is the devil's weapon.[15]

The village authorities took steps to rid themselves of Sánchez as quickly as possible. On Friday, several witnesses were rounded up and deposed, and on that same day Bachiller Barca sent Sánchez, the testimony, and a cover letter to the inquisitors in Cuenca. No material evidence could be sent because not a scrap of the sanbenito had survived Sánchez's personal auto de fe. Barca sold Sánchez's cape for eighteen and a half reals to pay for his transport and the notary's fee, and sent what was left over to Cuenca to be used by the court for its expenses. Sánchez was delivered in Cuenca the very next day, Saturday, April 11.[16]

3

A few days later, the inquisitors Dr. Diego García del Riego and Licentiate Miguel del Moral, with Juan de Ybaneta acting as secretary, called for their new prisoner. Sánchez did not posture as he had done in the past, and readily took an oath on the courtroom cross to tell the truth. Upon questioning, he explained how he had been arrested for burning his habit and brought to Cuenca a few days before. When asked why he had burned his sanbenito, Sánchez explained how he had felt unhappy during Easter and told the inquisitors the lengthy story of his escape. Halfway through his account, Bartolomé said he felt faint with a headache, and asked permission to continue his confession later. The inquisitors adjourned the hearing until the next morning, when Sánchez continued the story, embellishing it in his usual way with many details and snatches of conversation. He also told them how he broke his vow of secrecy during Carnival and had spoken against the clergy.

Riego and Moral had read Sánchez's dossier, and when Sánchez concluded, they asked him the obvious question: Had his conversion in 1554 been sincere? Sánchez replied:

> Although I had been instructed and indoctrinated by Dr. Vergara and Their Reverences and reconciled for these propositions and the others that I maintained before the inquisitors, after I left these prisons, from that moment to the present I have always believed for myself that the cross is the devil's weapon . . . and concerning the propositions about the clergy, I also have held and believed [them] since I left the prisons. Since I left the prisons I have not once revered a cross in my heart or will; I only revere God Who is in heaven and crucified and Who will save me, because sticks and pieces of iron, although they are made into crosses and crucifixes, will not save me.[17]

The hour had turned late, so Riego and Moral lifted the hearing despite the fact that Bartolomé told them that he had more to say. They did not return to their prisoner until a week later, April 22. When brought to the courtroom, Sánchez began to explain to the inquisitors an entirely new theory of his, which he had not completely worked out in his mind.

> I believe that when God made Adam and He gave him Eve as his companion, He took her from [Adam's] body out of his side when He could have just as easily given her to him out of some other material, such as from a pine tree or pin oak. But He gave her to him out of [Adam's] own body, which meant that she came out of his body as both his daughter and sister, because both were and are the children of God. [God] gave

this daughter and sister to [Adam] for his wife, and this is the law that God made and ordered, that brother should marry sister, and father with daughter. The Church does not uphold God's law; rather it prohibits it from being obeyed, and it is true that God confirmed this law [against incest].

Sánchez was having difficulty explaining his thoughts, and stopped to correct himself. Ybaneta wrote it all down as it come out, a confusing history of how Cain killed Abel and God took back the law, but then He reinstated it, back and forth until He finally reconfirmed the original law endorsing incest when He caused His Son to be conceived in His daughter, the Virgin Mary. Sánchez concluded by accusing the Church of not upholding God's law to allow incest.[18]

Having got that off his chest, Sánchez continued on to more familiar ground, the subject of the Jews, who, as before, he maintained were unjustly killed by the Inquisition for believing that the Messiah had yet to come. Inquisitors Riego and Moral listened without interruption, and when Sánchez was finished, they asked him why he was going back to his original propositions, and who was putting him up to it.

Sánchez replied, "I am the Son of Man and Elijah, and God orders me to say it, because those who govern the Church are in error."[19] Could it be possible that nothing had changed; that for two years Sánchez secretly had nursed his belief that he was the Elijah-Messiah? It was more than possible—if anything, his belief had become even more grandiose, since Sánchez now dared to appropriate for himself the messianic term used to refer to Christ.

Like Cortes before them, Riego and Moral at first took a moderate course when confronted with such an implausible claim. Ignoring the first half of Sánchez's statement, that he was the Son of Man, they tried to reason with him. "We want to know from you and understand, so that we can give you credit that God ordered you to say the things you've said in this trial, how you can be Elijah, since you know and it's common knowledge that it has been many years since Elijah came to the world." Sánchez replied that he wasn't believed before and they did not have to believe him either.

Riego and Moral moved on to the central question, Sánchez's relapse into heresy.

You already know that during the time of your first imprisonment concerning these propositions and errors, you were released to the secular arm of justice as a heretic and person who fell outside the brotherhood of the Church. Thinking that you converted with a pure and truthful heart, [the inquisitors] ordered you returned to these jails [and reconciled]. Now we see in you the same errors and other ones. We want you to declare if you faked your conversion and if at present you continue in the same errors and with the same belief, and why, in detriment to your soul and conscience, did you deceitfully wish to be reconciled?

The answer was simple. Sánchez replied:

I said what everybody wanted and I carried out their wish in doing what they asked because they were going to burn me. I always believed what I said in my trial, and if I was reconciled for those propositions it was also faked because they had me in prison and they were going to kill me and burn me. Right now I am of the same opinion and belief concerning those propositions that I said in my first trial, as I have stated them now in my second imprisonment.[20]

As for disseminating his beliefs, Sánchez affirmed that he had spoken of them a few times while he was working, but he had no particular memory of doing so. The inquisitors warned him for the love of God to look carefully at what he was saying and to repent so that they could treat him with clemency, but Sánchez, back to his old defiant ways, refused the advice because he believed that God would save him.

Another week went by before Riego and Moral called for Sánchez again. On April 30 the wool carder surprised them by announcing that for the past four years the devil had walked with him, and he retracted everything. "Crying and shedding many tears," Sánchez now claimed that he had said the things he had said without realizing what he was saying and without anyone teaching him. But while he was in prison, his cellmate had talked to him and made him see God and the light of day. On and on he went, blubbering and stammering that the devil had made him do it, he was not responsible for his actions, and he wanted to repent and return to the Holy Catholic Church.[21]

It was a remarkable performance and about-face. Who was this cellmate who had wrought such a miraculous change of heart in Sánchez? Not even Vergara had achieved as much. Alonso Sánchez was a public notary from the town of Minaya in La Mancha. He was in prison on charges of bigamy, which had recently been placed under the Inquisition's jurisdiction.[22] Public notaries in Castile were men of considerable legal training, and Alonso clearly had spent the week giving Bartolomé some free legal advice and coaching. First, he probably explained to Bartolomé the mortal danger he faced. If he were convicted of heresy a second time, there could be no question of reconciliation; the penalty for relapsed heretics was death, and Bartolomé Sánchez did not want to die. Next, he considered a defense strategy for the wool carder. An insanity plea would not work because in his first trial Sánchez had been found to be sane. Blaming his mistakes on the vision wouldn't work either, since Cortes had never really accepted that explanation. What other excuse could Bartolomé offer that would shift the blame from him to someone else? Bartolomé had always maintained that no one had taught him; to claim now that someone had indeed taught him would lead to a perjury charge. No, the ideal defense would be to claim that the devil had made Sánchez do it all; it was all the devil's fault.

Sánchez was a fairly good student. In his confession on April 30, he never once mentioned the original vision or even his imagination, the two excuses he had offered interchangeably in his first trial when he was trying to convince Cortes that he was not responsible for his beliefs. When Riego and Moral asked Sánchez directly if he had experienced any bad visions or if he had been ill since he was reconciled, in a rambling answer the wool carder emphasized his personal unhappiness but finally worked the devil into his excuses at the end of his statement.

Since I was reconciled, no visions from the devil have appeared to me nor was I instructed in these errors by anyone. Nor have I been sick since I was reconciled with any illness that would make me lose my mind. Since I got out with my [sanbenito] I have been very unhappy because when my own wife and brother saw me in it, they ran away from me and they didn't want to see me in Cardenete. So I haven't had a greater executioner than my wife, who didn't want to see or hear me because they told her how I was against everything that everyone held and believed. I don't know what other reason to give other than the said unhappiness or that the devil got inside of me.[23]

The inquisitors did not remark on the flimsiness of this explanation. Sán-chez had already confessed to them at length that he had been unhappy *before* he went back to Cardenete; his wife may not have been pleased to see him, but her disapproval was not the cause of his troubles. Instead, they asked how returning to his heresies could be a solution to his prob-lems. Sánchez didn't know; the devil had blinded him. Riego and Moral asked Sánchez if he now felt free of the devil's influence, or if he said what he did out of fear of punishment.

"Certainly at present I feel free of the devil's power, and I say what I do in good faith and good motives, and not out of any fear. God has come into me, and I believe firmly in what the Holy Catholic Church believes, and no one has made me say it."[24] When questioned, he also denied that anyone had put him up to burning his sanbenito; he had done that also on account of his unhappiness.

The inquisitors did not find Sánchez's performance very convincing, yet they too had fallen under the spell of this odd peasant. They ended the hearing by giving Bartolomé a heartfelt lecture. Referring to Cortes and Cueva, they began:

> Now, you see the love with which your person has always been treated by Their Reverences. We have the same wish to treat you with com-plete love and charity. Thus we warn and charge you that you entrust yourself to God and Our Lady with your whole heart, and to the Holy Spirit so that it will always guide your understanding so that you will not let yourself be conquered by the devil. You know that he does not take possession of anyone except those persons whom he finds lacking in faith. Run through your memory so that if you have offended God in something, you confess it and we can give you the remedy and con-solation that are necessary for the salvation of your soul. Always be-lieve and hold firmly everything that the Holy Mother Church of Rome holds and teaches.[25]

Sánchez promised to take the inquisitors' advice and warnings to heart, and still in tears he was returned to his prison.

Riego and Moral were in no hurry to try Sánchez's case; they let an-other three weeks pass before they called for the wool carder again. This strategy often was used to give recalcitrant heretics a chance to reflect on their sins, but if this were the inquisitors' intention, it backfired. When Sánchez arrived in the courtroom and they asked him if he had remembered anything else he should confess, Sánchez told them that he deliberately had put the whole case out of his mind. He didn't want to be reminded of what he had done since the devil had been chasing after him.

The inquisitors tried a different tack. They told Sánchez that in order to understand his case thoroughly, they needed to know if, when he believed in his errors, he was in possession of his wits and free will like any other man. Sánchez began to explain how he had been under the influence of his "errors" for four years until his cellmate, Alonso Sánchez, had made him understand his situation and the Holy Spirit enlightened him. When he realized how mistaken he had been, he was too ashamed to call the jailer himself, and asked Alonso to do it. He played the scene for what it was worth. Sobbing, he told the court:

> Throughout those four years when I found myself free of those anxieties, imaginings, and persuasions, I would fight with myself, saying, "God help me, how do I believe this? It goes against what I and my parents always believed before and is against the doctrine given by the Holy Mother Church." During the times when I was free of the said anxieties and temptations, I well understood that what I had said was contrary to what the Church held, and then, when those temptations came to me, I would say everything that I said above about my errors. . . . I don't know who made me say it because nobody taught me nor did I hear it from someone, nor did I read it. Instead it seems to me that it all came [out of nowhere?] to my mouth to say it like I have. I also remember that during the times when I was more or less free [of those temptations], I would fight with myself and I would get down on my knees to beg to God to enlighten me as to what was in His holy service. I would say to myself, "God help me, I'm crazy. Who is making me say this?" [26]

Sánchez's confession had made the hour late, and the inquisitors decided to leave it at that. At any rate, they seem to have heard enough, because the next time they met, it was to vote on how to handle Sánchez's trial. On June 6, Riego and Moral met with other members of the tribunal, the vicar general of Cuenca and two canons from the cathedral, one

of whom was Dr. Vergara. The question of Sánchez's sanity began to loom
in the forefront of their deliberations. Having seen enough of him in
several hearings to assess his state of mind and competence, they unanimously concluded that at the present time they were not convinced that
the defendant was sufficiently in possession of his understanding and free
will to be responsible for the crimes of which he was accused. Therefore,
they did not dare to use with him the full weight of the law. They decided,
as had an earlier tribunal, to see how things would develop. They would
go through with the trial, but stay the verdict and sentence until they had
a better understanding of Sánchez's mental condition. As for breaking his
prison sentence and burning the sanbenito, the tribunal had no doubt that
Sánchez was responsible for those crimes, and condemned him to a public scourging.[27]

A second trial for heresy! Strangely, Sánchez did not fight it. The peasant's former fire and defiant ways had disappeared. When the prosecutor,
Bachiller Serrano, presented him with the indictment, Sánchez had nothing to say except that it was all true, he was sorry he had been deceived,
and he hoped that God would pardon him.[28] The court gave him the choice
of three defense lawyers, and although Sánchez remarked, crying, that
God was his lawyer, without further theatrics he picked Dr. Muñoz and
accepted a copy of the indictment so they could prepare a defense.

On June 15, Sánchez returned with his lawyer to begin his defense.
Dr. Muñoz adopted the same strategy as had the notary Alonso Sánchez:
not to deny anything, but to shift the blame to the devil. Because Muñoz
was university educated, he added some legalistic and scholastic subtleties
to the description of Sánchez's loss of self-control. In a written statement
prepared by Muñoz, Sánchez asserted that his relapse into heresy was not
premeditated or voluntary, the conditions necessary for a finding of cul-
pability. Further, as soon as he realized what he had done, he had repudiated it and returned to the faith.

> It never was my deliberate intention to consent to those said crimes and
> errors, or to leave the Holy Catholic faith and evangelical law, because
> the things I have committed and have confessed to, I committed and
> said them while I was out my mind and natural reason on account of di-
> abolical imagining, fantasy, and illusion. When it ceased and I returned

to my full wits and remembered them, I was pained, and I repented and retracted [them], recognizing my error, returning to and affirming Our Holy Catholic faith.

With this statement, Muñoz was building a defense for Sánchez based on the concept of temporary insanity, which the law allowed.[29] Next the lawyer, still writing for Sánchez, gave the standard medico-theological explanation for how the devil was capable of causing temporary insanity.

The devil, who is so subtle, goes through the air and offends our bodies and goods. With God's permission, on account of our sins, through every means possible he harms and tempts a man's faculty of the imagination [potentia imaginativa], impressing upon it various imaginings to make him sin because [the devil] is the doer of evil. And thus, by his suggestion or inducement he has oppressed me through my imagination and harmed me in such a way that he took me right out of my mind.

The prosecution responded ten days later with a demand to hold a second inquiry into the defendant's mental condition. Bachiller Serrano's intention was to prove that Sánchez was sane and thus responsible for his crimes. Witnesses were to be asked if they considered Sánchez to be sane, without any sign of insanity or madness; if they had seen him work and support himself and deal with other people like a reasonable man; if they had seen him ask and answer questions like any sane person; if they had ever heard him rant[30] about anything other than his heresies; and if other people considered him to be sane. A second series of questions asked particularly if the witnesses had seen Sánchez behave like a sane and Christian man in the time since he was reconciled, without exhibiting any signs of madness or rantings that might appear to be due to lack of sanity; and a final question asked if the witnesses knew that it was common knowledge that Sánchez was a sane man.[31]

The testimony of the first witness, Sánchez's own confessor, was particularly damning. He remembered that during the time of the first trial, when the inquisitors had assigned him to confess Sánchez, the wool carder

did not want to confess or kneel; instead he said that he would confess only to God, and he said all of this with a lot of pride and vehemence but I didn't think that he might be crazy; instead [I thought] that he was in his right mind like any other man . . . and after they took him to be burned and he converted to the faith of Jesus Christ, which was more than two years ago in April of 1554, this witness . . . has always found Sánchez to be in his right mind, during confession as well as outside of it, and I never saw or understood from him that he might be out of his mind.[32]

The priest repeated several times that Sánchez had behaved since his reconciliation in a most Christian manner, confessing frequently, going to Mass and sermons, and working at his trade.

The next witness, Juan de Gaviria, one of the tribunal's two secretaries, had been living in private quarters set up in the secret prisons, which were nearly empty at the time, and knew Sánchez as a neighbor. He had employed him to card some wool, and found Sánchez in all of his dealings to be rational, straightforward, in his right mind and understanding. He had seen him get up at dawn to go to work, and had observed him going to Mass and listening to sermons like a good Christian.[33] Gaviria's wife was also called to testify, and confirmed her husband's report, but did mention that she had heard from a neighbor that sometimes Sánchez did not seem to speak in a very orderly fashion.[34]

The remaining two witnesses, Diego de Tapia and Juan Gómez, had nothing to add to their original depositions of two years before. All five witnesses were in conformity: Sánchez was sane and had behaved like a Christian man for two years. Thus Riego and Moral were left in the same quandary as Cortes before them: they doubted Sánchez's sanity, but no one else did.

At the same time that Sánchez's sanity hearing was being conducted, Riego and Moral cleared up the business of the obscene gestures that witnesses claimed to have seen the wool carder make to the Virgin. Sánchez denied the charges and argued, again with the help of his lawyer, that it didn't make sense that he would confess to far more serious things and deny this. He also pointed out that the instigator of the charges seemed to have fabricated the story, and then, to give it more credibility, spread it around to others. Riego and Moral were inclined to believe him, and dismissed the charges. Finally, on July 15, the court issued its decision. The intervening month had not served to change the judges' opinion about

Sánchez: they were still as perplexed as before. For breaking his prison
sentence, Sánchez was condemned to one hundred lashes to be adminis-
tered while he was paraded through the city streets seated backward on a
donkey. As for the relapse into heresy, the inquisitors reserved judgment
until they understood more perfectly the state of the defendant's mental
health.[35]

4

After his second scrape with the Holy Office's justice, Sánchez once again
kept out of trouble—for a while. When a year had passed, he petitioned
the judges to allow him to work during the harvest season outside the city
of Cuenca, returning occasionally to hear High Mass and sermons as he
was ordered. The inquisitors granted the petition, which raised the ire of
the prosecutor, Serrano. He pointed out that the judges had suspended
sentencing pending further information on Sánchez's mental health. A
year had passed and they had seen no evidence of insanity, yet the man
was allowed to come and go freely without punishment for his crimes.
Serrano demanded that the tribunal either find Sánchez guilty or let him
go. Riego and Moral responded that they would pass judgment when they
were ready, an answer that further incensed the prosecutor. Taking matters into his own hands, Serrano appealed the case to the Suprema. In
their own defense, Riego and Moral wrote to the Suprema explaining that
they had far more contact with the defendant than did Serrano, and thus
knew him much better. On the basis of that knowledge, they were extremely reluctant to try Sánchez as a sane man.[36] To support their position, they asked the secretary, Juan de Ybaneta, who had worked on the
trial since its beginning, to submit a statement giving his opinion of Sánchez's case. Such a request was highly unusual, but Ybaneta complied and
wrote the following

> Report by the Secretary on What He Feels about This Defendant.
> I, Juan de Ybaneta, royal secretary and notary in the Inquisition of
> Cuenca, mindful that the trial of the said Bartolomé Sánchez is to be
> sent to the members of His Majesty's Council of the General Inquisi-
> tion and that many of the hearings that the Lord Inquisitor Licentiate
> Pedro Cortes (may he rest in Glory) held with the defendant took place

before me, so that Your Lordships, better informed, may administer justice and so that I may discharge my conscience and any scruple that could form if I were not to make this report before Your Lordships, just as I have to the Lords Inquisitors who at present reside at this Holy Office, with their permission I say and declare the following.

The said Lord Inquisitor Cortes, having received word of the things that this Bartolomé Sánchez did and said, gave the commission [to take depositions] which is at the beginning of this trial.[37] Once the information was received and the defendant was brought as a prisoner to this Holy Office, in the very first hearing that was held with him, he entered the courtroom like a madman or someone possessed, striking many poses with his person and talking a lot of nonsense. Calmed down a bit by the Lord Inquisitor and asked for the account of his life and the origin of the errors he spoke of, he began to go on with his follies. Among the things he recounted, I remember that he said that he had seen a celestial vision in a pasture, and that he was terrified by this and even fainted. After this vision, while he was tied up in his own house there appeared to him something like cats out of the night [gatos de noche; also a colloquialism for thieves] and they gave him the most extreme anguish and left him tormented and spiritless. He freed himself and began to talk and say the things he said because God ordered him to. Mindful of his insanities and the things he said, since in this defendant there was not to be found enough competence or reason requisite for such a serious affair, I asked the Lord Inquisitor to put off the prosecution of this case until we could see and understand more completely if he were possessed or had lost his mind. The Lord Inquisitor answered me that later on everything could be decided and so he went on holding hearings with [Sánchez], taking down in them those of his words which formed the core of his propositions, and going along organizing them without removing or adding anything in their substance. Many of the things that he said were left out because they were nonsense and more nonsense. From what I could understand of this defendant, I always held him to be possessed or insane, and that he did not have control over what he said, and I said so to the consultors and the bishop's ordinary [Dr. Vergara]. They talked and communicated with him in a few sessions and were left with considerable doubt about his reason. Since he said in those [sessions] that although they were to throw him into the fire, the fire would not hurt him, and if it did burn him he would take back everything he had said, they agreed to vote on this trial in the way that they did. I heard Dr. Vergara, who was the ordinary of the city and who at present is in the city, say that if he had not been convinced that when this defendant got to the [Campo de San Francisco] he would return to God and retract his craziness, there was no way that he would have voted the way he did, because he was convinced that [Sánchez] had some demon or was crazy. Even at present this defendant goes around the city like a man possessed and out of his mind, begging for God's sake and working on a few things. After he was reconciled, I heard him say in this courtroom that he did not know what was wrong with him and that he was so tormented that he would throw himself off the city bridge into the river. They asked Dr. Vergara to treat him and to take away those imaginings, and Dr. Vergara took it over and worked very hard on it. And because this is the truth I signed it with my name, today, Wednesday, July 14, 1557.[38]

According to Ybaneta, from the very beginning Sánchez's first trial had been a sham. Ybaneta, who officially was not supposed to intervene in the cases he recorded, had persuaded Cortes to adopt a "wait and see" attitude toward the trial. Cortes, who already had his own suspicions regarding Sánchez's sanity, had never wanted to try the wool carder, and was just waiting for the evidence he needed to suspend the case. He had stretched out the hearings, made a note of whatever Sánchez said of a theological nature that made sense and was indictable, and left out the rest. Whatever those rantings and behavior were, they were suppressed, so that the trial transcript paints only half a portrait of Sánchez, one that shows a man with considerable skill in debate and no sign of irrational thought other than the belief that he was a second messiah. On paper, everything pointed to Sánchez's guilt, but Cortes and the others could not bring themselves to convict. Indicative of the difficulty of the case, at the end of Ybaneta's report, another hand has written: "Gaviria says the opposite in his statement" (now lost). Later in August, the Suprema sent back its verdict: they upheld Riego and Moral's decision of June 6, 1556.[39] Serrano (who later would be censured by the Suprema for being "hotheaded") we might imagine was infuriated by his inability to bring Sánchez to justice.

Bartolomé received his permission to leave Cuenca and headed home to Cardenete. He spent the summer working and minding his own busi-

ness, and in September, according to the inquisitors' orders, returned to
Cuenca with a letter from one of the clerics in Cardenete. Juan de Gallego
reported that Sánchez had behaved well, attended sermons and Masses,
acted like a Christian, and wore his sanbenito wherever he went. At his
interview, Sánchez asked the inquisitors to give him permission to live
out his sentence in Cardenete, for he would surely die of hunger in
Cuenca. Riego and Moral replied that they wished to see him consoled
and would take the matter under consideration. They eventually gave
Sánchez leave to live in Cardenete for six months, from October 1557 to
March 1558.[40]

Sánchez's original descent into heresy and subsequent outbursts had
all occurred during the Lenten season. It was as if the annual season of
penance and intense preaching pushed the wool carder over the edge, and
ideas that had lain dormant would burst forth once again. On March 21,
1558, Dr. Vergara showed up at Riego and Moral's afternoon session and
handed them a letter that Licentiate Jiménez, the assistant priest in Cardenete, had written to him three days before. The letter read:

> Here there is a man who has been punished by the Holy Office and
> wears a sanbenito, and I certify to you that he is an evil man, because
> one day this week I went to correct him for his outbursts and heresies,
> and he said even worse ones in front of me. He denies the sacrament of
> the Eucharist; he says that Christ is in the River of Stones; he winks and
> laughs when the word of God is preached; he doesn't want the kiss of
> peace; he never goes to Mass during the week; the houses that he visits
> he scandalizes with his words; he told me that Christ did not come
> to save the world but to condemn it, and so many other things that I
> promise you that I cannot bear it. . . . If this man is crazy or possessed
> one wouldn't know it because I cannot fathom or understand the things
> he does.

Jiménez concluded by begging Vergara to arrange for some solution because he no longer knew what to do.[41]

Jiménez's letter only touched the surface of the difficulties he and the
village were having with Sánchez, who in the fifth year of his troubles had
turned belligerent. Sánchez had begun to bait Licentiate Jiménez during
Mass by saying in a loud voice *"que se seque el evangelio"* ("let the Gospel
dry up") when the priest said *"sequencia sancti evangelio."* He quarreled

with his wife for wanting to confess with Jiménez and finally snapped at her, "Then go confess with the devil, at the synagogue and temple of the Jews, since the church is the devil's vine!" When Jiménez came to his house to see him, Sánchez told him to get out because on account of priests the whole world was condemned to death. The two men began quarreling over whether Sánchez would confess with the priest, and finally Jiménez asked him if he believed in the sacrament of the Eucharist. Sánchez replied he didn't have to tell him that because it was already written down in the Inquisition, and then accused Jiménez and the other priests of not understanding the Gospels. Sánchez quoted the line from St. Matthew that prophesied the arrival of the ruler from Bethlehem and challenged Jiménez to tell him who and where the promised ruler was. When Jiménez refused, Bartolomé declared triumphantly, "If I say this and where he is, then you don't know it or understand it!" With a little goading, Sánchez announced that the promised ruler was to be found in the River of Stones, but he wouldn't say where that was.

Sánchez's quarrels were not limited to the priest Jiménez. After he mocked the priest publicly in church, he went to watch some gambling in progress at Juan Martínez's house. Word of the scandal traveled fast, and the gamblers asked him why he had said those things in church. Sánchez replied they were well said. The men began to berate and threaten him, saying that if he didn't learn better, they would shave off his beard. Like Christ, Sánchez dared the group, "Whoever is without sin, let him cast the first stone," and with that, Juan Martínez and his brother pushed and shoved Sánchez out the door.

A few days later, Bartolomé had a second run-in with Juan Martínez, this time in the main square. Sánchez taunted him with being a heretic, and Juan and his brother told him again that he deserved to be stoned and have his beard cut off. Sánchez replied once more, "*Noli me tangere*, whoever is without sin, let him cast the first stone!"

Word of this public dispute got back to the town's alderman, and on Palm Sunday he and two other men took Sánchez outside the village (where no one could overhear them) and asked him what the quarrel was all about. Bartolomé answered, "I am a man who, like Christ, because of preaching the truth, doesn't fit in with other people until they kill me." As Bartolomé became more agitated, the truth came tumbling out. He wasn't just like Christ; he *was* the Saviour. He exclaimed, "I have come to burn the Church of Rome and to confound it. I am the one who I say I am—look at me!" [42]

No wonder the village and Licentiate Jiménez were at their wits' end. As soon as Riego and Moral read the letter, they ordered Sánchez's arrest. A full month later, they received a second, apologetic letter from Jiménez. When he had received the order to arrest Sánchez, he went to his house to ask for him, but Sánchez had already disappeared. Jiménez wrote, "His wife told me that the second day of Easter, before dawn, he left and she doesn't know where to because he never confided in her a thing, but many times she heard him say that he had to go to the River of Stones and the Curdled Place [*a la cuaxada*] and many other crazy things." Jiménez was worried that Sánchez might have spread his ideas to some people of little understanding, so he had spent the entire Lenten season preaching against Sánchez's ideas. He thought he had managed to prevent anyone from being touched by the heresies. [43] Jiménez promised he would continue to watch over the parish and would arrest Sánchez as soon as he turned up again.

About eight weeks after his mysterious disappearance, Sánchez appeared in Cardenete on a Saturday night in June. Jiménez lost no time in arresting him as soon as word of the wool carder's arrival reached him. Sánchez was sent to Cuenca by horseback on Sunday, June 5, and was delivered to the inquisitors the next day, having covered the distance of thirty-six miles in less than twenty-four hours.

Two days later, Riego and Moral sat down again to deal with Bartolomé Sánchez. Under the circumstances, their patience was remarkable. To test his mental condition, they asked the wool carder who had arrested him and brought him to Cuenca, and why he had been arrested. They also wanted to know what faith he really believed and lived by, and the whole story of what happened since the last time he left the Holy Office. Bartolomé was able to answer all of the questions about his arrest with great precision, and gave a detailed account of the events in the village that led up to his disappearance. That took up the entire hearing, but rather than reschedule Sánchez to continue his confession the next morning, Riego and Moral forgot about him. Finally, two weeks later Sánchez asked for a hearing. Inquisitor Moral, who was alone in court that day, asked him what he wanted. Bartolomé said abruptly, "Have what I said in the last hearing read back to me, or the last part of it, so that I can start where I left off in the last hearing and tell you the remainder of what I have to say."[44] The inquisitor complied, and having heard the transcript, Sánchez picked up the thread of his story.

> On the second day of Easter I left Cardenete on a pilgrimage to Our Lady of Guadalupe [200 miles away in Extremadura]. When I left Cardenete for Guadalupe, it was with the intention that wherever I went, God would free me of all the bad things and all the bad stones and adversities that I would run into. (The bad stones are the people who are in mortal sin or who put themselves in mortal sin.) So I went to Guadalupe begging on the road for the love of God. I was in the town of Guadalupe for one day and I didn't talk about a single thing in the town or the monastery except to beg for some shoes for the love of God. They gave them to me and I turned back to Cardenete, and coming and going I did not say a word of what I have in my heart. When I arrived in Cardenete they arrested me and sent me to this Holy Office.

Licentiate Moral asked Sánchez if he had anything else to say, and he most certainly did. He declared that the church was the synagogue of the Jews and, twisting the concept of asylum, he said that churches were not the temples of God but hiding places for evildoers, because if someone commits a crime, he can go to a church and they protect him. Sánchez concluded that he continued to believe everything he had said in his first trial with Inquisitor Cortes, but like St. Peter, he had to deny it all out of fear of being burned; they made him deny his faith—"But now is not the time to deny the faith of God."[45]

Inquisitor Moral could hardly believe his ears. He told Bartolomé that to be sure just what faith he held, he would have the entire transcript of his trial read back to him, from beginning to end, so that once he had heard it, he could confirm what he said. Sánchez agreed, and they began reading the transcript. This took the remainder of the day and part of the next, and when they finished on June 23, Sánchez said he remembered well having said the propositions just as they were written down, and that was what he believed. Sánchez went out of his way to explain, "And what I said in the hearing of April 30, 1556, in which I retracted my propositions, saying that I wanted to hold and believe what the Holy Mother

Church believes and holds, saying that the devil had deceived me, etc., I did that through the persuasion of the notary Alonso Sánchez, who was with me in prison at that time, but not because I held as true what the Roman Church holds and believes."[46]

Sánchez had fooled the inquisitors not once but twice. He had never given up a single one of his beliefs, and if what he said outside of Cardenete in March were any indication, he never had stopped believing he was the Elijah-Messiah (although he was more careful to hide this conviction from others). Moral decided that they would have to send to Cardenete for depositions to confirm Sánchez's account of what he did during March, and wrote to Licentiate Jiménez detailing what questions were to be asked which witnesses. Jiménez was able to track down all of the witnesses except for Juan Martínez and sent back the testimony on July 25. The eight witnesses' memory of the events coincided substantially with Sánchez's; there could be no doubt that the man had gone out of his way to commit heresy in the village.[47]

One of the witnesses was Catalina Martínez, Sánchez's wife, who was asked for the first time about her husband's behavior. Like her husband, she had a gift for telling stories, and gave a brief but vivid description of life with the heretic.

> I've spoken with my husband many times, and correcting him about the things he said to me or what I heard other people say about him, I watched him secretly to see what he did in the house, and I said to him, "You've talked to Beezelbub." On the second day of Easter he left two hours before daybreak, and I told him, "Come back here and tell me where you're going." He answered me, "Go back to bed and entrust yourself to God, Who will preserve you in His holy service, for I am going on a road both long and short." He was away for eight weeks, and he came back very thin and lost [perdido], and I said to him, "Have you been stuck in some cave [i.e., like a hermit] since you've come back so thin and lost?" He answered, "I can carry a dead body that I wore out. I took ship in Alicante." He went to Seville, and there he left the sea because he was tired out, and from there he went to Granada and to Our Lady of Guadalupe,[48] and from there he came home on Saturday, the evening before the holy day of the Trinity. When he finished supper, he told me, "Do not be sad that later I must go, because my steps are nothing but mystery and I cannot help but go, because just as you ask me

now, the disciples asked Christ when they asked him to stay with them in the village of Emmaus."[49] He said so many things that I don't remember. I never saw him do anything at home or any ceremony besides walking around as if he were on a special mission. He would get out of bed saying that there were many dogs and he never slept at night. He said that the clergy were Pharisees and devils, and that God wasn't in the Host, but in His Word.[50]

On August 1, 1558, the tribunal of Cuenca met to vote once more on the case of Bartolomé Sánchez. The recording secretary was Juan de Ybaneta, who had been the principal secretary throughout Sánchez's trial. As he started to write down the names of those attending, he began with Licentiate Pedro Cortes. Ybaneta caught himself, crossed out the name, and began again with Licentiate Moral. The only other member of the tribunal to attend the meeting was Dr. Vergara, the bishop's ordinary. The other members, canons in the cathedral, may have been on vacation, as was the chapter's custom in August, or perhaps Moral and Vergara saw no need to involve anyone else.

At this late date, Moral and Vergara were still puzzling over the truth of Sánchez's case. As the minutes of their meeting reveal, they acknowledged that the trial had reached an impasse; it had gone beyond the possibility of arbitration. They noted that they had conducted an exhaustive investigation into Bartolomé's relapse and that they could not find any reason why he should remain so fixed in his propositions. Although Sánchez appeared to be sane in some ways, nonetheless they were truly convinced that he was insane and possessed. Once they decided irrevocably that Sánchez was insane, there was no question of continuing the proceedings against the wool carder. Although they used the word "possessed" in the same breath as "insane," clearly the inquisitors did not believe that Sánchez was possessed, at least in any way that could be helped by priestly intervention; that is, an exorcism. Instead, they thought that the explanation for Sánchez's madness was to be found in medical science. His sickness was not in his soul but in his body. Moral and Vergara could not help the tormented man, but they were not without ideas about a remedy. They ordered the wool carder to be placed at one of three hospitals for the insane, not just so that he could be confined but in order that, as they put it, the humor afflicting him could be removed and he could be cured of his insanity. Twelve days later, Sánchez, well shackled so he would not escape on the journey, was handed over to a man who had contracted to deliver the prisoner to the Inquisition of Zaragoza, which would take charge of admitting him to the Hospital of Nuestra Señora de la Gracia in Zaragoza.[51] And so, after five years of legal and theological battles, Sánchez passed out of the inquisitors' hands and into those of the doctors.

8

MADMAN

1

BY THIS POINT, WE SHOULD NOT BE TOO SURPRISED BY RIEGO AND
Moral's decision that Sánchez was insane. For several years they had been
inclined to regard Sánchez as not entirely in his right mind; before them,
Pedro Cortes had always doubted his prisoner's sanity but had lacked the
proof to dismiss the case. By the spring of 1558, Sánchez's condition had
deteriorated to the point where further proof was no longer needed. He
had lost the ability to moderate his behavior in public and at times lapsed
into a private language whose meaning was known only to himself. He
believed that he was surrounded by sinners—"stones," as he called
them—whose depraved moral state would prevent him from achieving
his purpose; by journeying to the River of Stones, he would overcome
these obstacles, these stones in his path. Once, many years before, he had
carried five stones in a saddlebag on his shoulders as a penance, one for
each of Christ's wounds. Sánchez's private world of personal sin had become externalized to all sinners in his path, whose existence threatened to
undo him. Convinced that he was the Elijah-Messiah, he could not avoid
drawing parallels between his experience and that of Christ. Despised and

rejected by all, he was on a lonely journey that quite possibly could end in his murder.

The secretary Ybaneta wrote that he recorded only those of Sánchez's statements that made sense to them; how do we reconstruct the state of mind of a man whose most anguished and ambiguous utterances have been systematically suppressed?[1] Although Cortes and Ybaneta were interested only in Sánchez's theological ideas, not every single stray comment was repressed, and there remains the testimony of Sánchez's neighbors in Cardenete. Sánchez could fix precisely the date when his troubles began: Midsummer's Eve (June 24), 1550, when he saw a vision while walking home after spending the day reaping in the fields—hot, exhausting work, to be sure. At moments in his trial when it was convenient for his defense, he attempted to deny that the vision had been real to him, and instead blamed the experience on either the devil or his imagination. However, several of his neighbors mentioned in March 1553 that Sánchez had told them about the vision, and Ybaneta recalled that it was the first thing that Sánchez said to the court when he arrived in Cuenca the following October. When it occurred, Sánchez had no doubt as to its reality or its significance; sixteenth-century Spaniards were raised in a culture pregnant with the miraculous and the inexplicable. No one thought that the vision by itself was proof of madness; the only question in their minds was its origin: divine, diabolical, or a trick of the mind.

At first Sánchez told no one about the vision, despite the fact that he had found it comforting. Six months later, as he recalled, he began to doubt his faith, and then, in March 1551, Sánchez found the vision reproduced in his book of hours. At that point he became obsessed with finding out what the vision meant. Sometime between Lent in 1551 and Lent in 1553 Sánchez found the answer in the belief that he was the Elijah-Messiah, as a few isolated remarks scattered over the course of two years indicate:

> *Herrero:* [Sánchez] wanted to go back to Albacete and when we asked him what for, he replied that he was going because St. Peter was supposed to give him the keys so he could guard Paradise.
> *Bartolomé de Mora:* [Sánchez said,] "You have got me tied to the column just like the Jews had Christ—which of you is to give me the first lash?"

Sánchez: The men were frightened—"Who let me out?"—and I told them, "God. . . ."

Miguel Caballero: [Sánchez said] he would defend himself since the chains that they've put on him to imprison him are roses and flowers. . . .

Alonso Sánchez: When some people told him that they had to take him to Cuenca, Bartolomé Sánchez replied that they wanted to take him like they carried away Christ Our Lord, and they were some Pharisees.[2]

With the exception of the first statement, one could argue that all of these utterances were merely similes and metaphors. In a culture that drew naturally on the Bible to illuminate all of life's experiences, Sánchez's resort to such language to comment on his own predicament would not have been seen as unusual. He followed up these statements, however, by an explicit declaration in court on October 24, 1553, that he was the Elijah-Messiah, and several statements to the effect that through God's protection he was invincible. In May 1554, to save his life, Sánchez eventually retracted his claim to divinity as part of his recantation, but two years later he declared openly to the court that he was the Son of Man and Elijah (Apr. 22, 1556), and in March 1558 Sánchez predicted that he would be killed as Christ had been because he preached the truth and he had come to burn the Church of Rome. Two explicit statements and half a dozen oblique references over the course of seven years—not much for an individual who believed he was the Messiah and enjoyed God's protection. Whatever the nature of Sánchez's illness, it did not prevent him from keeping a secret when it seemed necessary to do so.

Throughout these years we catch glimpses into Sánchez's emotional and physical state. For some months before his fit in the church (March 1552) until about Christmas of 1552 Sánchez underwent a phase of intense physical stress and emotional instability. At times during that period he was so tense that it seemed his heart "would leap right out of his body." At other times his emotions were so intense that he was no longer aware of his surroundings; it was as if he were spinning.[3] The word for "anguish" (*congoja*) appears frequently in his speech. Sánchez's cousin remembered that the wool carder spent an entire day out of his senses, crying because he was convinced that some men (wearing yellow hose, no less) were coming to kill him. Several times it was necessary to restrain him physically by tying him to a post. He could be hostile and argumentative. Symbolic of Sánchez's turbulent emotional state as well as his private conviction that he (of all people) was the Elijah-Messiah who would destroy the Church, Sánchez would remove his left shoe when he entered a church and say that the world had turned topsy-turvy.[4]

After Christmas in 1552 Sánchez's emotional crisis cleared and he entered another phase. Gone are the references to mental anguish and physical distress (aside from headaches, which almost seem to be a defense tactic); instead Sánchez fearlessly began to express many of his heretical notions to his neighbors. Although Sánchez had no fear of what could happen to him, he still kept his identity a secret from his family and neighbors. His attitude was one of exaltation; lifted by the secret knowledge that he was God's chosen messenger, the Elijah-Messiah, he confidently defended his ideas to anyone who would listen to him. His arrest and removal to Cuenca reinforced his conviction that God had singled him out, and he operated on the assumption that with God's protection he was invulnerable. During the first two weeks of his trial, in a state of high emotion he challenged Inquisitor Cortes at every step, at times hardly allowing the inquisitor to speak and certainly not believing a word of what Cortes had to say to him. Secretary Ybaneta remembered that when Sánchez first appeared in court he was highly agitated, went on about some vision he had had, and that they had to calm him down before they could begin to talk to him. During this phase of his illness, in the presence of his persecutors, Sánchez finally revealed his identity and explained his theology and, by extension, his delusion in their complete form.

As an intelligent man, Sánchez knew that he could not be *the* Messiah without disposing of the other Messiah, Jesus Christ.[5] He was not so out of touch with his surroundings as to ignore the opinion of virtually the entire world. Thus he developed an elaborate but logical explanation for Jesus' election and failure. To distinguish himself from the failed Messiah, Sánchez called himself "the Elijah-Messiah," and supplied the biblical proofs for his coming. Sánchez's conception of his mission, however, differed drastically from Jesus' and seems to have been molded primarily by his fear that the Inquisition would kill him. With merely a nod to the notion of salvation, the defining purpose of his mission, which he repeated several times, was to announce that God would punish the Inquisition for murdering innocent people like himself. Sánchez even set a deadline—All Saints' Day—for his release.

Sánchez's prayers to God reveal the extent to which he was in the thrall of his grandiose delusions. What he could not dare to say directly to the inquisitors is expressed indirectly in his prayers, which go far beyond any psalmist's plea for assistance or revenge. In the Lord's Prayer, Sánchez called on God to bestow His kingdom on the wool carder and to work His will through Sánchez. In a prayer adapted from Psalm 110, Sánchez called on God to make a footstool of his enemies and to give him the strength to overthrow the powerful. In his prayer delivered on November 6, the wool carder called on God to enlighten him and others, and again to give him the strength to overcome his adversaries. He thought of his trial as the burden of the Antichrist and the devil. As Elijah, the lowly wool carder saw himself at the center of an apocalyptic struggle between God and the Antichrist. The Antichrist/devil/inquisitors might try to stop him, but ultimately he, like Elijah, would prevail, even though he might be killed in the process.

When November 1 came and went without his release, Sánchez entered the next phase of his illness—denial and depression. He refused to engage in any more debate, dared the inquisitors to work their will, and placed his fate in God's hands. Intuitively Dr. Vergara realized that the way to break through Sánchez's defenses was to prove to him that the core belief—that God had chosen the wool carder as his messenger and would protect him from harm—had no basis in reality. Hence the auto de fe and death sentence. Afterward, during several interviews with Pedro Cortes, Sánchez appeared to be a broken man, abjectly retracting all of his heretical statements, saving for last his conviction that he was the Elijah-Messiah. Some of this surely was an act; Sánchez proved later that he was fully capable of lying and feigning remorse when it suited his purpose to do so. But the stake and crowd had been real and God had not intervened, just as He had not blasted the Inquisition to hell on November 1. It was enough to give Sánchez pause. Ybaneta remembered that after his penancing the wool carder had become so depressed that he said he wanted to throw himself off the city bridge, and the court had assigned Dr. Vergara to his case to help him through this period.

From spring 1554 to spring 1558 we have little information about

Sánchez's emotional state, but it would appear that his condition gradually worsened. He continued to believe secretly that he was the Elijah-Messiah, and each Lenten season, with its focus on that *other* Messiah, would send him into a crisis. The pattern is quite clear:

March 1551: buys book of hours and sees his vision reproduced in it.
March 1552: breaks down in Cardenete's parish church.
March 1553: arrested in Cardenete for heretical speech.
Carnival–Holy Week 1556: breaks conditions of penance; returns to Cardenete to burn sanbenito.
March 1558: picks quarrels with his village over religion; during Easter, disappears for eight weeks.
March 1560: resumes heresies in Cardenete.

During this period, Sánchez seems to have pulled back from his belief in his own invincibility; he began to lie when necessary to save his life, a development that complicates our analysis somewhat. Nonetheless, his references to considerable mental torment appear sincere and are consistent with previous statements; only the professed desire to convert is false. By March 1558 his behavior had become hostile and his speech enigmatic; yet when he was arrested in June, he appeared coherent, if not repentant.

Sánchez's sense of tragic identification with Jesus Christ intensified during this period. Before leaving to search for Christ in the River of Stones and the curdled thing (*la cuaxada*), he told his wife not to get out of bed, even to say farewell to him. What he needed to do had to be accomplished alone. Sánchez seemed to be drawing parallels between Christ's isolation toward the end and his own social and spiritual isolation. Saying paradoxically "I am going on a road both long and short" lent an aura of hidden significance to his search for the truth. When Sánchez returned from his trip to Guadalupe (if indeed he ever went there), he seemed to think that he had changed somehow, for he told his wife, "Do not be sad that later I must go, because just as you ask me now, the disciples asked Christ when they asked him to stay with them in the village of Emmaus." In other words, Sánchez now saw himself as the risen Christ who revealed himself briefly to His disciples and then disappeared. The River of Stones was his metaphor for all the people trapped in sin; Christ had been killed by such people, who refused to see the truth of what he said and mend their ways.

One possible tradition for Sánchez's enigmatic words "the curdled thing" can be found in a seventeenth-century history of the Carmelite Order, which venerates Elijah as its founder. The author described Mount Carmel as a "mountain curdled in sanctity, it is called Carmel by the Sea." He in turn is echoing Psalm 68:16, which in the Vulgate refers to the *mons coagulatus* (*monte cuaxado* in sixteenth-century Spanish). At Mount Carmel the prophet Elijah triumphed over the 450 prophets of Baal and secured the worship of Yahweh among the Israelites (1 Kings 18); both Jews and Christians regard Elijah as the prefigurer of the Messiah.[6] Given these traditions and the fact that there was a Carmelite monastery just down the road in Requena, Sánchez probably heard a preacher use the term in some sermon and understood that the "curdled thing" had something to do with his identity as the Elijah-Messiah.

2

From our vantage point, with access to the entire trial transcript, it seems clear that Sánchez was deeply disturbed. Yet not a single witness who was asked directly about Sánchez's mental state and behavior stated that he believed the wool carder to be insane. Only two expressed any doubt at all—Bartolomé de Mora, who had witnessed most of Sánchez's breakdown in 1552, and Juan de Gaviria's wife, who reported that she had heard from neighbors that Sánchez had a tendency to "rant." A common element in many witnesses' observations about Sánchez was that he worked and behaved perfectly normally except when he got onto the topic of religion. Since only the inquisitors heard him actually say that he was the Elijah-Messiah, what the witnesses heard from Sánchez was a torrent of heretical abuse of the Church, sacraments, and sacred images, without the underlying, improbable idea that gave it all meaning.

By examining the testimony from similar contemporary cases of Inquisition defendants whose sanity is in question, we can come closer to the popular understanding of madness and appreciate why Sánchez's neighbors regarded the wool carder as sane.[7] The Inquisition dealt with such cases often enough: the most common scenario was that an individual while delirious or in the grip of some fit would make religiously offensive remarks. A bystander without familiarity with the person's condition, or in spite of it, would complain to the Inquisition. When the

defendant could point to a preexisting medical condition and produce witnesses who would confirm his illness, this usually would be enough to get
the case suspended. In 1539, for example, Juan de Herreria, from the village of Valhermosa (Sigüenza), made some stupid remarks in Francisco
Ruiz's water mill, where evidently Juan was not well known. Ruiz denounced Herreria for saying that "God came down to earth three times
a year, and he knew which days He came down and which days He went
back up, and he knew that [God] had to die on Good Friday and His
wife[!]one day later, and that God the Father had come down to [Herre-
ria] while he was sick and He had prolonged his life." In his defense, Herreria called five witnesses, who all confirmed that Herreria had been ill,
and since that time suffered regular relapses. One witness said that he had
seen Herreria go mad while sick and lose his reason, and he had helped
another man to tie Herreria by the hands to keep him from doing harm.
Herreria had remained tied up and out of his wits for many days, and he
was never the same afterward.[8] Several men mentioned that Juan's sickness was so grave that for a while they thought him possessed. Pedro de
Arriba also had seen Juan lose his mind while he was sick and noted that
his condition came and went with the moon. His episodes were so severe
that it occurred to Arriba that it could be caused by a "spirit" or a stomach disorder.[9] The village priest's testimony corroborated the villagers'
impressions. He recalled that it was on his orders that Herreria had been
tied up and on account of his illness he was now considered a "lunatic."
Finally, Herreria testified on his own behalf. He did not remember having
said what was contained in the accusation and said,

> . . . they say that while I was sick I said many injurious and vituperous
> words against the people who came to visit me, and for fear of that,
> many people stopped coming to visit. They tied my arms so I would not
> cause any harm and I don't remember a single thing except the pain I
> felt in my arms while I was tied up.

The inquisitors on this case, Licentiates Gongora and Cortes, were satis-
fied that Herreria was not legally responsible for his actions at the time
he committed the heresies in question and suspended the trial.

Epileptic fits also were easily understood by the community for what
they were, although they did not guarantee compassionate treatment. In
1563 Hernando de Madrigal, of the village of Tebar, to the south of

Cuenca, was denounced for some remarks he had made against papal indulgences. Several villagers were hostile toward Madrigal, whom they viewed as a know-it-all, contemptuous of everyone else. Key to Madrigal's defense was that while he suffered his seizures he was insensible and remembered nothing of what he did or said. He produced many villagers who had witnessed him undergo one seizure or another, sometimes right on the street. During the fits he foamed at the mouth and flailed about uncontrollably. The fits occurred regularly, but no one suggested that Madrigal's illness was supernatural in origin. One man even suggested *gota coral,* the popular term for epilepsy. Clinching his successful defense was the testimony of the village doctor:

> I have diagnosed [Madrigal] as suffering from *gota coral,* which is otherwise called elpilepsy [*sic*], which illness deprives one of one's reason for a certain amount of time. . . . I think that because of the nature of this illness, while Hernando de Madrigal is sick he could have said some crazy things to those who spoke to him. Those who have this illness usually do not remember what they say because they are not in control of their senses. . . . It seems to me as a doctor that because of the illness Hernando de Madrigal is changed in his expression and in the vitality of his person and senses.[10]

The testimony delivered in the case of Juan de Santaren, an epileptic who lived in the small city of Huete, provides more detail about how the fits appeared to onlookers and the callous treatment that the epileptic could experience at the hands of some individuals. Apparently his fits caused Santaren to be regarded more as the village fool than as someone who was ill. In 1582 the archdeacon of Huete described how on many occasions he had seen Santaren

> taken by his madness in the plaza and in church during Mass, shouting and striking at those around him, calling them "goddamned buggers" and other words along these lines, and spuming foam from the mouth. The bystanders not being able to restrain him, he falls on the ground and lies stunned for a while and he wounds himself on his face and in other places.

As a consequence of his madness, the archdeacon said, people would come up to Santaren in the middle of the street when he was not suffering a fit and call Santaren barbarian and pigfat[11] and Jew and grab him by the beard and make him sing and recite couplets and verses along with madmen's sayings. Juan de Santaren calls them Jewish faggots and barbarians and other idiotic things along these lines, and the boys and people gather around him in the squares and streets and they shout at him and he threatens that he will have them burned. This shouting goes on every day in the gaming houses where they gamble.

The archdeacon concluded with a story that was meant to demonstrate Santaren's charitable nature but underscored the man's precarious sanity in the eyes of the community. Santaren would give freely to the city's beggars until he had nothing left. The poor would follow him around, hoping for a handout. One day he took pity on a poor boy, led him to a bakery, and loaded the boy down with bread. Finally, the boy being unable to hold any more, he placed a last loaf in the boy's mouth. This incident became the subject of many a joke at Santaren's expense.[12]

Clearly lay people were willing to tolerate aberrant, religiously offensive behavior and excuse it as madness when there was an obvious physical explanation. Likewise, inquisitors quickly applied the principle of the insanity defense to dismiss such cases. Even with a preexisting medical condition, however, when the behavior was grossly offensive or hostile to religious symbols, the Inquisition had more difficulty deciding on an appropriate sentence. Gonzalo Hidalgo, a petty nobleman from the town of Horcajo in La Mancha, was arrested by the civil authorities in nearby Uclés in 1572 for indecent and insulting words against the Virgin.[13] Seven witnesses all agreed that occasionally Hidalgo appeared crazy or said mad things, especially when he drank too much wine, but at other times he was sane and said perfectly rational things. They were more inclined to call him a wicked man (*bellaco*). Gonzalo's brother, Diego, learned of his arrest and wrote to the authorities, explaining that Gonzalo had been crazy, mad, and out of his mind (*loco, furioso, y . . . fuera de juizio*) for some eight years and that, as his brother, he had been given legal permission in writing to keep Gonzalo chained at home. Gonzalo's madness primarily took the form of verbal abuse, which his neighbors could not tolerate, and he had been arrested many times, only to be released each time on account of his insanity. His loose tongue eventually landed him in the king's galleys (repeating some rumors, he had said that the royal secretary Eraso and the king's favorite, Ruy Gómez, had murdered Don

Carlos, the crown prince), but he was sent home after three months because, once again, he was found to be mad. The prior of Uclés also wrote on Gonzalo's behalf, and expressed his opinion that Gonzalo's condition had no remedy. Although he had periods of sanity (he used the legal term *aliqua lucida intervalla*), they did not last long, and he was not competent to be punished. Despite this testimony, the inquisitors in Cuenca had Gonzalo brought to the city for questioning. He told the court that he was twenty-eight years old, was married, and had lost everything. Sometimes when he went mad,

> it seems to me that my heart is being eaten, and then I start shouting and I can't eat or sleep, only drink, and I hit myself a lot and I don't feel it, and I'm like that until they chain me. After I'm chained, I don't do anything but shout. This usually happens at intervals, most commonly when the hot weather comes in around St. James's [July 25], and it keeps up until around Christmas. This year around Michaelmass [Sept. 15] when I was chained up in my house, I cut the chain with an ax and I picked up a roasting spit and the ax that I used to cut the chain and I jumped over some half-fallen-down walls of my house. I lived next to the cemetery and I went into the church to pray, then I went out in the village, and I walked around with the ax and spit, shouting the whole way, and then the guards arrested me and put me in a cart and took me to Uclés.[14]

After telling how he was imprisoned and sent to the galleys, Gonzalo mentioned that he had once been put in a cage, from which he would throw rubble at his tormentors. He concluded by praising the Virgin and the Lord, and asking Him to return him to his wits because "going around like this is the worst thing in the world; I want to rip out my heart and I tear my clothes instead."

In all of this testimony, no one offered a reason for Gonzalo's behavior beyond his insanity or wicked nature, and probably to his own detriment, he could remember what he did while insane. In the successful defenses seen earlier, the defendants all contended that because of some physical ailment they were out of their minds when they said the damaging words, and they had no memory of their actions. In such a situation, lack of criminal intent or guilt was easily proved. In this case, however, despite all the indications that Gonzalo was suffering from some form of illness, the inquisitors thought that he bore some guilt. Perhaps they felt that gross insults to the Virgin could not be tolerated under any circumstances; on this occasion Gonzalo was sentenced to be gagged and given fifty lashes, and to pay the court's expenses.

Cases in which there were no physical symptoms at all, only irrational or delusional speech, were the most difficult of all for casual observers to evaluate. The case of Juan García, who came to the attention of the inquisitors in Toledo in 1541 for his visionary dreams, provides a telling counterpoint to Bartolomé Sánchez's case.[15] Like Sánchez, García was poor; he worked as an unskilled laborer on the construction of the cathedral of Toledo. Despite his low class, he had a smattering of education and liked to talk about religious and political affairs. His dreams drew clumsily on the prophetic, millenarian traditions of the day. On September 16, 1541, Juan Martínez, a mason's assistant, appeared in the tribunal's rooms and denounced García for the suspicious content of his dreams.

> I heard García say that in his dreams he knows more than all the learned people in the world and even the inquisitors, and that he dreams there's going to be the greatest lord who's ever been in the last 300 years and he is going to do things that those already born never have done, and God shows these things to him more than to any man of all those who have been born in the last 300 years, not to judges, lawyers, or clergy.

On the same day, Mateo Hernández, a plasterer, also came to the court. He told the inquisitors that García had said he knew what God was doing through his dreams, and when it rained it was for the injustices that were done by those who were entrusted with doing justice and when the Pope gave people what they asked him for (implying that the Pope's favors were corrupt as well). García bragged that he knew more than anyone in the world, even the inquisitors, who had summoned him before and found him blameless.

Later in the day Juan García was called to the court, and after the preliminary fact finding, was asked if he knew if God had revealed Himself to any person. Without hesitation, García admitted that it had happened to him a few times, but taking a defensive position, he dismissed the experiences by calling them "fantasies," and he asked God for forgiveness. It didn't take much questioning, though, before Juan changed his story and claimed that his revelations did come from God, but he would not say in what they consisted. A few days later, when the inquisitors tried to interview him a second time, they got no further than before. García spoke in such "a clever and underhanded way" that they couldn't understand him.[16] In frustration, Inquisitor Yañes warned him that if he had anything to say, to say it clearly, and García answered that he had so much to say that it would take five or six years to say it all.

A few weeks later, García's cellmate denounced him for some things he had said in prison that did not seem right to him.

> I heard him say that he knew by night what the Holy Inquisition and the civil authorities did by day and that if he wanted to get into really deep things [si quería entrar en hondura], he would set all of Spain spinning, and that Inquisitor Juan Yañes was imprisoned every night and Inquisitor Sandoval had withdrawn from his case and had gone to Valladolid or Madrid, and if he [García] wanted, he could make Our Lady of Guadalupe come to wherever he was and if he wished, he could make Our Lady of the cathedral of Toledo come to where he was with the chasuble of St. Ildefonso[17] . . . and he knew what kings and great lords did among themselves, and he knew what the Great Turk [the sultan] did . . . and that the Lord Inquisitor had gone to [García's] hometown and taken from him more than ten thousand ducats from his estate. . . .

Further talks with García still got nowhere with the worker, so finally he was asked which he preferred, one hundred lashes or internment at the local insane asylum known as the Casa del Nuncio. Juan wouldn't choose, so they sent him back to his cell. The jailer reported that on the way back Juan complained, "What a choice—if I want to be crazy or one hundred lashes—sane and free is what I want to be!"[18] This comment prompted the inquisitors to conduct an inquiry into García's sanity.

Six of García's co-workers from the cathedral building site were called in to depose. There was little agreement among them. The first witness, when asked what sort of reputation García had among the men, and if he thought García was mad, sane, or simple-minded, stated firmly that he believed him to be a rational man (honbre concertado), of sound judgment and understanding, and they had never seen him do anything crazy. Once he had criticized García for saying bad things, and García had answered back that they were the crazy ones for interfering and they didn't know what he knew.

Asked the same question, Miguel Ramírez said that he thought García was more crazy than sane because he wanted to argue with the inquisitors (a reasonable assumption!). Ramírez repeated things he had heard García say that were similar in content to what other witnesses had deposed. The inquisitors pressed Miguel for a more definitive evaluation of García's mental state, but Miguel could not make up his mind. "[García] said some things that made me think he was drunk and I thought he was crazy and crude, and other times it seemed to me that he talked sensibly." Asked if he thought García should be sent to the local asylum, Miguel could not say.[19]

Mateo Gómez, in response to the question, also gave a good summary of García's various ideas. He and his companions had reprimanded him, telling him (as Sánchez had once been told) that he was either crazy or a heretic for saying those things, and García had answered back that they were the crazy and wicked ones. When the inquisitors asked Gómez if he thought García spoke well, in an articulate and sensible way, Gómez agreed that he did, except for the things he had mentioned, and that sometimes García talked to himself. In the end, though, he too could not decide if García was sane or insane.

Another witness, a stonemason, had no doubt whatever that García was sane. More than that, the mason, who also was called Juan García, thought that the defendant spoke like a learned man, and the things he had said seemed to be the words of a man of some training, he knew not in what. The remaining two witnesses, on the other hand, thought just the opposite, that García was crazy.[20]

Despite the improbable and fanciful content of García's revelations (compared to similar prophecies of the time) and the occasional odd comment that suggested that García was far from completely rational,[21] the jury of popular opinion leaned toward tolerance. García's statements did not contradict the faith; only one of the six witnesses suggested that he might be a heretic. Perhaps talking to himself was a bit odd, but in his favor, most of the witnesses pointed out that he was a good worker and spoke coherently enough by their standards. Insanity, for these witnesses, was nothing less than the complete absence of reason. Some three hundred years before in Córdoba, the Jewish philosopher Maimonides had pointed out the inadequacy of such a definition:

> We should not consider demented solely the person who runs naked through the streets and throws stones at his household belongings but also the *one whose consciousness is obliterated by a single idea, even while he remains normal in every respect that is not related to that idea.*[22]

Obviously, Maimonides' insight had not reached the popular level in sixteenth-century Castile, or Sánchez and García would have fared differently in witnesses' opinion.[23] Many witnesses stated that Sánchez was normal in every respect except when he talked about religion, and like García, Sánchez was considered sane because he was a good worker and did not behave in a demented fashion. His bizarre get-up and public breakdown in the parish church of Cardenete were not enough to tip the balance of public opinion in favor of insanity; instead, witnesses were shocked by his aggressive attack on the principles of their faith.

3

Despite the lack of subtlety in local people's understanding of mental illness, the testimony in these Inquisition cases points to the pervasive influence of Galen's medical principles, even at the popular levels of society. Pedro de Arriba, for example, noted that Juan de Herreria's sickness came and went with the moon, an ancient notion that linked the influence of the moon's humidity on people's own wet and cold humors. Arriba thought that Herreria's insanity could be caused by either some spirit or an upset stomach. This latter suggestion was not a random shot at a diagnosis but also recalled humoral theory, according to which the stomach's natural state is hot and dry while the brain is naturally cold and wet. When the stomach becomes upset, the excess of hot and dry humors upsets the balance of humors in the brain, resulting in some form of madness.[24] In one epilepsy case, a layman provided the diagnosis of *gota coral* for Hernando de Madrigal, and in Juan de Santaren's case, another witness, a priest, thought that Santaren suffered from heart disease, which was considered to be the cause of epilepsy, by virtue of the same humoral theory.

In several of the cases, witnesses noted that the ill person's mad behavior was associated with drinking wine. They were saying more than that the person had been drunk. In the medical thinking of the day, wine, as a chemical agent, was known for its ability to provoke mental disorder by sending its hot vapors up to the brain and causing delirium.[25] Thus Lucas Verdugo, a priest who knew Gonzalo Hidalgo, commented that because he drank and talked a lot, in addition to having a weak cerebrum (he used the word *celebro* [*cerebro*], a more educated term for the brain than the common word, *seso*), these things all came together to produce his illness. Alonso Martínez de Allende, from Villaescusa de Haro, claimed in his own defense in 1526 that when he drank wine, he would so completely lose control over himself that he would go out of his mind and say many ugly and disorderly things. Once his *furor* (a technical term for violent loss of self-control) was over, he had no memory of what he had done or said.[26] One desperate husband in Huete denounced his wife for heresy, explaining that "to her misfortune and mine, she is out of her mind and on top of that she drinks. Many times she has said that she is the daughter of the emperor Charles and that half the kingdom is hers, and that she is better than Our Lady and she doesn't believe in God."[27]

Conspicuously absent from these several cases was the belief that some spirit or the devil was the cause of the aberrant, often frightening behavior and words.[28] The closest anyone would come to a supernatural explanation was to suggest that the victim's actions were due to his insanity *or* some spirit or demon, but the materialist explanation would prevail in the end. It is quite possible that the sixteenth-century revival of Galenism led people to downplay the influence of the supernatural when they dealt with extreme, inexplicable behavior.[29] In the works of Pedro Ciruelo and Martín de Castañega, written in the 1520s to educate parish priests and literate laymen about popular superstitions, both authors took the position that most apparent cases of possession were actually caused by some sickness of the brain or heart. Castañega wrote that even though the precise nature of the illness was unknown to doctors, with luck, eventually both a cause and a cure might be found. Before proceeding with an exorcism, Ciruelo advised parish priests, they should always consult with a doctor so that medical causes could be ruled out.[30]

We often can see this neo-Aristotelian rationalism at work in minor exchanges between the educated parish clergy and the lower classes.

While a few of Juan de Herreria's neighbors thought that a demon just might be involved in his illness, it was the village priest in Valhermosa who issued the definitive diagnosis, calling Herreria a "lunatic" and ordering his restraint. Early in his illness, Bartolomé Sánchez went to visit a shrine to Our Lady in the nearby village of Monteagudo, where he hoped to receive relief from a supernatural source.[31] But the village priest there found no trace of a supernatural ailment and gave Sánchez some medicines.

4

In view of the cases we have analyzed, the inquisitors' decision that Sánchez's delusional heresies were the result of some humoral imbalance appears unremarkable. In reality, their ruling stems from a gradual change in the Church's dealings with false messiahs. Despite the teaching of Roman law concerning crimes committed by the insane, theologians and religious judges had not always been so charitable toward those who claimed they were God, the Messiah, or the disciples of such persons. The position of the Church was that there was only one Messiah, Jesus Christ, and to announce the coming of another, for whatever reason, was the worst form of heresy, not insanity. Even if the culprit were indisputably insane, some theologians and jurists maintained in the sixteenth century that certain crimes were so heinous (such as attacking a consecrated Host, claiming to be God, or treason) that they could not go unpunished, whatever the circumstances.[32]

The medieval Inquisition's unforgiving approach to religious insanity may be seen in the following case from Barcelona. Exactly two hundred years before Sánchez's breakdown in Cardenete, the Catalan inquisitor Nicolau Eimeric tried Nicholas of Calabria as a disciple of Gonzalo de Cuenca, who claimed to be nothing less than the son of God. Apparently Gonzalo had granted himself more extensive powers than Sánchez had ever dared to claim as the Elijah-Messiah. Although he admitted he was born of earthly parents, Gonzalo believed himself really to be the son of God and to have been conceived eternally in heaven. He was immortal, and when the Holy Ghost came to be incarnated in future times, Gonzalo would convert the whole world. On Judgment Day, Gonzalo—the true savior of mankind—would pray for all those who had died in mortal sin and were damned to hell, and save them. Unlike Sánchez, who had never revealed himself to anyone except the inquisitors, Gonzalo preached his mission and recruited a collaborator and disciple, Nicholas of Calabria, and together they co-authored a book called *Virginale.* In 1352 Nicholas was arrested, tried, and reconciled. Eventually, after a relapse and a second arrest in 1357, Nicholas was burned along with his book.[33]

According to Eimeric, Gonzalo de Cuenca was never caught; but, had he been, the possibility of an insanity defense was out of the question for the false messiah. Eimeric took the position that there was no such thing as an insane defendant or religious insanity, a topic that only fifty years before had received sympathetic treatment by a fellow Catalan, the physician and philosopher Arnold of Villanova (1250–1313). Eimeric knew Villanova's work well enough to condemn it for its prophecies and magical tendencies. Writing in his famous manual for inquisitors, Eimeric declared those who try to claim the insanity defense

> laugh while answering, and mix into their answers a quantity of irrelevant, comic, and idiotic words. Thus they hide their errors. They frequently do this when they see that they are going to be tortured or handed over to the secular arm of justice. All this to escape torture and death! I have seen it a thousand times: the accused pretend to be completely crazy or to have only moments of lucidity.[34]

At the beginning of the sixteenth century, the Holy Office was under the direction of the Spanish crown, but inquisitorial attitudes about false messiahs still had not changed. Mossen Urbano, a friar and native of Florence, was arrested in Barcelona in 1507 for spreading the teachings of his master, Barba Jacobo, who claimed to be the equal of Jesus Christ, and that at the end of the world he would judge both the quick and the dead. According to Urbano, Jacobo was a shepherd who dressed in sackcloth and preached the standard prophecies concerning the apocalypse and imminent end of the world—beliefs widely shared at the time.[35] It is not clear from Urbano's testimony where Jacobo was and what Urbano was doing in the city. After a great deal of persuasion and emotional upset, Mossen Urbano renounced his master, only to return to his convictions a few months later, just as Nicholas of Calabria had done. The inquisitors burned Urbano as a relapsed heretic without any apparent discussion regarding his state of mind.[36]

Admittedly, in these two cases the messianic figures had mysteriously disappeared and were never captured, so the Inquisition was able to try only their followers. The two disciples were treated as fully responsible for their apostasy, and in the surviving commentary the inquisitors never seem to have questioned the sanity of the would-be messiahs or of their disciples, or to have doubted the danger they represented.

Yet fifty years after the execution of Mossen Urbano, Bartolomé Sánchez and Luis de San Pablo (discussed in chapter 5) were treated with compassion. During those fifty years, the Inquisition's theologians had come to revise their methods of dealing with prophets, mystics, and witches whose activities challenged the Church's orthodoxy.

The immediate origins of the change in theological approach can be traced back to the beginning of the fifteenth century. As the French theologian Jean Gerson (1363–1429) explained in his treatise on visions, his investigation into the problem of the discernment of visions was inspired by the unsettled religious times in which he lived, which were full of speculation over the coming of the Antichrist, the identity of the future pope, and an abundance of fantasies, illusions, dreams. According to Gerson, there were even many who went about saying, "I am Christ."[37] In that situation, earlier discussions on the nature of revelation and prophets were inadequate: theologians needed something that gave more useful guidance than the categorical pronouncements of John Chrysostom and Thomas Aquinas, who had either discounted the possibility of insanity or ignored it in their treatment of false prophets. Gerson wrote two treatises on the subject, *De probatione spirituum* and *Tractatus de distinctione verarum visionum a falsis,* the latter specifically intended for both the contemplative laity and religious.

In both treatises, while establishing a method to prove whether a vision came from God, Gerson advocated evaluating the motives, health, and social status of the person who was experiencing the vision or revelation. Here we see a sensitivity to the human condition that was completely lacking in Aquinas, who accepted that virtually all persons, regardless of condition, could become prophets and limited himself to discussing the prophetic gift in relation to Aristotle's tripartite division of intelligence.[38]

When he dealt with a person who was susceptible to visions, the first thing that Gerson wanted to know was the individual's physical and mental health—not merely whether the person had been seriously ill, had suffered a head injury that would disturb his reason, or was suffering from outright madness, but whether he suffered from melancholic and illusory fantasies.[39] Introducing melancholia in this context reveals that Gerson thought of mental illness as not one absolute condition but several, each with its own diagnosis and prognosis. This was an extremely important first step toward a more nuanced view of mental illness, with many implications for developments in the sixteenth century for dealing not only with false messiahs but with witches, alumbrados, and mystics.[40] In his treatise written specifically for religious and contemplative laymen, Gerson also warned against excessive penances and deprivations, which could cause the penitent to fall mentally ill and become susceptible to fantasies.[41]

At the time Gerson wrote his treatises, there were few mystics in Spain; the foremost religious issue of that time was the presence of the large Jewish minority on the peninsula. A hundred years later, however, shortly after Mossen Urbano was executed in Barcelona, interest in mysticism and prophecy took Spain by storm, and there was also an outbreak of witchcraft cases. Taken together, these forms of religious extremism challenged the Inquisition's methods, since the judges were far more experienced in prosecuting the statements and actions of purported Judaizers than they were in dealing with the shifting forms of religious inspiration and the devil's tricks. The infamous case of Magdalena de la Cruz, a celebrated visionary who confessed her frauds in 1543, sent a collective shudder through the ranks of inquisitors, spiritual advisers, nuns, and believers. Henceforward, Magdalena would be invoked as the cautionary tale par excellence for those who aspired to the mystic life. In helping judges find their way through these difficult cases, Gerson's work was pivotal. Although Gerson wrote in the early fifteenth century to address the conditions of northern Europe, his methods could help sixteenth-century Spaniards deal with the rising numbers of mystics and ascetics whose meditations went awry.[42] In the seventeenth century his opinions formed the basis for a set of instructions to be used by the Spanish Inquisition to aid in the discernment of visions.[43]

In the case of witchcraft, the Suprema adopted in 1526 a compromise position that allowed for the reality of witchcraft so that the tribunals would gain jurisdiction over the heresy. At the same time, though, the Suprema demanded such a high level of proof that few cases could be proved if judges followed its instructions. The long-term result was that few women or men were executed for witchcraft by the Inquisition; most were reprimanded for holding superstitious beliefs. As we have seen, in the 1520s two theologians writing in Spanish suggested that possession was a psychological-medical problem; they also advanced the theory, held by the theologian Martín de Arles, that witches traveled only in their imagination with the help of drugs. This had been the medieval position, but it was giving ground in most parts of Europe to the "modern" theories of the *Malleus maleficarum*, published in 1487, that witches' powers were real. In Spain, however, the theological establishment was never completely won over by the *Malleus,* just as inquisitors never gave up their standards of proof for trying such cases.[44]

5

Gerson's psychologically astute approach to religious extremism was reinforced by Spaniards' growing interest in society's responsibility for the mentally ill. Before 1400, although Galenic medicine was well known, the knowledge that dementia was a disease like any other had not translated into any particular public responsibility for the mentally ill, who were left to fend for themselves and suffer the abuse and prejudice that came their way. The city of Valencia dealt with dangerous cases by paying one of the trading vessels in the harbor to transport madmen to some far-off destination. In 1409 Gilabert Jofré, a Mercedarian friar in Valencia who was moved by the miserable condition of the mentally ill living on the city streets, organized a hospice for their care and protection. "Protection" went both ways; the ill needed to be sheltered from the abuse they received on the streets, and the city's residents needed protection from the violently insane. Perhaps Jofré had heard of the hospitals for the insane in

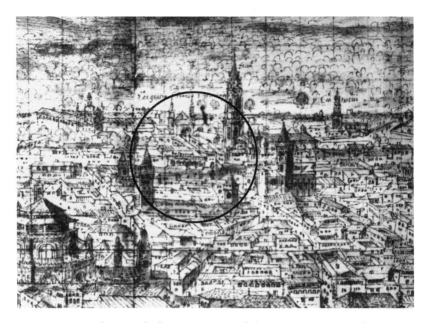

12. Royal Hospital of Nuestra Señora de la Gracia, Zaragoza. The hospital is in the center of the circle. (Drawing by Anton van den Wyngaerd. Bildarchiv der Österreichische Nationalbibliothek, Vienna; Zaragoza [F], Vienna 10)

North Africa, where his religious order worked at ransoming Christian captives; in 1375 a similar hospital had been founded in Muslim Granada. The original foundation in Valencia was conceived as a place for the insane to be housed and restrained if necessary; interest in treatment would come later.[45] By 1500, hospitals or wards for the insane were in operation in Zaragoza, Barcelona, Palma de Mallorca, Seville, Toledo, and Valladolid. In the mid-sixteenth century, the hospitals in Toledo, Valencia, and Zaragoza enjoyed varying degrees of fame or notoriety: the Hospital del Nuncio or "Inocentes" in Toledo had a reputation for receiving the most difficult cases; Valencia caught the imagination of the literary world, for it had been founded first and was the grandest; and Zaragoza was admired for its therapeutic work.[46]

The Hospital Real y General de Nuestra Señora de la Gracia of Zaragoza was founded in 1425 by King Alfonso V of Aragon on the outskirts of the city. Originally dedicated to care for the poor, by 1561 the hospital cared annually for some 500 abandoned infants, 200 mentally ill, and

400 to 500 patients in general admissions (organized into subspecialties). The ward for the mentally ill, which was separate from the rest of the hospital, was spacious, with men's and women's dormitories with individual beds for the inmates (a luxury for the period) and a separate salon for the mentally impaired, where the fireplace was protected by a safety grille so that the patients would not injure themselves. Patients who had to be physically restrained were kept in cells. After admission, mentally ill patients were given green and brown shifts and were supervised by five salaried "fathers" and "mothers." Inmates who were not dangerous were given various tasks to do around the hospital: the women spun, sewed, washed lengths of cloth, and made pastries; the men worked the hospital's kitchen gardens, did domestic service, and labored in the workshops. According to one account, the more insensible ones were employed in tasks that no sane person would do because the work was too revolting or demeaning. The patients' diet included meat every day, but they received less than other inmates so as not to overheat their already unbalanced brains.[47] In short, Our Lady of Grace was one of the best hospitals in Spain, particularly noted for its treatment of the insane. When Cuenca's inquisitors decided to send Bartolomé Sánchez there, they were not sending him off to a different kind of imprisonment; they acted out of the charitable hope that the doctors there actually would find a cure for him.

At the end of August 1558 Licentiate Moral received a letter from his colleagues at the Inquisition of Zaragoza advising him that they had managed to place Sánchez at Our Lady of Grace. This was a feat, as the hospital normally did not accept patients from outside the kingdom of Aragon. The inquisitors advised Moral, "There's only one thing—they are not so successful in curing [the insane] of their illness as is commonly thought, but we will try to make sure that they do more with [Sánchez] than with the others."[48] For Sánchez, a man accustomed to extreme poverty and hard labor, Nuestra Señora de la Gracia must have seemed like a palace. He would be well fed there, given a clean hospital gown, and examined periodically by doctors. The hospital's church was even staffed with musicians to grace divine services. Given his skills, Sánchez probably was put to work in the gardens and carding wool for the women to spin. On Corpus Christi he would be expected to participate in the hospital's observance of the holiday, which by the end of the century would become a

sight to behold. The streets were festooned with banners, a large number
of clergy participated with precious crosses and relics, and the mad (who
were considered innocent of sin and Christ's special wards) marched along
with the city confraternities. They were dressed in their shifts and each
one had a musical instrument, which he played "according to his understanding"; in other words, there was total cacophony.[49] After Christmas, on Twelfth Night, the mad had another special holiday, which they
celebrated with "much happiness and many hurrahs, wearing capes and
costumes made of *guardamanil,* and playing tambourines, cymbals, and
flutes."[50] For whatever reason, though, Sánchez did not take to his new
life, and sometime during the next eighteen months he escaped and
headed home.

The residents of Cardenete were not happy to see the heretic, now
certified insane. Sánchez lost no time in picking up where he had left off.
Licentiate Jiménez sent another report to Cuenca, but no reply came from
the inquisitors (in fact, the report never found its way into the file). The
village elders wrote another letter to the Inquisition on March 26, 1560,
to complain that Sánchez was back to his old heresies and that a man so
heretical should not be allowed to remain among the people. By coincidence, the bishop's inspector arrived in Cardenete just as the village council was preparing to send its letter. Armed with the new awareness of the
threat of Protestantism in Spain (whole cells of Lutherans had recently
been uncovered in Valladolid and Seville), he examined Sánchez, declared
him to be a "knavish" Lutheran, and ordered him sent as a prisoner to
Cuenca together with the council's letter.

The letter is entered into the file just before the very last entry in Sánchez's dossier, which reads as follows:

> In Cuenca, March 28, 1560. While the Lord Inquisitor Padilla was pres-
> ent during the morning session, a man entered the courtroom and de-
> livered a letter to the Lord Inquisitor and said that along with it he
> brought prisoner Bartolomé Sánchez, resident of Cardenete. The Lord
> Inquisitor saw the letter and looked at Bartolomé Sánchez's trial, and
> having seen it, it seems to him that it contains the same propositions as
> the letter refers to, and that the Lords Inquisitors and consultants voted
> that they did not hold Bartolomé Sánchez to be a man in his entire wits
> and understanding, and as such they removed his sanbenito and sent

him to the insane asylum in Zaragoza. Having seen that, he directed Bartolomé Sánchez to remain in this city and to stay in the perpetual prison until something else is decided.[51]

Ybaneta concluded hopefully, "When the inspection [of this Holy Office] was carried out, a report concerning Bartolomé Sánchez and this affair was made [to the Suprema], and it could be that Their Lordships will soon send a decision as to what should be done. This took place before me, Juan de Ybaneta, notary."

The letter never came, and the ultimate fate of Bartolomé Sánchez, wool carder and secret Messiah, remains unknown.

CONCLUSION
Forgotten Endings

AFTER MARCH 1560, BARTOLOMÉ SÁNCHEZ DISAPPEARS FROM THE documents as a protagonist. His family struggled on, and in September of that year, Catalina Martínez petitioned the court to remove her husband's sanbenito from the parish church in Cardenete. From another source we learn incidentally that before Bartolomé's final arrest the couple had been quarreling and Sánchez had locked himself in the house and refused to let anyone in. Catalina's petition gives no hint of the whereabouts or status of her husband; by that point, Catalina probably did not want to know where he was. On his account, no one wanted to marry their daughters, and as long as his sanbenito hung in the church as a perpetual reminder of his dishonor, their daughters would never marry. She pointed out that since an earlier court had found Sánchez to be insane, he was excused from wearing a sanbenito and so its duplicate in the parish church should be taken down as well. Dr. Vergara, who had been involved in Sánchez's case since the beginning, took it upon himself to relay the petition to the Suprema.[1]

No decision seems to have been taken. At that point, the Suprema was conducting a review of the conduct of the tribunal of Cuenca and the council was not happy with what was coming to light. The two inquisitors, Riego and Moral, had become enemies and the entire tribunal had split into two factions, more or less divided between those who fraternized with Cuenca's high nobility and those who, contrary to all policy, kept company with conversos. Because of the tribunal's perpetual poverty, officials engaged in various illegal or prohibited activities to supplement their salaries, which were several months in arrears. The charges began with the inquisitors, whose crimes were relatively slight: they accepted gifts of chickens, capons, trout, and other foodstuffs sent to them at Christmas by Cuenca's prominent citizens. To preserve the Inquisition's dignity and avoid complications, officials were not supposed to engage in trade or menial labor of any sort, yet Secretary Ybaneta was noted for spending his free time weaving cloth and trading in pork fat and fresh fish. He sold the cloth he wove through conversos who had been penanced by the tribunal. (In his day, Bartolomé Sánchez had carded wool for another Inquisition functionary.) Ybaneta and Dr. Muñoz, who had served as Sánchez's defense lawyer, accepted "gifts" in exchange for good news about the fate of the donors' loved ones. They carried on this commerce in good news through their servants, who competed with one another to be the first to arrive at the family's home and win a reward. Some officials lent money at interest. All of this activity, shocking though it seems to the modern observer, was typical of bureaucracies at the time, as officials could not count on regular payment of their salaries to cover their living expenses and had to invent alternative sources of income.[2]

Various irregularities were noted in the way the tribunal handled its secret papers and maintained procedural protocol. Inquisitor Moral was blamed particularly for this laxity on the part of his subalterns. The worst offense of many was that defendants were given the original transcripts of their trials, which contained such confidential information as the names of their accusers. Inquisitor Riego was chastised for allowing Juan de Ybaneta to speak his opinion freely about the court's cases, even to resist or change what the tribunal's judges and advisers had decided. Having seen Ybaneta's conduct in Sánchez's trial, we cannot be surprised by this indictment.[3] Two inquisitors in a row, Cortes and Moral, had found Ybaneta's advice indispensable, and the secretary abused their confidence by flouting the Holy Office's rules. Another official, the prosecutor Bachiller Serrano, was criticized for his impetuous temper, gambling, and womanizing. He survived the inspection and went on to a distinguished career, but Ybaneta lost his job and was permanently barred from working for the Inquisition again.[4]

With these meager final notes, the past we have reconstructed in the course of this book (we—because the reader is a participant in this process as well) fades from view and finally disappears beyond further recovery. Despite the apparent immediacy of the events as recounted here, Bartolomé Sánchez, as we have come to know him in these pages, owes his existence to the note-taking skills of Juan de Ybaneta, what I have written, and the reader's imagination. Yet he also was his own creation, as he wove stories, confessions, and lies in his efforts to save his life. His very identity as the Elijah-Messiah was a fiction, a delusion, or, more charitably, a product of his overstimulated "ymaginaçion," as he sometimes put it. Somewhere, between these things and the unrecorded irruptions of his madness, exists the failed farmer, sometime wool carder, and secret Messiah.

The problem of Sánchez's trial lies not in what was documented but in what was *not* asked or recorded, which composes as it were the negative spaces of the historical text. Because Pedro Cortes and the other inquisitors did not believe in Sánchez's sanity (and therefore his guilt), they failed to interrogate the wool carder rigorously to discover everything they could about his heretical notions, how he might have learned them, and if he had "infected" anyone else with them. We can appreciate the difference in the result by picking up the trial transcript of Domenico Scandella, better known as Menocchio, and seeing how the questioning in that trial proceeded and what it produced. Menocchio, like Sánchez, was essentially a cooperative defendant because he was proud of his intelligence and wanted an audience. The Italian inquisitors' questioning of their prisoner was relentless, to the point of employing torture. They made no attempt (on record at least) to convert Menocchio to more orthodox beliefs. The result was that the range of information elicited from Menocchio was far greater—the miller was something of a natural philosopher and there were few things he had not reflected on. We find out his thoughts about creation, the nature of God, the soul, other peoples in the world, the Church, the more orthodox aspects of doctrine, and his sources and with whom he conversed.[5] By contrast, Sánchez's interrogators did not track down every lead offered to them. His judges do not appear to have been interested in his other theological views or "heresies" derived from folklore. Sánchez was never interrogated regarding his ideas on the transmigration of souls, their peculiar punishment in purgatory, the seven-headed serpent, or the location of the Virgin Mary, who he once claimed lived in a palm tree.[6] And these are only the stray remnants of Sánchez's more offbeat declarations to the court that managed to survive Ybaneta's strict editing. We cannot begin to imagine what else he may have said.

Just as the deliberately incomplete trial challenges our trust in the sources, Sánchez's unexplored statements challenge historians of Spanish popular culture to ask more of their texts, especially of those negative spaces, the less obvious leads, such as Sánchez's odd statements about the souls of the dead. Out of curiosity, let us follow one of these leads just briefly.

There is ample documentary evidence recording a lively belief among early modern European peoples in the transmigration of souls, the wandering dead, and the hordes or armies of the night. Despite this evidence, historians who have studied Spanish attitudes toward death during the early modern period have uniformly considered only the manifestation of orthodox belief found in testaments, sermons, and devotional literature, and have ignored the occasional condemnation of folk belief concerning the status of the soul after death that can be found even in these eminently conformist sources. It was commonly believed, for example, that at death some souls were condemned to wander the earth to haunt the living until an adequate offering of masses was made for the repose of the suffering spirit; a case of such a haunting took place in seventeenth-century Cuenca.[7] Nor was Bartolomé Sánchez the only person in the bishopric of Cuenca to propose the transmigration of souls. In 1499 Andrés Borrachero (his name, meaning "drunkard," is an evocative indication of the contempt in which he was held by the community) apparently held a metaphysical discussion with some people about the nature of the earth, heaven, and hell. While talking about these things, he allegedly said that "there was no, nor is there any, purgatory, paradise, or hell.

There is nothing but to be born and to die." Although scandalous and heretical, this statement ("No hay una cosa sino nacer e morir") was nothing new, either to the inquisitors or to Andrés's audience, as it frequently appears in inquisitorial trials. But Andrés did not stop there; according to the indictment, "To better affirm his evil purpose and cursed error, he said that they should not believe that the souls of the dead purged their sins except by going through the air and inhabiting other bodies and going about in the shape of dogs." Remarkably enough, this proposition echoes the popular quasi-religious-philosophical beliefs of the ancient Pythagoreans, which continued to circulate after the end of the classical world. It is a challenge to investigators to trace the genealogy of such ideas, despite the difficulties involved.[8]

Similarly virtually unexplored by Spanish historians are the related notions of the hordes and processions of the dead, which survive in medieval and Renaissance Spanish literary sources and in modern anecdotal evidence.[9] Outside of Spain, the legends, which have been extensively studied, appear most consistently in Teutonic settings, but variations have been found in medieval France and Renaissance Italy.[10] One version involves phantom armies seen in ethereal battle; the other describes processions of the dead marching through the landscape. The medieval Spanish poets El Berceo and Count Fernán González describe processions of "very many people with candles in their hands and burning torches, ugly but not shining, with their king in the middle."[11] Centuries later, Cervantes picked up on the theme and incorporated it into one of the most eerie scenes in *Don Quixote*. Are these mere literary tropes or reflections of popular belief? The sixteenth-century humanist Diego de Mendoza described in *La Guerra de Granada* how "the local inhabitants see squadrons meet in the air; voices are heard as when people join battle: common Spaniards call such apparitions or phantasms *estantiguas*."[12] Though skimpy, the literary evidence is intriguing; combined with the odd inquisitorial case, clearly investigations less strictly focused on evidence of Christianization will turn up more vestiges of non-Christian belief.

Like the wandering dead, the question of would-be messiahs is equally fascinating and elusive. In all periods of history there are scattered references to individuals who have claimed that they were the Messiah; in extraordinary circumstances, one of these men might attract a following.[13]

Before the seventeenth century, rarely does enough documentation survive to cast light on the personality and motives of the individual, whose memory is obscured by legends and official hostility.[14] Only thirty years before Sánchez's trial, two messianic figures attracted considerable followings on the Iberian Peninsula: El Encubierto, who revived the failing Germanías Revolt in Valencia, and Luis Dias, "the Messiah of Setubal," who roused the hopes of conversos living in southern Portugal.[15] Their success was made possible by the generalized apocalyptic fears of the time, and more specifically by their followers' feelings of hopelessness and persecution. Of these men, or of other contemporaneous messianic figures such as David Reubeni and Solomon Molcho, almost nothing can be said with certainty about their true intentions. Their chroniclers were not interested in understanding the mentality of such persons, whom they regarded with loathing. They were variously condemned as madmen, scheming adventurers, and dangerous heretics. Hence the extraordinary nature of Bartolomé Sánchez's case. Hatred and fear did not blind Inquisitor Cortes, Dr. Vergara, and Secretary Ybaneta to Sánchez's humanity; rather, their compassion for the struggling wool carder led them to strive for the necessary comprehension to save his life. Through their deliberations and investigations, we gain some insight into the life experience and thought processes of one man who came to believe in his own messianic destiny. And in the end, in an ironic twist of fate, through the papers of the Holy Office of the Inquisition, Bartolomé Sánchez, failed farmer and secret Elijah-Messiah, is reborn.

NOTE ON THE EDITING OF
THE SPANISH TEXTS

The texts have been edited slightly to make them more accessible to readers not familiar with sixteenth-century Spanish. All abbreviations have been written out in full. Original spellings have been kept, but capitals and some accents have been added. At the time, Spanish handwritten texts were composed with a minimum of punctuation, even after printed texts had adopted the conventions of periods, commas, and interrogatives. Some additional punctuation has been added to improve the texts' readability.

APPENDIX A

Excerpts from Bartolomé Sánchez's Trial

1. Bartolomé Sánchez Explains the Origin of His Heresies, June 20, 1556 (Chapter 1)

[120v]* Preguntado quando començó a tener estos herrores que ha confesado y qué le movio a ello pues dize que nadie se los ha enseñado, dixo que por San Juan de Junyo que abrá çinco o seys años venyendo este confesante de segar de la vega de Yemeda que es junto a Cardenete que puede aver asta media legua, en acabando de ençerrar el sol que aun no era anocheçido allegando que allegó junto a vn hermyta que se dize San Sebastian, en el ayre se le representaron en figura de lumbre o de cleridan figuras de dos honbres y una muger, y la muger se le figuró que estaba en medio de los honbres y ençima de la dicha muger se le representó que estaba una abe que con la punta de una ala tocaba del otro, y viendo esto se yncó de rodillas y rezó alli çinco Pater Nosteres con çinco Ave Marias, y despues luego tres Pater Nosteres con tres Ave Marias y todo de rodillas suplicando a Dios que si aquello era cosa buena se lo declarase y sy no se lo apartase, y que en este medio se desapareçió aquello que vido y que le paresçio que quedó su coraçon consolado y asy se fue a su casa y nunca lo dixo a nadie, y andubo siempre ymaginando entre sy qué sería aquello asta que vino la quaresma que se fue a confesar con Martyn de Almaçan cura viejo de la villa de Cardenete, y en este medio conpró vn libro de Hernan Çomeño, que eran unas romanas que tenyan su matilbojo [martirlogio?] en romançe y este confesante leya por aquellas oras. Y donde encomençaban las oras de la Conçepcion de Nuestra Señora alló en una oja pintada la figura que se le representó en el camyno venyendo de segar, y confesandose con el dicho cura le mostró la figuraba que estaba en las dichas oras y tanbien le dixo lo que se le avia representado en el camyno que por esa como lo que estaba pintado [121r] en las oras, y el dicho cura abrio las oras y vio aquella figura pintada. Y vista y lo que este confesante avia dicho le dixo, "No te la puedo tachar ny abonar porque no lo

*All folio numbers in appendixes A and B refer to ADC, Inq., leg. 126, exp. 2216.

alcanço; ¿qué sé es? no digas a nadie nada." Y confesado y absuelto se fue a su casa y siempre este quonfesante no podia caber en sý asta saber de personas dottas y sabias qué era aquello, y despues las vezes que veya algunos frayles o persona docta luego se yba a sus pies y se confesaba y se lo dezia todo lo que arriba dicho es y amostraba la figura de las oras y ansi lo dixo a fray Piçarro e a fray Sebastian lo que dicho tiene y les mostró las dichas oras para fin que le dixiesen qué podia sinyficar aquello e que despues de muerto el cura de Cardenete el biejo lo comunycó con el cura moço que es agora que se llama el bachiller Barca. Un dia despues que se avian leydo unas escomunyones en la yglesia le dixo que él que las daba y él que las leya merezecian ser apedreados, y el dicho cura le dixo "Veys, aveys yncurrido en esas escomunyones" y este confesante le dixo que no, y ansy el dicho cura le tornó, "Pues, ¿qué se os da a vos? Me aveys de pedir vos esas cuentas." Y entonces este confesante le dixo al dicho cura que el Hijo de Dios no vino a ganar aziendas syno anymas y que los que escomulgaban por allegar azienda mataban las anymas y con tanto se despidio dél. E dende a ciertos dias vino a Cardenete a predicar dia de Santo Tome antes de Navidad un frayle de Carboneras, y este confesante, como no podia caber en sý de las cosas que ymaginaba fuera de lo que manda la Santa Madre Yglesia, se fue a confesar con el dicho frayle y le dixo todo lo arriba dicho y le mostró la dicha figura de las oras. El qual dicho frayle le dixo que aquello que se le avia representado era el diablo y no le quyso absolber [121v] y le mandó que se fuese con él a Carboneras a comer y que no dixiese a nadie nada y tambien le dixo que poco sería la vida de este confesante. Y con esto quedó este confesante muy trasboleado y fue este confesante a su casa e hizo una soga de esparto crudo y luego se la çinyó por el cuerpo en la carona de la carne y se dio con ella çinco o seys bueltas para yr ansy ante el dicho frayle como en penytençia syn que el dicho frayle le oviese mandado nynguna cosa desto. Y quando se huvo de yr allá avia aparejado çinco piedras y las metio en unas alforjas que pesarian una arroba poco más o menos para llevar a cuestas tanbien en penytençia al dicho monesterio de Carboneras donde avia de yr a ablar al dicho frayle para que le avsolbiese. Y la noche de antes del dia que avia de yr que tenya su soga ceñyda y las piedras aparejadas para el dicho hefeto, porque su muger no las viese en las dichas alforjas metidas debaxo de un tryllo, y mandó a Bartolomico su hijo que leyese por las dichas oras las oraciones que este confesante tenya en devocion porque este confesante estaba tan elevado y trasboleado que no podia él rezar. Y estando rezando la Pasion el dicho muchacho, este confesante cayó en el suelo de una silla en que estaba asentado, dando bozes y diziendo, "¡Vete maldito Lucifer, no te di gracia que entres aca!" encomendandose a Dios y a los santos. Y visto esto la muger e hijo de confesante salieron a los vezinos dando vozes como agollantados viendo las cosas que este confesante dezia y ansy se llegaron muchos vezinos, honbres y mugeres, e vn clerigo que se llamaba Juan Gallego y le preguntaban a este confesante qué era aquello que avia que se espantaban dello y le levantaron y asentaron en su silla, y este confesante les dixo que se fuesen en orabuena [122r] a sus casas, que no sabía lo que se hera ny que avia avido, y asy se fueron a sus casas excepto Garci Perez, texedor, que dixo que se queria quedar con este confesante para que a él le dixiese lo que avia. Y asi se quedó y este confesante se acostó y el dicho honbre Garçi Perez se asentó junto a él, preguntandole qué era aquello y este confesante le dixo que no sabía más de que el frayle que avia predicado el dia de Santo Tome confesando con él no le quyso avsolber y que avia de yr a Carboneras. Y el dicho Garci Perez le dixo que no fuese asta que él ablase con el cura, y que otro dia de mañana el dicho Garci Perez vino de mañana a donde estaba este confesante y le dixo que no se fuese que aun el cura no estaba levantado y este confesante le dixo que si avia de venyr, vynyese presto porque no podia dexar de yr a Carboneras para que el dicho frayle le ausolbiese. Y el dicho Garci Perez cerró el palaçio por de fuera porque este confesante no se pudiese yr e que ydo el dicho Garci Perez este confesante llamó a vn muchacho y le abrio y tomó las alforjas a cuestas donde estaban las dichas piedras y tira camino de Carboneras, y allegando bien fuera del pueblo el dicho Garci Perez tras él y le alcançó y le quytaba las alforjas y no le dexó yr e hizo tornar asta que hablase con el cura, y le llevó a su casa y truxo el cura alli. Y el dicho cura dixo a este confesante, "Andad, acabamonos la mysa a la yglesia y despues de dicho mysa platicaremos," y ansy se fueron a la yglesia y el dicho cura dixo la mysa y este confesante la oyó y despues el dicho cura [dixo] a este confesante, "Salgamonos aqui a la cuesta de la torre que es junto a la yglesia," y le preguntó qué era que lo que avia e a dónde yba, y este confesante le dixo que yba a Carboneras con aquella soga y piedras en penitencia para que el dicho frayle le avsolbiese. [122v] Y el dicho cura le dixo que no tubiese pena que él le avsolbia de todo aquello e ansy le hizo quytar la dicha soga y quytar las piedras delante dél y le dixo que se fuese a su casa y que trabajase como solia para dar de comer a su muger e hijos y ansy este confesante se bolbio y todo el dia estaba elevado y trasboleado. Y vispera de pasqua de Navidad vino el dicho cura a casa deste confesante a verle y le pidio las oras que este confesante rezaba y las llevó, y otro dia de pasqua de Navidad su muger deste confesante le dixo que se levantase y se fuese a mysa y este confesante le dixo que no queria yr, y ella le respondio que ¿de quándo aca no queria oyr misa? y fue a llamar a sus hermanos y otros. Y como este confesante oyese el remor de la gente que venya, huvo myedo que le venya a hazer más y se levantó y tomó vn bordon en la mano para defenderse dellos y que le dexasen en su casa y se fuesen, y ellos arremetieron a este confesante con quytalle el bordon y se lo quytaron y viendo las cosas que dezia y desatinos que hazía le ataron a vn poste desnudo en camysa y descalço y salieron del palaçio y çerraron la puerta por de fuera. Y este confesante como no le queryan desatar su muger ny nadie con las dientes corta la soga que hera de esparto y se suelta y arremete a la puerta para dar con ella entera para se salir y los honbres se espantaron, que ¿quyén le avia soltado? y este confesante dixo que Dios y le hizieron vestir y le llevaron a mysa. Y por ser tarde çesó la audiençia. Gaviria, notario. [Unfortunately, Sánchez was not asked to resume his confession and the remainder of information about what occurred to him before his arrest is supplied by other witnesses.]

2. Why Men Should Not Worship the Crucifix (Chapter 2)

[23v] Dixo el dicho Bartolome Sanchez que pues él pedio a su Reverençia le declarase las çircunstançias del pecado y no se las declara, que él se las declarará. Y que en lo que su Reverençia le tiene dicho acerca que declare quales son los que él llama ydolos y a que no se tiene de creher y adorar, dixo que quando el Hijo de Dios vyno al mundo que nos se lo envió Dios Padre, nos lo envió en graçia que no nos costó nada y vino a darnos ley con que nos saluasemos. Y como que era que todos somos y desçendemos hijos de Dios primeramente y de Adan y de Eva y con ser hijos de los susodichos y somos de un linaje y somos hermanos, y predicando Dios su palabra evangelica verdadera a nuestros hermanos los antepasados y ellos, porque les reprehendia lo que mal hazian e yvan contra la ley de Dios, le calumnyavan y dezian que yva contra su ley porque yba contra su proposito dellos. Y le dezian, "Myra, ¡qué blasfemyas dize!, ¡myra que nos afrenta!" Pues, ¿quál sería mejor ley—la que el Hijo de Dios dava o el proposito que ellos seguian?, que no le quisieron creer ni adorar como a Dios y Señor verdadero, que si lo creyerian no era justa justiçia que a él que dize la verdad lo maten sino que lo aguardaran como a Dios y Señor. Y era y es mucha razon que si lo guardaran e seguieran y lo creyeran como syguen agora y aguardan un rey y esperan que haga Cortes e saque leyes a su [24r] proposito, que no lo mataran. Mas como no querian creer lo que él les dezia y se afrontavan dello, diziendo ansi, que vn hijo de vn carpintero, vn honbre synple e pobre les reprehendia lo que yvan contra la ley de Dios. E contrataron los nuestros hermanos antepassados de vendello y de conprallo, que vendieron la graçia y la conpraron en serviçio de xxx dineros, y a este Hijo de Dios y a su Padre y a la misma Madre y al Espiritu Santo que en ellos está se deve de honrar y adorar. Y como que era que nuestros hermanos los antepassados, hermanos de todo el genero humano, mataron a Christo en aquella cruz, no queriendo creer su ley evangelica y no quisieron creer su pasion ny su ley sino que todo la confundieron. Creen y adoran en el palo en que él fue crucificado y cosa más justa fuera creerlo a él en vida pues nos dava ley y declarava que no agora adorar y honrrar el palo que es la cruz, que son las armas del diablo con que los diablos

bisibles se defendieron de Christo y lo mataron en ella. Que como era y es el diablo enemigo de Dios, asy hizieron aquella cruz y palo con que de Christo se deffendieron desta vida humana porque se afrentavan de la ley que les dava. Asi como se defiende un honbre de otro enemigo suyo con sus armas, ansi se defendió el diablo o diablos con aquella cruz que la tiene por santa de palo o hierro, que con ello le mataron a Christo, y que a esta cruz y palo tiene él [i.e., Sánchez] por ydolo y que ansi este declarante no adora en el crucifixo que es un palo o hierro syno en él que crucificaron, en él que fue el Hijo de Dios.

3. How Christ Did Not Want to Die and How Elijah Is Coming to Avenge His Death (Chapter 2)

[24v] Dixo el dicho Bartolome Sanchez que en lo que tiene dicho se afirma que no adora ny cree en ny la quyere honrrar ny adorar a las cruzes de palo, hierro ny plata ny en las otras ymagines sino en el Hijo de Dios que fue en la dicha cruz crucificado y que por fuerça aquellos honbres, que son diablos que mataron a Christo, le hizieron padesçer y llevar la cruz a cuestas a renpuzones y en ella le mataron y ansi dixo al Padre por tres vezes, "Si posibile est, yo no mirera [mirara?] ni beba este caliz de amargura," y que dixo, "Padre no quiere que nynguno mate al justo," mas da lugar que cada uno cunpla su voluntad, como que si un honbre quiere hazer una cosa que no deva ir contra los mandamientos de Dios, le da lugar para ello porque por sý se tiene de condenar o saluar. Y Dios como es justo juez no puede dexar de hazer justa justicia y envia Dios un juez, el qual es Helias profetizado a vengar esta muerte de Christo, porque una sentençya que dio Pilatos contra el Hijo de Dios, que fue la mayor que se dio en el mundo, si aquella como se dio syn verdad y sin justicia fuera perdonada, todas las sentençyas mal dadas fueran perdonadas y ansi byene y es nacido Helias que viene a pelear y a conquistar [25r] con el diablo y con el Antechristo no para que viene, ny trae armas defensyvas, ballestas ny espadas ny tiros fuertes y gente para matar a nadie syno la fe verdadera de Dios con que se a de defender. Y ese Helias junto con él que dyzen rey de los judios y el Mezias prometido en la ley y el duque que dize el evangelio de San Mateo, do dize, "Tú Velem tierra de Juda no eres pequeña, que de ti saldra un duque que regira el pueblo de Ysrael," y estos quatro son todos una persona y trahe la palabra que dixo Dios, "Byenaventurado será aquel que no me viere y me creyere," lo qual escrivio San Juan que dixo, "Vendra la luz contra las tinyeblas y las tinyeblas no podran comprehender esta luz," y torna a dezir Sant Matheo, "Tú Velem tierra de Juda etc., que de ti saldra el duque que regira el pueblo de Ysrael," y sella el evangelista San Lucas, "Reynará en la casa de Jacob y de su reyno no será fin," y sobre esto habla San Marcos evangelista, "Que aunque a este duque le den cosas matiferas no le enpeceran nada." Todas estas çinco palabras, que son

"Byenaventurados son los que no me vyeran y creheran," estan confirmadas por quatro evangelistas y toda quanta maldad ay en el mundo se confundira y estas dichas palabras no pueden dexar de cunplirse porque dixo San Juan en otro evangelio, "Veran en él que traspasaron mas no quereran dél otra escriptura, etc."

4. Sánchez Declares that He Is the Elijah-Messiah
(Chapter 2)

[26r] Dixo que pluguyese a Dios por su infinyta bondad de juzgar a vno segun su merescimiento y a este declarante el primero y que él es mensajero y que el mensajero no ha de ser mentiroso y deve declarar la verdad de lo a que es venydo, y que despues de declarado es justa justicia diziendo la verdad le den liciençia para que se vaya a su casa a travajar y ganar de comer para él e su muger e hijos, y que ayer dixo a su Reverençia le declarase las circunstançias del pecado y no lo hizo, y que tanbyen le dixo que era venydo y nacido Helias y el Mexias y el rey de los judios y el duque que regira el pueblo de Ysrael de quyen tiene dicho, y como estos [26v] quatro son una mysma persona y que todo lo que dixiera sea en servicio de Dios, y que el Hijo de Dios quando vino al mundo no sentencyó a nynguno a muerte humana ny enterna, y que los que lo mataron porque les dezia la verdad, ellos mysmos se sentencyaron a muerte eterna porque él [que] mata a él que dize la verdad él mysmo se condena a muerte eterna, y que pues él dize que el Mexias es venydo y nacido (que él lo mostrará con el dedo y dira a donde está quando sea menester) y que si esto es ansi verdad y la Ynquisicion y sus oficiales han muerto e sentenciado y quemado mucha gente syn cuento, tenyendo por heregia e herejes a los que dizen que el Mexias ha de venyr, y que pues este declarante tiene dicho y dize que él que mata a él que dize la verdad muere muerte eterna, que pues los dichos de la Ynquisicion han muerto mucha gente como tiene dicho contra los que tienen dicho y dizen que no es venydo el Mexias, los han muerto mal. Y les requiere de pies de Dios y lo que enplaça [es] que antes del dia de Todos Santos que agora verna vayan con los dichos muertos que ansi han muerto al juzgado de Dios y que a los que tienen presos e aherrojado[s] los suelten, y dexandolo de hazer les protesta escandalos, muertes y daños que sobre ello vinyere, porque el Mexias que tiene la Ynquisicion, que es venydo haya myll y quinientos y tantos años, que éste que es ansi, y él lo quonfiesa que vyno y éste es el Hijo de Dios, encarnado en la Virgen Marya, y que este otro Mexias de quyen este declarante dize que viene, que es el Helias, es la justicia que envia Dios contra los que han muerto la Ynquisicion syn culpa y que este Helias y Mexias, que son los quatro nonbres que trahe, ha cinquenta años y dos más o menos que es nacido, y está en la tierra y es nacido y criado en el lugar de Cardenete.

5. Sánchez on the Word of God and Faith
(Chapter 3)

[34v] Dixo que las palabras de Dios dondequiera que se dizen son buenas y esas dize él y que tenyendo él consigo la palabra de Dios y estando Dios con él, que mediante su voluntad no piensa de perder el anyma ny el cuerpo porque su officio no es de matar ny robar, porque esto es officio del demonyo y ansi se haze en este officio que teneis por sancto de la Ynquisiçion, que han muerto e quytadoles sus haziendas a muchos syn cuento syn averles hecho [35r] prejuizio ny daño. Porque quando Dios vino al mundo y le dixeron blasfemyas, no mató ny robó a ninguno, que ¿por qué en la Ynquisiçion se hazen mejores juezes que Dios?, y que la Ynquisiçion myre el medio que ha de tener, que a esto viene y es enbiado de parte de Dios el Helias y el Mexias a pedir estas muertes que sin razon se han fecho, y que matando ansi a estos los de la Ynquisiçion y quitandoles sus haziendas, con justa razon les dira Dios y este declarante en su nonbre y dé malditos de my Padre al fuego del infierno.

Y en lo que su Reverencia le dize del baptismo, que teniendo la palabra que dixo Dios, "Byenaventurado será él que no me viere y me creyere," y que esta palabra y las otras quatro por él nonbrados las cree Helias con el Mexias como dicho tiene, y que con la dicha palabra se baptiza este declarante y con la fee que tiene declarada y no con agua sal de la yglesia, que la llamó Dios en su sermon synoga, porque la Sagrada Scriptura dize que si tanta fee los honbres tuviesen como un grano de mijo que un cerro se mudaria de un cabo a otro y que la fee sin las obras es muerta, y en otra parte dize que sola la fee salua, y que los de la yglesia que ¿qué fee les dan?, pues con la que les dizen no tienen ny alcançan hasta un grano de mijo, y que en la fee que tiene declarado se afirma y que estas cosas que ha declarado se han confirmado en él desde Sancta Marya de septiembre proxima passada [Sept. 8, 1553] hasta agora donde en este su processo las tiene declaradas, y que algunas dellas tenya de antes y no tan confirmadas como al dicho tiempo aca y se las ha confirmado Dios por su mysericordia, y lo mostrará su Divina Magestad quando él sea servido y que él con Dios lo dize e lo osa dezir y le suplica tenga por byen de librarle de todos los enemigos visibles e ynvisibles.

6. Inquistor Cortes Rebukes Sánchez for Believing He Is the Messiah
(Chapter 3)

[39v] Fuele dicho que ansi mysmo dixo en la dicha audiençia que allende del Hijo de Dios encarnado en la Virgen Marya ay otro Mexias de quyen este declarante dize que vyene, que es Helias y que trahe los dones y gracias de renonbres que tiene referido y que aún que es él, etc., que miente, que un honbre

como él syn letras y syn prudencia, y avn con ella hablar y dezir cosas semejantes es muy grande vicio y torpedad porque nunca se tuvo ny esperó más de
solo un Mexias y este vino que es Jeshu Christo Nuestro Señor como se le ha
dicho. Y Helias no es muerto, antes se dize que él y Henoc estan depositados en
el Parayso Terrenal para hazer a Su Divyna Magestad el servicio que les man-
dare, y Helias quando lo ubiere de hazer cosa que sea atribuyda a Su Magestad,
no se la atribuya asy, que este declarante siendo un honbre pecador y de tan
baxa materia y en semejante tribunal que el es en que está se atrebe e osa dezir
cosas semejantes e las otras demas que tiene declarado, que demas de ser hereti-
cas e reprobadas son locura y vanydad de que en esta dicha audiencia [40r] no
se tiene de pensar, quanto más tractar. E pues con zelo de le recoger e apartar
de sus herrores e libiandades se le disymula y dize lo que oye, si les encarga de
lo passado, tenga el arrepentamiento que debe, e se recoja e lo confiese por mal
dicho, tenydo, e creydo, y emyende su vida para delante e Su Divina Magestad
se sirvira de se lo perdonar.

7. Sánchez Escapes to Cardenete and Burns His Sanbenito
(Chapter 7)

[103r] Dixo que lo que pasa es que este confesante se confesó con Matheo
Sanchez clerigo e capillan deste Santo Officio en la yglesia mayor desta dicha
cibdad uno de los dias de la Semana Santa proxima pasada, e el primero dia de
pascua de Resurrecion syguiente se tornó a reconciliar e comulgar en la dicha
yglesia con el dicho Matheo Sanchez. Y en acavando de rescebir el Santisymo
Sacramento le tomó vn recozimyento y descontento que no cabia en sý e con el
dicho descontento anduvo los dias de pascua pensando e myrando de qué le podria suceder e qué podria ser, e estando ansy descontento acordó de se yr al lugar de Villar de Saz de Arcas con sus peynes para veer sy allaria a qué trabajar
porque le dixo un mançebo que pasadas las fiestas podia ser que en el dicho lugar hallase qué trabajar. Y ansi el postrero dia de la dicha pascua [103v] por la
mañana se levantó e tomado sus peynes se yva para el dicho lugar y salido desta
cibdad y llegando al camyno que se aparta para Arcas, que está medio quarto de
legua, le vyno otro pensamiento e congoxa de no yr al dicho lugar de Villar de
Saz y de yrse para su lugar de Cardenete a su casa. Y le dio luego un pensamiento estando en esto, que ydo al dicho lugar Cardenete quemase en la plaça
su habito penytencial, y ansi con este pensamiento e peleando consigo mysmo
y diziendo entre sý que si lo hazía que aun los niños le apedrearian porque yva
contra el mandamiento de los señores ynquisidores, toviase determyno de yr.
E llegó al dicho lugar de Cardenete myercoles en la tarde e se fue derecho a su
casa y estuvo en ella esta noche con su muger e hijos e que juebes de mañana

le dixo su muger que se fuese a cabar un hortezuelo de su muger porque avia que no se cavava todo el tiempo que este confesante andava por aca, e que allá le llevaria a almorzar. Y ansi tomó su açada y se fue allá solo y acavó de cabar su huerto e en el almorzó con su muger e hijos e le fueron a ver ciertas mugeres. E acavado de cabar el dicho huerto se vino para su casa e antes ya se avian venido la dicha su muger e hijos e venido que este confesante se vino a su casa, le dixo su muger que no estava cozida la olla, que se esperase un poco para comer, y ansi esperó e comyeron ya tarde. E en acavando de comer, tomó su capa e su habito encima como lo solia traer e salio del dicho lugar camyno de Cuenca y de alli con la congoxa y descontento que tenya le tornó al pensamiento de voluer al lugar e tomar leña en el camyno y quemar en la plaça el dicho su habito. E peleando consigo e viendo el mal que queria hazer e conjectarando consygo que quál era mayor pecado, quemar un poco de paño o vn christiano, e peleando consigo que aquello [104r] no era paño syno penitencia e que era desobediencia y que yva contra el mandamyento de sus Reverencias, e no podiendo vencer este pensamiento e descontento que tenya, tomó del dicho camyno por unas vyñas unos sarmientos e unos romeros devaxo del sobaco e se fue derecho a la plaza donde sacó de una bolsa yesca e pedernal, que syenpre lo trae consygo, e encendio lumbre con ello. E ya que ardian los manojos e romero, se quytó el dicho su habito penytencial de los honbros e lo arrojó en el dicho fuego e ansi arrojado se apartó del dicho fuego. Y en esto allegó un ve-cino del dicho lugar que se llama Madrid (que cree que es texedor e vibe de ju-gar) e el dicho Madrid sacó el dicho habito del fuego e se lo tornó a dar a este quonfesante diziendole, "O mal honbre, ¿qué aveis fecho? ¡que los regidores hos prenderan!" Y este confesante le respondio, "No hos fagais vos ynquisi-dor" o "No se haga ninguno ynquisidor pues no lo sois," y en esto este confe-sante tornó a hechar el dicho su habito en el dicho fuego para que se quemase, e hechado, se fue por una calle arriba hazia la fortaleza y despues se tornó a la dicha su casa. Y que al tiempo que este confesante encendia el dicho fuego en la plaza estavan tres honbres en la dicha plaza e se metieron en casa de Francisco Herrero que vibe en la dicha plaza, que este confesante no sabe sus nonbres más de que cree que el vno dellos es el mesonero del pueblo, y que luego pasado lo susodicho Anton de Barca, regidor del dicho lugar, vino a su casa deste confe-sante con quatro o çinco honbres e le dixo, "Yd preso." Y este confesante le dixo, "Pues mirad, ¿qué quereis? que yo lo he fecho e lo puedo hazer!" (aunque no está byen cierto sy dixo las dichas palabras o otras semejantes) e que tiene memoria que dixo, "Tomenlo por testimonio e llevenlo a los señores yn-quisidores," e no se acuerda sy dixo otras más palabras. E que ansi [104v] le lle-varon preso a casa del jurado donde le echaron una cadena e unos grillos e otro dia le enbiaron a este Santo Officio como lo tiene dicho. Y que porque le vino a este confesante vn dolor de cabeza o desvanecimiento, pedio se quedase esta audiencia por agora e sus Reverencias holgaron dello. Y le amonestaron que piense en lo demas que le quedar [sic] por dezir y que toque al descargo de su consciencia [y] fue vuelto a su carcel. Pasó ante my Juan de Yvaneta, notario que a lo susodicho fuy presente.

En Cuenca quinze dias del mes de abril del dicho año estando en la audiencia de la mañana los dichos señores ynquisidores mandaron traer ante sy al dicho Bartolome Sanchez preso e como fue presente le dixieron que ¿qué es lo que se ha acordado acerca del descargo de su consciencia?

Dixo que lo que se le ha acordado es que estando en el dicho lugar de Cardenete preso en casa del dicho jurado Anton de Sazedon luego agora como le llevaron preso los regidores para enviale aqui y estava alli tanbyen presente un hermano del dicho Sazedon, no se acuerda de su nonbre, e unos peones que venyan de cabar e un hierno de Sazedon, y estando ansi preso el dicho hierno de Sazedon començó a tratar y dezir de las cosas pasadas que este confesante solia dezir en el dicho lugar de la cruz e ymagines, e hablando en esto le dixo el dicho hierno de Sazedon, "Andad, ¿que no creeis en la cruz?" y a esto este confesante respondio publicamente que a él un palo ny un hierro no le avyen de saluar syno solo Dios que fue cruçificado, y que en él avya de creer e adorar y no en el palo ny en el hierro e syno que se abraçassen en ellos con un palo e un hierro fecho cruz e él con Dios e que verian qual se saluaria mejor. Y ellos todos como estavan alli le respondieron que aquellos eran ymagines [105r] de Dios e que se avian de adorar e que a esto este confesante respondio que Dios no hizo un palo ny un hierro a su semejanza syno al honbre e que por tanto el honbre se avia de honrrar, que un palo o hierro de qualquiera manera que le hagan cruz o crucifixo es vn palo o vn hierro. Y que a esto los sobredichos que alli estauan le repitieron ciertas palabras de que no se acuerda que a las quales este confesante les respondio que la cruz eran las armas del diablo y que este quonfesante preguntó a los susodichos que alli estaban que si vno matase a su padre o madre con una espada o palo, que sy aquella arma con que ansi le matase, que si le ternyan e adorarian por reliquya. E que el vno dellos le respondio, "na [ya?] sabe quyen que no," y otro dellos se quedó en dubda y no le respondio e que en esto este quonfesante les dixo, "Ya me aveis confesado que no la terniades por reliquya ny adoraiades a la espada o palo con que oviesen muerto a nuestro padre o hermano, pues desque uno os dize a vos unas palabras con que hos pesa, le dezis, "¡No me las digais porque hare un desconcierto contra vos!," y aquella persona se las torna a dezir para le más ynjuriar e yndignar, la persona ynjuriada en su vengança toma unas armas o le mata con ellas. Y que ansi el Hijo de Dios dezia e predicaba a aquellos diablos visibles, dandoles ley con que se saluasen, e que ¿quál sería mejor [ley], la que él les dava o la que ellos tenyan? (e que los diablos visibles este quonfesante tiene que eran los que crucificaron a Christo) y que los dichos diablos visibles le respondian a Christo, arguyendole, "No te queremos creer lo que nos dizes ny aún que tú lo creas tanpoco," diziendoles Dios, "Umyllaos a mí e seguidme porque hos vengo a saluar," y ellos no queriendo humyllarse a él ny creerlo hizieron una cruz para que se defendiessen destas palabras y doctrina que Christo les dava y en ella le crucificaron. E ansi con aquella cruz e en aquella cruz le mataron, [105v] y ansi con justa verdad se puede dezir que la cruz son armas del diablo pues con ella se defendieron de Christo por la doctrina santa que les daba, que los judios defendieron con la dicha cruz los cuerpos e no las almas, y que como él esto dezia se fueron los dichos honbres por ay e no le querian escuchar y que no se acuerda sy otra cosa alguna más alli passó ny se acuerda de otra cosa por el presente, e que si algo viene más en la probança se lo diga y que si se acordare, él lo dira, etc.

8. Secretary Ybaneta's Report (July, 1557)
(Chapter 7)

[143v] Relacion que hizo el notario de lo que siente deste reo.

Yo, Juan de Yvaneta, scriuano de su magestad real y notario del secreto de la Ynquisicion de Cuenca, atento que este processo del dicho Bartolome Sanchez se ha de lleuar a los señores del consejo de Su Magestad de la general Ynquisicion y que muchas de las audiencias que con este reo tuvo el señor ynquisidor el licenciado Pedro Cortes, que sea en gloria, se hizieron e passaron ante my, porque más ynformados sus señorias puedan admynistrar justicia y por lo que toca al descargo de mi consciencia y al scrupulo que podria formar en no hazer esta relacion ante sus señorias como la hecha a los señores ynquisidores que al presente resyden en este Santo Officio, con licencia de sus reverencias digo y declaro lo siguiente.

El dicho señor inquisidor Cortes, tenyendo relacion de las cosas que este Bartolome Sanchez hazía y dezia, dio la comysyon que está al principio [144r] deste processo, e rescebida la ynformacion e traydo este reo preso a este dicho Santo Officio, en la primera audiencia que con él se tuvo, entró en la sala de la audiencia como un hombre furioso o endemonyado, haziendo muchos personajes de su persona y diziendo e hablando muchos desatinos e apaciguado algo por el dicho señor ynquisidor y preguntado por el discurso de su vida y origen de los herrores que dezia, començó a proseguir en sus desatinos, y entre las cosas que contó tengo memoria que dixo que avia visto una vision celestial en una dehesa e que desta quedó muy atemorizado e que vino a perder el sentido e tenyendo en su propria casa despues desta vision atado se le aparescian unos como gatos de noche y le davan grandissima congoxa y le dexauan atormentado y syn spiritu e que se soltó y començó a hablar y dezir las cosas que dezia porque se lo mandava Dios. Y teniendo respeto a sus vanydades y cosas que dezia, supplique al dicho señor ynquisidor que pues en este reo no se hallava tan entera capaçidad ny el juizio que convenia para negocio tan grabe, se sobreseyesse en la prosecucion desta causa hasta veer y caler más enteramente si éste era endemonyado o avia perdido el juizio, y el dicho señor inquisidor me respondio que más adelante se podria proveer en todo y ansi fue con él haziendo sus audiencias y tomando en ellas de sus palabras lo que más hazía a la materia de sus proposyciones y las fue ordenando sin quytar ny añadir en la substancia cosa alguna y se dexaron de scriuir en ellas muchas cosas de las que dezia por ser desatinos e disparates. Y a lo que yo pude conprehender deste dicho reo siempre le tuve por honbre endemonyado o loco y que no tenya libertad en lo que hablaba y dezia, y ansi lo di a entender a los [144v] consultores y ordinario y ellos le hablaron e comunicaron en algunas sesiones y quedaron con harto scrupulo de su juizio. Y porque en ellas [sesiones] dezia que aunque le hechasen en el fuego, el fuego no le enpeceria, y que si le quemasse que él se disdiria de todo lo que dezia, acordaron que este proceso se votase en la forma que le votaron, y oý dezir al doctor Vergara canonigo de la magistral (que era el ordinario e está al presente en esta ciudad) que si no tuviera por cierto que en llegando al campo este reo se volviera a Dios y se retractara de su locura, que en ninguna manera vinyera en lo que votó porque tenya por cierto que tenya demonyo o estaua loco, y aún al presente anda este reo en esta ciudad pidiendo por Dios y trabajando en algunas cosas para su sustentamiento como honbre envelesado y fuera de sí. Y despues de reconciliado le oý dezir en la sala desta audiencia que no sabía qué se tenya, que era atormentado porque se hechase de la puente desta ciudad en el rio, y rogaron al dicho doctor Vergara que le tractasse y quitase destas ymaginaciones y el dicho doctor lo lleuó a cargo y en ello ha trabajado harto, y por que esto es ansi verdad lo firmé de my nonbre oy, miercoles xiiii de jullio de myll e quinientos e cinquinta e syete años.

APPENDIX B
Sánchez's Prayers (Chapter 5)

PRAYER OF SUPPLICATION

{52v} Señor Dios Padre, vos sois pan, Señor Dios Hijo, vos sois vino, Virgen Sancta Marya vos sois carne. Señor, por vuestra sanctissima Trinydad no me dexere caer, y si cayere, vos me levantad. Señor, enseñad vuestro saber, descrubid vuestra bondad. Vean todos en my las maravillas de vuestra santisyma claridad para que en vuestro nonbre pueda vençer y conquistar este cargo que me aveis dado con el Antechristo y con el diablo.

[Secretary's note] Y que el cargo que dize Dios le ha dado es el que este su proçesso tiene dicho y declarado.

Compared to Their Equivalents from the *Horas de Nuestra Señora* (Toledo: Juan de Ayala, 1565)

SÁNCHEZ'S HAIL MARY	AYALA'S HAIL MARY
Ave Marya llena soys de gracia. El Señor es en vos, bendita soys entre todas las mugeres y bendito es el fee fructo de vuestro byentre, que es Jeshus. Sancta madre de Dios, tened por byen de rogar por my e por todo el pueblo de Ysrael por syempre jamas, amen.	Dios te salve maria llena de gracia: el señor es contigo. Bendita tu entre las mugeres. Y bendito el fruto de tu vientre Jesus. Sancta Maria virgen madre de Dios ruega por nosotros pecadores. Amen

SÁNCHEZ'S OUR FATHER

Padre myo que estais en los
çielos, sanctificado sea
vuestro nonbre. Venga en my
vuestro reyno. Hagase en my
vuestra voluntad asi como se
haze en el çielo, sea fecho en
my que es a tierra. El pan
vuestro Señor tened por byen
de darmelo oy y cada dia, a my
y a todo el pueblo de Ysrael,
y a quien vos Señor tuvyere dél
por byen, y libradme de
tentacion por syempre jamas,
amen.

AYALA'S OUR FATHER

Padre nuestro que estás en los
cielos sanctificado sea
el tu nombre. Uenga a nos
el tu reyno: hagase
tu voluntad, assi
en la tierra como en
el cielo. El pan
nuestro de cada dia
danoslo oy. Y perdona nuestros
deudos: assi como nos las
perdonamos a nuestros
deudores. Y no nos traygas en
tentacion: mas libranos de
mal. Amen.

SÁNCHEZ'S MAGNIFICAT

Señor myo, vos dixisteis que
él que hos tenyese hariades
fortaleza en su poderio, ansy
vos tened por byen de hazer
fortaleza en mi poderio, y
tened por byen de derramar los
soberbios con voluntad de su
coraçon y de derribar los
poderosos de la sylla y
ensalçar los humyldosos y a
los hanbrientos cumplillos de
byenes y a los ricos dexallos
vazios para que rescibamos el
pueblo de Ysrael que son los
legos, a Dios, que es su saluador.

AYALA'S MAGNIFICAT

Hizo
fortaleza en el su poderio:
derramo los
soberbios con voluntad de su
coraçon. Derribó los
poderosos de la silla: y
ensalzo los humildosos. E a
los hambrientos cumplio de
bienes: y a los ricos dexó
vazios. Recibio
Israel a su saluador: acordose
de la su misericordia.
Assi como dixo a los nuestros
padres Abrahan y su linage por
siempre. Gloria sea al padre
y al hijo y al spiritu sancto.

SÁNCHEZ'S MATTHEW

Dixo heli heli lamaza
batani.

Ven Helias ven Helias a vengar
mi muerte que me han matado.

AYALA'S MATTHEW

Llamó el señor con gran voz.
Et dixo. Heli / heli / lamaza
bathani: que quiere decir Dios
mio: Dios mio, ¿por qué me has
desanparado? E algunos que
alli estaban y lo oyan dezian.
A Helias llama este.

NOTES

Introduction

1. The literature (pro and con) spawned by this debate is vast. Appleby and Hunt try to steer a middle ground in *Telling the Truth about History*, as do Spiegel, *Past as Text*, and Chartier, *On the Edge of the Cliff*. For a lively attack, see Windshuttle, *Killing of History*.

2. Some of the problems confronting historians who use the Inquisition's records to gain access to the words and thoughts of the illiterate do not apply to this document. Outside of the Castilian Inquisition, records were kept in Latin, and the inquisitors did not necessarily speak the language of the defendant. In Sánchez's case, all proceedings were conducted and recorded in Castilian, and were read back daily to Sánchez for his approval. For a further discussion of inquisitorial record production, see Del Col's introduction to Scandella, *Domenico Scandella Known as Menocchio*, pp. xli–l.

3. ADC, Inq., 196, leg. 2216. The manuscript is 164 folios long, complete, and in a good state of preservation. Virtually all of it was prepared by the secretary Juan de Ybaneta.

4. Ferrazzi, *Autobiography of an Aspiring Saint*, recovers the voice of a seventeenth-century Venetian woman.

5. Examples of such inventions are Wunderli's *Peasant Fires*, 1–4, and Schama, *Dead Certainties*, 3–8.

6. Full Spanish transcriptions of Sánchez's lengthier statements to the court are reproduced in the appendixes.

1. The Breakdown

1. ADC Inq., leg. 196, exp. 2216 (henceforth Proceso), various witnesses, ff. 2v–18r; e.g., Juan Caballero (f. 7r): "Este testigo vido al dicho Bartolome Sanchez andar con un bonete colorado y con un pie calçado y otro descalço y con un bordon y le preguntó este testigo que por qué traya un pie calçado y otro

descalço y que respondio el dicho Bartolome Sanchez y dixo que porque andaba el mundo al reves."

2. The witnesses recall snatches, all slightly different.

3. Proceso, f. 14r.

4. Pablo Herrero: "hera labrador y que agora por su neçesedad y no poder sustentar la labor deprendio ofiçio de peinador el qual es al presente" (Proceso, f. 3v).

5. Pinel y Monroy's *Retrato del buen vasallo* remains one of the best sources on this region. See also the collection of articles in *Moya: Estudios y Documentos I,* and Alvarez Delgado, "Repoblación y frontera en la Sierra baja de Cuenca."

6. Proceso, f. 50v: "otros hermanos se le fallescieron chiquitos."

7. Because the marquisate's archives have disappeared, many details about Cardenete must be gleaned from such diverse sources as royal, civil, and inquisitorial documents. These sources were used to create a check list of Cardenete's residents from 1480 to 1580. The inquistorial trial of Angelina Montero (ADC, Inq., leg. 57, exp. 839 [1497–1515]) records the testimony of Basque immigrants against Angelina, herself an immigrant from Valencia.

8. AGS, Contadurias Generales, leg. 768, "Recuento de 1528–36." My thanks to Régulo Algarra for this citation. The two noblemen were Don Alonso Pérez Serrano (ARCG, Hidalguía, cab. 301, leg. 4, no. 51. [1527]; and Francisco de Villaviciosa (ibid., cab. 304, leg. 586, no. 181 [1539]).

9. Catastro de Ensenada, AGS, Dirección General de Rentas, leg. 80, f. 707. Cereal lands were measured in *fanegas,* the amount of land necessary to produce one bushel of wheat. Income was often stated in terms of fanegas as well.

10. ARCG, Comunales, El concejo de Cardente, 1552, cab. 3, leg. 1142, no. 3.

11. Details on Sánchez's family history come from the genealogy and account of his life that he gave orally to the inquisitors on Nov. 4, 1553 (Proceso, ff. 50r–51r).

12. Bartolomé de Mora: "Le vido tomar un jarro y hechar dentro de él un ponçal y que santiguava el jarro y dezia que aquel ponçal significava la mançana que tenia Dios Padre. . . . De noches salia de su casa con una baçina de las aguas que él orinava y las vaziava en la calle y que este testigo le preguntó al dicho Bartolome Sanchez que, ¿para qué lo hazía? y que le respondio y dixo que le dava una fantasia en la cabeça que las animas de los condenados se vañavan en aquellas aguas que él sacava y que se ahogavan y que las animas de los buenos que se vañavan en agua clara y no se ahogavan" (Proceso, ff. 14r, 15r).

13. The priest acted correctly. See chapter 8.

14. Proceso, Mora's deposition, ff. 14r–16v.

15. I.e., June 24, or Midsummer's Eve. The summer solstice was a magical time, celebrated by bonfires recalling pre-Christian beliefs. Many spells were effective only if performed at this time.

16. Proceso, ff. 120v–21r (June 23, 1556). Sánchez gave this lengthy statement to the court at the request of the prosecution, which overheard him explaining to his own lawyer the origin of his troubles. See appendix A for the Spanish original.

17. Proceso, f. 121r. Sánchez's statement is reminiscent of the apocryphal Luke 9:52, "I was not sent for the destruction of souls," and John 12:47, "I did not come to judge . . ." The sentence of excommunication, meant to be the worst spiritual punishment of all because it entailed exclusion from the sacraments, was so abused in the sixteenth century that people did not take the sentence seriously.

18. Proceso, ff. 121r–v. "Con esto quedó este confesante muy trasboleado." *Trasboleado,* literally "bowled over," was probably a term borrowed from the popular game of bowling. Sánchez consistently uses this word together with *elevado* ("high") to describe his mental and physical state during this time.

19. Proceso, statement of June 23, 1556, ff. 121v–22v.

20. Ibid., f. 122v. Note how the notary has forgotten to keep Sánchez's testimony in the past tense: "Viendo [los vecinos] las cosas que dezia y desatinos que hazia le ataron a un poste desnudo en camysa y descalço y salieron del palaçio y çerraron la puerta por de fuera, y este confesante [i.e., Sánchez] como no le queryan desatar su muger ny nadie, con las dientes corta la soga que hera de esparto y se suelta y arremete a la puerta para dar con ella entera para se salir y los honbres se espantaron."

21. St. Julian and the Veronica of Jaén both were popular relics that attracted pilgrims from all over New Castile.

22. Clearly, a reference to his confiscated book of hours.

23. Proceso, ff. 5r–6v. Sánchez's evaluation of a vision's authenticity according to its emotional impact is typical of the age.

24. Proceso, ff. 7r–v.

25. Proceso, ff. 7v–8v. Note that Sánchez believes in an apocryphal gospel of St. Peter, which purportedly is the true gospel, deliberately kept from the people by the Church.

26. Proceso, ff. 9v–10v: "Vos sois el dañado y yo soi el salvo porque tres leyes ay debaxo la capa de el çielo que son christianos y moros y judios y la peor ley de todas estas es la de los christianos, la que vosotros teneis y guardais."

27. These depositions form the first 17 folios of the trial and much of the basis for the description of Sánchez's breakdown.

28. Proceso, f. 19v, letter dated Oct. 15, 1553.

2. In the Secret Prisons

1. The Inquisition occupied several locations between 1489 and 1583, when it constructed its own building. In the 1550s, it occupied the quarters of what today is the Provincial Museum, across the street from the episcopal palace (Pérez Ramírez, "Archivo de la Inquisición," 863.

2. Sánchez Gil, "Tribunal de la Inquisición," 29, 34.

3. AHN, Inq., lib. 574, f. 309v (Feb. 26, 1553), responding to Cortes's letter of Feb. 8, 1553. Unfortunately, in all of the correspondence between Cortes and the Suprema, no one bothered to mention the actual name of Cortes's hometown or his age.

4. If convicted in the worst degree, the deceased would be burned in effigy, his or her remains removed to unconsecrated ground, and a sanbenito (a penitential garment) hung in the parish church to the perpetual shame of the person, family, and community. The convicted individual's descendants faced the confiscation of property inherited from that person and important legal disabilities.

5. I reconstructed Cortes's activities by going through all of the paperwork he generated from January 1552 to his death in June 1555, and putting it into calendar form. When holidays are added, a pattern emerges of periods of work and absenteeism.

6. This is exactly the doctrine of the "Quaternity" as described by Milhou in *Colón y su mentalidad mesiánica*. See below, chapter 4.

7. Proceso, f. 20r.

8. Proceso, f. 20v, "Dios padre no tuvo más de un hijo encarnado en las entrañas de la Virgen Marya y que de dos personas, padre e hijo, no puede hazer tres, sy no ponen la sustancia y el amor de la madre donde se fraguó."

9. The secretary writes, "con ynportunydad de palabras que Su Reverencia le hizo . . ." (Proceso, f. 21r).

10. Proceso, f. 21r.

11. Proceso, f. 21v: "Su Reverencia le hizo señas con el dedo se ynclinase de rodillas hazia el sobredicho altar. . . ."

12. Proceso, f. 22r.

13. Proceso, f. 22v.

14. Ibid.: "como entró en la dicha sala alçó la cabeça a myrar hazia arriba y se santiguó e syn más de humillar hazia el sobredicho altar se llegó a la mesa de la dicha audiençia y dixo que ¿qué le mandava?"

15. Luke 23:39–42. One thief said, "Si tú eres el Cristo, salvate a ti mismo y a nosotros," but the other said, "Señor, acuerdate de mi cuando estuvieres en tu Reino" (*Santa Biblia* [1569]).

16. Proceso, f. 23v.

17. This analogy is a correct description of how law was made in Castile at the time.

18. *Proceso*, ff. 23v–24r. Note that Sánchez does not rely on the Commandments to justify his attack on idols. See appendix A for the Spanish original of this sermon.

19. Here Cortes slips into a common error by using the word *adorar* ("worship") rather than the theologically correct *venerar* ("venerate").

20. *Proceso*, f. 24v: "ansi dixo al Padre por tres vezes *si posibile est*, yo no mirera ni beba este caliz de amargura, y que dixo Padre no quiere que nynguno mate al Justo." A reference to Matt. 26:39–42, "Pater mi, si possibile est, transeat a me calix este." Sánchez has twisted the original Scripture's meaning, that Christ did not want to die but he accepted his Father's wish, to an expression of defiance. Covarrubias writes in the *Tesoro de la lengua castellana* (1611) that Jesus called his Passion *caliz* (chalice), and for this reason death is commonly referred to as the "cup of bitterness" (s.v. "caliz").

21. Here Sánchez is drawing on the popular notion of a just judge who will save individuals from the authorities. See Fajardo Spínola, *Hechicería y brujería*, 152. My thanks to William A. Christian Jr. for this reference.

22. *Proceso*, ff. 24v–25r. See chapter 4 below for a discussion of Sánchez's use of the meaning of Elijah in Jewish and Christian eschatological thought, and appendix A for the original text of this prophecy.

23. See n. 20. Either Cortes or the secretary has slipped here and written *cruz* (cross) when he meant *caliz* (chalice) (*Proceso*, f. 25v).

24. *Proceso*, f. 25v.

25. *Proceso*, ff. 26r–v. See the appendix for the original. Note in these passages how well Sánchez uses legal terminology and concepts such as *emplazar, protestar, requirir, justo juez, justa justicia*: he is well informed about the system.

3. The Elijah-Messiah

1. *Proceso*, f. 27r.

2. *Proceso*, f. 27v.

3. The reference to St. Alexis (San Alejo) as one of the first Christians makes little historical sense, but the saint's legend was very popular in the Middle Ages. In sixteenth-century Spain there existed an *Oración de San Alexo* (mentioned in Juan de Timoneda's *Entremes de un çiego y un moço y un pobre, muy gracioso*, cited by Rodríguez-Moñino, *Diccionario de pliegos*, 87) and at least one print version of his life (*La vida de sant Alexo* [Burgos: Philippe de Junta, 1562]).

4. *Proceso*, f. 28v.

5. Note that Sánchez balks at the points when it is explained to him that God does things through his omnipotence. So, even though he could resist his crucifixion, he submitted to it and overcame death; or the Host turns into the real body because Christ wills it.

6. Proceso, f. 29r: ". . . entró en la dicha sala, alçó la cabeça y manos hazia el çielo y se santiguó syn hazer humyllicaçion alguna al dicho altar y ansi se llegó a la mesa de la dicha audiençia. Y oyendolo scriver, dixo que él no tiene otro altar ny se humylla sino a Dios que está en el çielo, y a él se ofresçe y entrega."

7. Proceso, f. 28v. Cortes: "se lo dize apiadandose de su opynion mala y deseandole reduzir a la buena para que salue su anyma y no la pierda."

8. Proceso, f. 29v.

9. Ibid.

10. Proceso, f. 30r. ". . . Dios es el santo sacramento donde quiera que está, y que la Hostia que toman los clerigos, que es una poca de harina masada, y que de la dicha Hostia ninguno es bastante a hazer carne ny sangre syno solo Dios."

11. Proceso, f. 31r.

12. Ibid.: ". . . si [el] templo fuera de Dios, que no echara della como hechó los canbiadores, y que pues la dixo synoga que ansi la dize él . . . que si casa de Dios fuera, no vendieran en ella a Christo como Lo vendieron, que Dios es el templo suyo, que no los cantos y palos que se haze la yglesia y la teneis vosotros por templo de Dios."

13. Proceso, f. 31v.

14. The conclusion to this audience provides a good example of Cortes's style: before letting Sánchez go, he read back the transcript of the session and asked him if it was corrrect or if he desired to correct anything. Sánchez indicated he had nothing to change; it was all true (ibid.).

15. A small fortune—more money than Sánchez would see in his lifetime.

16. Proceso, ff. 32r–v.

17. Proceso, f. 33v: "Dixo que el Hijo de Dios tanbyen fue criatura humana, nasçida y criada en la tierra como su madre lo fue e lo tiene declarado, y que él no quita la sustançia de donde Dios Padre la puso syno cada uno habla a su proposito, y que para declarar la verdad de esta question él dexa a Dios por juez."

18. Proceso, f. 34r.

19. Proceso, f. 34v.

20. Ibid.: ". . . su officio no es de matar ny robar, porque ésto es officio del demonyo y ansi en este offico que teneis por sancto de la ynquisiçion. . . ." Here, Sánchez plays on the various meanings of the word *oficio*, which can mean occupation, business, and office.

21. Proceso, ff. 34v–35r. See appendix A for the Spanish original. With

"faith without works is dead" and "faith alone saves" Sánchez goes straight to one of the contemporary disputes between Catholics and Protestants. It is astonishing that Cortes did not challenge the wool carder at this point to reveal his sources. Did he not appreciate the danger of Protestantism, or did he disregard the citations because he did not take Sánchez seriously?

22. The text reads "*sacramento* de la vid," but this must be the court secretary's slip for *sarmiento* (vine cutting).

23. Proceso, ff. 35v–36r. See the appendix for the Spanish original.

24. Proceso, f. 36r.

25. Proceso, f. 36v. Legally, at this point the hearing was closed, but Ybaneta remained in the room and continued to take notes of the informal conversation.

26. Proceso, f. 37r: "[God sends] . . . su juzio final para matar los muertos, que son los muertos los que están encenegados y encarnicados en pecado mortal, y que los que ansi estan encenegados y encarnicados en pecado mortal son la ynquisicion y todos los sus acessores."

27. Proceso, ff. 37r–v.

28. Matt. 27:46–47: "And about the ninth hour Jesus cried with a loud voice, 'Eli, Eli, lama sabachtani?' that is, 'My God, my God, why has thou forsaken me?' And some of the bystanders hearing it said, 'This man is calling Elijah.'"

29. Proceso, f. 38r: ". . . vosotros los de la ynquisiçion matais a quyen no hos ha ofendido haziendo vosotros justiçia y si hos han ofendido declaradmelo." Here the court recorder, Ybaneta, became so wrapped up in Sánchez's speech that he forgot to convert Sánchez's words into the customary third-person past tense.

30. Proceso, f. 39v.

31. Proceso, ff. 39v–40r. See appendix A for the Spanish original.

32. Proceso, f. 40v. Cortes: ". . . no le puede dar syno muy grande congoxa, negando lo que él los nyega. . . ."

33. Ibid. At this time (mid-1550s), few people knew the Ten Commandments as part of their catechism (Nalle, *God in La Mancha*, chap. 4). In the Muslim *Breviario Sunni*, written in *aljamía* (Arabo-Spanish written in the Arabic script) by Ice de Gebir in the fifteenth century, a similar conflation of the Ten Commandments occurs. He counsels, "Do not kill, do not steal, do not commit fornication with any creature" (Harvey, *Islamic Spain*, 88–90). There were plenty of Moriscos in Cuenca, including Cardenete itself.

34. Proceso, f. 41v. Cortes: ". . . myre que se le açerca el ynfierno si no haze penytencia confesando sus pecados, tomando fe a Dios."

35. Ibid.

36. Proceso, f. 42r. Sánchez uses the word "trunk" to refer to humankind's

descent from Adam; the term is borrowed from contemporary genealogies, which were literally drawn as trees.

37. *Proceso*, f. 43r. Sánchez's ecumenism, although unusual, is not unique for the time. See chapter 4. "Church" is meant here in the sense of organized religion.

38. *Proceso*, f. 43v. Legally, the Inquisition had no authority over persons who had not accepted baptism, but one can see from this conversation how little importance this legal technicality held for both Judge Cortes and Bartolomé Sánchez. Despite their baptism, New Christians were not accepted as bona fide converts.

39. Ibid.: "Dixo que agora es ya tarde y que él responderá para la primera audiençia y que no ay neçesidad se le lea lo que en ésta esté scripto pues se le ha leydo muchas vezes lo que en esta dicha audiençia se ha scripto y no ay en ello por agora que corregir."

4. Lessons Learned at Home

1. An example is Guevara, *Menosprecio de corte y alabanza de aldea* (1539). A study of village life as depicted in Golden Age literature is Salomon, *Villano*. A review of the scholarship, maintaining that villages were very much tied to the outside world, is Vassberg, *Village and the Outside World*.

2. On conversos in Cuenca see Jiménez Monteserín, "Hermanos Valdés," and Rábade Obradó, *Elite de poder*.

3. ADC, Inq., L-351, "Relaciones de causas," and L-353, "Lugares del distrito de esta Inquisicion de Cuenca donde en cada uno se hallaran los procesos. . . ." It is impossible to be more precise than this; the tribunal of Cuenca lost many of its documents from the early years of its existence.

4. Ibid., leg. 698, exp. 14 (Alonso); leg. 57, exp. 839 (Angelina); and leg. 55, exp. 815 (Fernando de Cuenca). In 1517, on the children's appeal, the Suprema ordered their release and removal of their sanbenitos.

5. Rokiski Lázaro, *Arquitectura del siglo XVI*. Notice of the tower comes in the form of a 1333 royal order to destroy it because it was the cause of much "theft and harm" (RAH, Abella, leg. 2, no. 4).

6. AGS, RGS, Nov. 21, 1520.

7. ARCG, Pergaminos 36, f. 6r; *Catálogo de los duques de Frías*, no. 129 (Sept. 25, 1448); Pinel y Monroy, *Retrato del buen vasallo*, 203; García, *Virtudes de la Reina Católica*, 396.

8. Gutiérrez Nieto, *Comunidades*, 198–209; AMC, Libro de Actas del Cabildo, leg. 235, ff. 141r, 151v, 154r (city council meetings of Sept. 14, 25, and 27, 1520).

9. AGS, RGS, Nov. 21, 1520. Cabrera's letter is incorporated into the royal order authorizing Don Jorge Ruiz de Alarcón to wage war against the rebels. The capture of Cabrera's storeroom was no small matter; in it the rebels would find supplies of grain and weapons. Pinel y Monroy, *Retrato del buen vasallo*, 403, notes that Juan Fernández de Cabrera spent most of his life in poor health.

10. The revolt was forgotten until it was researched by Gutiérrez Nieto, *Comunidades*, 200–204. See also Nalle, "Moya busca nuevo señor," for further details.

11. AHN, sec. Nobleza, Frías, 674:30.

12. So writes the marquis's personal secretary and accountant in a memorial concerning his service to the marquises of Moya (ibid.).

13. AGS, RGS, Nov. 7, 1524; Cooper, "Nueva aproximación." Cooper's article on the fortress in his magisterial *Castillos señoriales* (vol. 1, pt. 2, p. 869) first alerted me to the intrigues in Moya after the Comunero Revolt.

14. The royal judge, Licentiate Montalvo, gave the sum in his report about the rebellion to the crown (AGS, CC, 138:77, May 6, 1522). Cabrera later forgave half of the sum (AGS, RGS, Nov. 7, 1524).

15. By November 1524, the village claimed to have paid in reparations in excess of 300,000 maravedis (approx. 1,500 maravedis or 4 ducats per family) (AGS, RGS, Nov. 10, 1524). A workman's daily wage at that time was about 20 maravedis.

16. Dánvila, *Historia crítica*, V:469; ADC, Inq., leg. 86, exp. 1271.

17. AGS, RGS, Oct. 24 and 29, 1524; AHN, sec. Nobleza, Frías, 674:30.

18. AHN, sec. Nobleza, Frías, 674:30. The marquis's former accountant provides a colorful (and biased) narrative of his attempts to scuttle the lawsuit. The two parties' legal motions in the case are scattered throughout the unindexed records of the Cámara de Castilla and Registro General de Sellos sections of the AGS.

19. AGS, RGS, July 12, 1526. Sánchez's wife may have been a relative of the Comunero inquisitor Juan Martínez de Mariana, who had relations in Cardenete. Sánchez's uncle by marriage, Juan de Mora, appears in the village' petition to the crown in 1524 (ibid., Oct. 24 and 29).

20. In case he needed a refresher course, one was available. In 1552 the village of Cardenete was involved in an important lawsuit with the city of Cuenca over the lease of Yémeda (ARCG, Comunales, cab. 3, leg. 1142, no. 3).

21. *Proceso*, ff. 120v–21r (June 23, 1556).

22. For a discussion of aspects of pricing and availability of cheap religious texts, see Nalle, "Printing and Reading."

23. By comparison, it was not unusual for more well-to-do farmers in La

Mancha to own several books, and in Italy, the miller Menocchio Scandella owned or had read eleven or more books (Nalle, "Literacy and Culture"; Ginzburg, *Cheese and the Worms*, chaps. 12, 13). Sánchez's learning was primarily oral, reinforced by the one book of hours.

24. Judging by an inventory of his shop, Juan de Ayala specialized in cheaper editions. In 1556 he had on hand 700 copies of "Spanish hours from Toledo in 16°" valued at 25 maravedis each. He had another 260 hours in seven editions as well (Blanco Sánchez, "Inventario de Juan de Ayala"). None of this production survives except a 1565 reprint edition, *Horas de nuestra señora en romance*, conserved at the Biblioteca Nacional, Madrid.

25. For discussion, with illustrations, see Milhou, *Colón y su mentalidad mesiánica*, 80–87.

26. Milhou tells of a preacher who met a well-educated lady in the 1580s who assumed that even schoolchildren knew that the Trinity consisted of "God the Father, Son, Holy Spirit, and the Virgin Our Lady" (ibid., 81, n. 203bis).

27. For a comparison of Sánchez's prayers with texts from the book of hours, see appendix B.

28. For a balanced survey in English, see Hamilton, *Heresy and Mysticism*.

29. Márquez, *Alumbrados*, 273–83. A study of the propositions in the edict is Ortega, "Proposiciones."

30. Flecniakoska, "Propagation des idées protestantes."

31. A complete list of the diocese's religious foundations may be found in Nalle, *God in La Mancha*, app. 2. According to the 1591 "census," there were 773 male religious in the royal administrative districts of Cuenca and Huete; 388 of them were Franciscans, 72 were Dominicans, and 33 were Carmelites (F. Ruiz Martín, "Demografía eclesiástica," in *DHEE*, 2:707).

32. For a good overview of trends in traditional and Renaissance sacred oratory, see Redondo, *Antonio de Guevara*, chap. 4. More generally, see Herrero Salgado, *Oratoria sagrada española*.

33. Beltrán de Heredia, *Corrientes de espiritualidad*; Cátedra, *Sermón*.

34. Quoted in Fuster, *Rebeldes y heterodoxos*, 21. See also Cervera Vera, *Francisco de Eiximenis*.

35. Asensio, "Fray Luis de Maluenda"; Blanco Sánchez, "Inventario de Juan de Ayala." Today there is only one surviving copy of the book in question, *Leche de fe para el príncipe christiano* (Burgos: Juan de Junta, 1545), condemned by the Inquisition in 1559.

36. Milhou, *Colón y su mentalidad mesiánica*, 97.

37. Sainz Rodríguez, *Siembra mística*; Kinder, "'Ydiota y sin letras.'"

38. Reeves, *Influence of Prophecy*; Pou y Martí, *Visionarios*.

39. An overview of the situation may be found in Nalle, "Millennial Moment."

40. Nieto, *Juan de Valdés*, 73, n. 83.

41. McKendrick and MacKay, "Visionaries," 94.

42. On the situation in Andalusia, see Edwards, "Elijah and the Inquisition." In 1519 an eighty-year-old conversa called Isabel Sánchez remembered "that she heard many Old Christian and converso people in the town of Alcázar publicly say how there was a goddess in Herrera and that she saw God and knew His secrets and she said that the Messiah was not come and he would come and he would remove the conversos from the captivity in which they were and he would carry them to good lands . . ." (ADC, Inq., leg. 73, exp. 1065).

43. Proceso, f. 3v. Pablo Herrero stated that "long ago he heard from old and ancient persons of whom there is no memory because they're now dead that the said Bartolomé Sánchez is part converso."

44. "*Libro de profecías*," 107; Ginzburg, *Cheese and the Worms*, 43.

5. Trial Motions

1. On Nov. 20, Sánchez declared that after death people's souls go into animals or the air; there is no hell, only this purgatory (Proceso, f. 64r). For a further discussion, see the conclusion.

2. Proceso, f. 52v. See appendix B for the Spanish original of this and all the prayers that follow.

3. Alonso Ramírez de Vergara was the canon magister in Cuenca, as well as the bishop's ordinary. At this time he was deeply involved in the founding of Cuenca's first Jesuit college (Nalle, *God in La Mancha*, 77, 87).

4. Proceso, ff. 47r–48v. The conversation between Vergara and Sánchez was not recorded. We know it occurred because a few days later Cortes reminded Sánchez that he had seemed close to converting when he talked to Vergara ("parescia que se ablandava") (Proceso, f. 52v).

5. Proceso, f. 49r–v.

6. Proceso, f. 50r. In the margin of the trial transcript is written a note about the testimony from Cardenete indicating that Sánchez may have had converso ancestry. The inquisitor chose not to pursue the issue, however. Note the reference to instruction in Sánchez's statement; first, off the record, he was instructed about what would be asked, and then he was asked it for the record.

7. Proceso, ff. 49v–51r.

8. Proceso, f. 51v.

9. Proceso, f. 52r.

10. Sánchez is quoting Luke 20:42–43, based on Psalm 110:1: "Sit at my right hand, / till I make thy enemies a stool for thy feet" (Proceso, f. 54r–v).

11. Proceso, f. 54v.

12. Proceso, f. 55r. Cortes: ". . . lo que de presente con el dicho señor dotor

se trata es solo lo que para el descargo de su consciencia debe tener, entendido lo que tiene declarado en este proceso y no para otro effecto, y que como honbre ydiota no se vaya al ynfierno."

13. Proceso, f. 55v.

14. Proceso, f. 56r.

15. Proceso, f. 56r–v.

16. Proceso, ff. 57r–58v. As a religious court, the Inquisition could impose only spiritual penalties. Because the commission of heresy was also a capital offense in Spanish criminal law, unrepentant or recidivist heretics could be handed over to the civil authorities for execution. Lesser offenses, such as blasphemy and sacrilege, could be punished by scourging for the same reason.

17. Proceso, ff. 59v–60r.

18. Proceso, f. 60r. Sánchez's assertions concerning his proselytizing never provoked a response from the inquisitor, an indication that Cortes did not take them seriously.

19. Proceso, f. 69r: "las anymas de los que mueren honbres y mugeres que estan en los cuerpos de los anymales y otras andan en los ayres por donde Dios es servido hasta que ese dé la sentencia por Dios que es la que pide este Helias que es este declarante."

20. Proceso, f. 69v. As part of the court's practice of keeping defendants in the dark about who had spoken against them, the testimony from Cardenete would have been censored so that Sánchez in theory would not be able to identify the witnesses.

21. Proceso, f. 70v.

22. Ibid.

23. Proceso, f. 71r. Cortes: "algun ruyn maestro le ha enpuesto en semejantes libiendades."

24. Ibid. Cortes: "pues es honbre de tan poco saber y no leydo y está en su dezir tan porfiado que otra o[sic] otras personas le han enpuesto en ello o que él lo ha leydo en algun libro."

25. Proceso, f. 72r.

26. Proceso, f. 72v: "Sanchez dixo que él ha pensado anoche y oy sobre ello y lo ha encomendado todo a Dios y Él le dize que como letrado que es suyo que no haga ninguna cosa."

27. In fact, this is the first surviving case of a Protestant in the Cuenca tribunal (ADC, Inq., leg. 198, exp. 2228, Pedro Baleta). It is studied in Flecniakoska, "Propagation des idées protestantes," and Jiménez Monteserín, "Luteranos."

28. The most famous case was that of El Niño de la Guardia, in the late fifteenth century. It was publicized in 1544 by Licentiate Vegas in a *Memoria*

muy verdadera de la pasion y martirio, que el glorioso martir, inocente niño llamado Cristobal, padescio . . . en esta villa de la guardia (Haliczer, "Jew as Witch," 151). Cortes had some direct experience as well, in a case of a "crucified child" in 1542 (ADC, Inq., L-224, f. 130). See also ADC, Inq., leg. 145, exp. 1771, and leg. 152, exp. 1811.

29. The Inquisition's unthinking prejudice against conversos generally is not justified by the facts. Recent scholarship suggests that most of the people accused of Judaizing were true converts to Christianity, and trials of conversos were the equivalent of witch hunts. On the tragic consequences of one inquisitor's overzealous interpretation of his role, see Contreras, *Sotos contra Riquelmes.*

30. Proceso, f. 73r. In the absence of indoor plumbing, many houses in Cuenca were equipped with small privies built out over back alleys or the cliffs. Waste was eliminated straight onto the street or the rocks below. It is a bit surprising that prisoners had such easy and potentially dangerous access to fire; before this incident, Sánchez also burned his indictment.

31. Proceso, f. 73v. Cortes: "él syendo un honbre desbaratado e syn letras que ¿qué razon tiene para de por sý solo hazer e ynventar lo que él haze y dize?"

32. Ibid. The meaning of this comment is not clear. Did Cortes mean that he would listen to Sánchez with more understanding than ordinary people, who would just see a madman?

33. Proceso, f. 74r.

34. Personal communication from A. Manuel Pinedo, while he was researching the city parish death registers.

35. Cortes's rooms were located in the Inquisition's quarters; one of Sánchez's cellmates describes the wool carder at the time as doing nothing but pacing and talking.

36. Realgar: arsenic monosulfide, a red mineral prized in some cultures for its supposed medicinal qualities, despite its toxicity. As the mineral burns with an intense white light (hence its use in pyrotechnics), there are interesting connections to alchemy and Luis's sun imagery. See Covarrubias, *Tesoro de la lengua castellana,* s.v. "rejalgar."

37. ADC, Inq., leg. 186, exp. 2107. See also chapter 8.

38. Eimeric and Peña, *Manual de los inquisidores,* 150; Diego de Simancas, *De Catholicis Institutionibus,* f. 139.

39. Proceso, f. 74v.

40. Proceso, ff. 76r–77r.

41. Proceso, f. 77v (April 13, 1554). Esquivel: "no estaba loco ny en nynguna cosa le hallava fuera de él ny tal que por alguna cosa se devesse tener por loco . . . e que de los dichos sus errores no se puede defender por loco."

6. Acts of Faith

1. ADC, Inq., leg. 199, exp. 2243. A tailor from Almazán (Sigüenza), Luis was penanced for Judaizing in 1554.

2. This question contradicts the practice that Kamen describes in *Spanish Inquisition*, 187, whereby prisoners were denied the sacraments and access to Mass. No visitors were allowed in the prison, whose occupants effectively were lost to the world until their release.

3. Proceso, f. 78r–v. Cortes: "Dios se sirva de se lo perdonar y goze de su muger e hijos y muriendo de yr al çielo . . ."

4. Proceso, f. 79r.

5. According to Pérez Ramírez, *Catálogo del Archivo*.

6. Proceso, f. 80r.

7. Proceso, f. 80v.

8. Ibid. Note the completely ahistorical explanation Cueva offers for the origin of religions. Is this deliberate simplification for Sánchez's benefit?

9. Encapsulated in this discussion between Sánchez and Cueva is the very complex issue of the assimilation of the former Jews into Spanish life. One might begin with Domínguez Ortiz, *Clase social de los conversos*, and Edwards, "Conversos."

10. This simple statement reveals that Sánchez has some notion of arithmetic: "old enough to understand" (7–9 years) + 40 years + 2 = about 50, Sánchez's approximate age.

11. Proceso, f. 81r.

12. Proceso, ff. 81v–82v.

13. No special account of this particular auto de fe has appeared in the record, but a great deal about it can be learned through a close reading of Sánchez's trial transcript. I assume that the familiars and prisoners were dressed according to custom and that the cathedral appeared as it did. Cuenca's autos de fe customarily were held either inside the cathedral or outside in the plaza mayor.

14. Proceso, f. 85v.

15. The text of Sánchez's sentence and the summary of his case occupy ff. 82v–85v of the Proceso.

16. According to Inquisition handbooks, the execution was not supposed to take place on a Sunday. This tribunal liked to do things its way, it would seem (*HIEA*, 2:490).

17. Proceso, f. 86r: "Pidio mysiricordia a Dios Nuestro Señor y parescio tener señales de christiano y arrepentimyento y que se queria convertir . . . y . . . lo baxaron del asno en que yba." A notary present at the auto de fe recorded what transpired and a copy was sewn into the transcript of Sánchez's trial. The Virgin had appeared to him on Sept. 8.

18. Proceso, f. 86v. Although Sánchez could read, he could not write. Reading and writing were taught separately, and the acquisition of full literacy was expensive.

19. ADC, Inq., L-356, "Registro primero de votos d'este Sancto Officio," f. 190v. Vergara suggested "'que sea relaxado e que hasta el palo se le espere para que queriendo se admyttia, sea admitido [a reconciliación].' Al cabo todos los señores en conformydad dixieron que por las causas que les mueven y la seguridad de sus conciencias e confiando en la misericordia de Dios le reduzira al dicho Bartolome Sanchez a su servicio. . . ."

20. Proceso, f. 87v.

21. Proceso, f. 88r. Cortes: "honbres cuerdos y de buen entendimiento . . . con sobrevenyrles semejantes luz e ymaginacion. . . ."

22. Proceso, ff. 88v–89r.

23. Proceso, f. 89r–v. ". . . so color de aquella claridad, que dize que tiene dicha . . . desde vido la dicha vision, se elevó y alteró, y ansi con aquella alteracion de la dicha vision ha dicho y sustentado todo." Note that Sánchez only now repudiated his conviction that he was the Elijah-Messiah; he held on to the idea as long as he could, until he realized that if he was to be reconciled, that core conviction had to go as well.

24. Proceso, f. 89v: "el dicho elevamyento le ha nacido y procede de la ymaginacion de la claridad que dicho tiene."

25. ADC, Inq., leg. 685, exp.51, and leg. 199, exp. 2244, statements from Diego de Villanueva (the murderer) and Alonso Alvárez de Ayala, city councilor and witness. The murdered man worked as a servant in the home of Diego de Villanueva, where he seduced and impregnated the familiar's sister. When the man refused to marry the girl, her brother secretly swore revenge; the other familiar involved in the crime was Diego's uncle by marriage, who happened to be near the church when the attack took place and spontaneously went to the aid of his kinsman (or so he claimed).

26. AHN, Inq., leg. 574, f. 342v. Valladolid, May 12, 1554.

27. Proceso, f. 90r: "[Cortes] viendole estar a la mesa de la dicha audiencia llorando e limpiandose las lagrimas de sus ojos con vn panzuelo, le demandó que, ¿por qué llorava?"

28. Proceso, f. 90r. ". . . lo que él dezia eran boberias y locuras."

29. Proceso, f. 90v. Cortes is playing a game here with Sánchez in order to get a complete confession from him. Even though he privately believes that Sánchez probably is insane, he reveals no hint of his conviction to the wool carder.

30. Proceso, f. 91r–v.

31. Proceso, ff. 91v–92r.

32. Proceso, f. 92r. This is reminiscent of the prophecies of Maestro Uray

(Juan d'Alamany), which circulated earlier in the century, as in "Sant Joan que dize que uido una vestia con siete cabezas" (Alba, *Acerca de algunas particularidades*, 183). Sánchez seems unaware that his serpent is the beast from the Apocalypse.

33. Proceso, f. 92v: "Dios sabe su corazon quan asado le tiene e ronpidas sus entrañas de averle ofendido en aver quebrantado sus mandamyentos."

34. Proceso, ff. 93r–94r.

7. Déja Vu

1. See Martz, *Poverty and Welfare*, and Flynn, *Sacred Charity*. Sánchez continued to live in the prisons while he worked in the city.

2. Letter dated May 24, 1554 (ADC, Inq., leg. 199, exp. 2248, Ana la Roa and María la Parra). The Spanish Inquisition's cautious approach to witchcraft cases is commonly recognized. See Monter, *Frontiers of Heresy*, 255–75.

3. Since inquisitorial law required two eyewitnesses for conviction, torture was permissible when there was only one witness to a crime other than the accused, who by law was presumed guilty. Torture could also be used to obtain a complete confession from the defendant when the evidence was conclusive but the accused refused to admit guilt or implicate accomplices. In either case, testimony obtained through torture was not valid until the defendant ratified it later in the courtroom. See Kamen, *Spanish Inquisition*, 187–90.

4. Their punishment was to suffer 100 lashes applied "lightly" and banishment from the area. The lashes were to satisfy the perjury conviction; banishment was probably for everyone's protection. Caro Baroja, *World of Witches*, charts the introduction of northern European theories into Spanish manuals of witchcraft during the sixteenth century.

5. Shortly after Cueva left for Molina de Aragón, he received a letter from the Suprema asking him to return to Cuenca to help run the court because Cortes was ill (AHN, Inq., L-574, f. 343r, letter dated May 12, 1554).

6. Ibid., L-573, f. 346v, letter dated July 31, 1554.

7. Ibid., L-574, f. 355v–56r (Dec. 4, 1554). Cueva's crime seems to have been fleecing his victims and accepting gifts. His servant, Francisco Beltrán, was arrested in Cuenca for murdering a man on the street, and was arrested a second time in Molina de Aragón for creating a public disturbance late at night (ADC, Inq., Civiles, leg. 685, no. 52). He resisted arrest and would have drawn his sword against the law officials had he not been prevented from doing so. He escaped punishment each time by claiming the protection of the Holy Office.

8. AHN, Inq., L-574, f. 353r, letter dated Nov. 5, 1554.

9. Attempts to locate a will or an exact date of death have met with failure. Cortes's last appearance in the court records is June 1, 1555.

10. Proceso, f. 123r–v. Heras describes exactly the manner in which Sánchez made the gesture: "Vio que tenya el dedo pulgar metido entre los dos dedos . . . a la manera que bulgarmente llaman 'yga.'"

11. Proceso, ff. 125r–28r, 133r.

12. Proceso, ff. 105v–6r.

13. Meals were taken much earlier in the day than at present; having risen at dawn, Sánchez would have eaten "lunch" [almuerzo] around 9:00 A.M. and "dinner" [comida] sometime around noon. See Alcalá-Zamora, Vida cotidiana, 61, 308–12.

14. Proceso, f. 103r–v. See appendix A for the original Spanish.

15. Proceso, ff. 104v–5r. See appendix A for original Spanish.

16. Proceso, f. 99r–100r. The five witnesses confirm in substance Sánchez's account of burning his sanbenito and conversations with the other villagers.

17. Proceso, f. 106r.

18. Proceso, ff. 106v–7r. In its reference to Adam and Eve as sexual partners, this curious statement recalls the heresies of the Brethren of the Free Spirit, which re-emerged among some of the alumbrados of Sánchez's day. Sánchez never showed any mystical tendencies, however, and in two statements to the court vigorously condemned sex outside of marriage. Once again he appears to have been repeating uncritically ideas he had heard during his wanderings.

19. Proceso, f. 107v: "Dixo que él es hijo del honbre e Helias, e que se lo manda dezir Dios."

20. Proceso, ff. 107v–8r.

21. Proceso, f. 108v.

22. ADC, Inq., leg. 203, exp. 2296. Alonso did not actually maintain two wives; "bigamy" frequently occurred when a man abandoned one wife, moved to a new community, and remarried without obtaining an annulment.

23. Proceso, f. 109r.

24. Proceso, f. 109v.

25. Ibid.: "Sus Reverencias le dixieron que ya vee el amor con que siempre su persona ha seydo tratado por Sus Reverencias e que la mysma voluntad tienen para le tratar con todo amor e quaridad. . . ."

26. Proceso, f. 110r–v: ". . . que por espacio de los dichos quatro años que se hallaba libre de aquellas congoxas, ymaginaciones y persuasiones, peleaba consigo diziendo, 'Valame Dios, ¿Cómo tengo yo esto?' . . . le paresce que se le venya todo a la boca para dezir como lo dezia. . . ." The confession seems to have

been coached by the cellmate; this was the first time Sánchez blamed his actions so directly on his insanity.

27. Proceso, f. 111r.

28. Proceso, f. 115r.

29. Proceso, f. 117r. Diego de Simancas (d. 1583) provides a good analysis of the insanity defense in relation to heresy in *De Catholicis Institutionibus,* f. 139.

30. This was the first time a word [*desvariar*] that has connotations of insanity was used in connection with Sánchez's behavior.

31. Proceso, f. 135r–v.

32. Proceso, f. 136r: ". . . todo esto lo dezia [Bartolomé] con mucha soberbia y con furor pero no conosco dél que estubiese loco syno con su juyzio. . . ."

33. Proceso, f. 137r: "siempre le ha visto tener buen juizio y como honbre de buen juyzio y entendimyento le ha visto ablar y tratar. . . ."

34. Proceso, f. 138r: "algunas platicas que no tenyan concierto." As a report of hearsay, this evidence was not admissible in court, just as it would not be today.

35. Proceso, f. 141r. It is hard to believe that the lashes were applied at full force.

36. Proceso, ff. 141v–43r.

37. The letter of commission has since disappeared.

38. Proceso, ff. 143v–44v. See appendix A for the Spanish original.

39. Proceso, f. 145v.

40. Proceso, f. 146r–v.

41. Proceso, f. 147v.

42. Proceso, ff. 150r–51r. Note that Sánchez stopped short of saying outright that he was the Messiah. He confessed that belief only to the inquisitors.

43. Proceso, f. 148r. This is the first reference to anyone's being swayed by Sánchez's arguments.

44. Proceso, f. 151r.

45. Proceso, ff. 151r–52r.

46. Proceso, f. 152r–v.

47. Proceso, ff. 155r–57v.

48. A somewhat improbable itinerary.

49. Luke 24:29.

50. Proceso, f. 158r. Catalina: " 'volveos y dezime a dónde vays,' y que le respondio, 'tornaos a [a] costar y encomendaos en Dios que os conserva en su santo servicio que yo voy un camino largo y corto' y que estuvo allá ocho semanas y que vino muy flaco y perdido, y que le dixo, '¿En alguna cueba aveys es-

tado metido pues venis tan flaco y perdido? . . . nunca le vido fazer cosa ninguna en su casa ni serimonia mas de andar ablegado . . .'"

51. Proceso, ff. 158v–59v.

8. Madman

1. In the pages that follow, readers doubtless will form opinions of their own about the precise nature of Sánchez's illness. Although some forms of mental illness have been proved to be organic or genetic in origin and thus potentially can occur at any time in any society, how madness is expressed, interpreted, and treated is thoroughly conditioned by the culture in which it occurs. To label Sánchez with a modern diagnosis will teach us more about twenty-first-century medicine and medical fashions than it will about sixteenth-century Spain. On this point, see the introduction to Midelfort, *History of Madness*.

2. Proceso, ff. 4v, 14r, 122v, 10v, 13r.

3. Of the words that Sánchez used to describe his emotional state (*congoja*, *excancosto*, *elevado*, and *trasboleado*), only two, *congoja* and *elevado*, are readily defined as "anguish" and "high," respectively. *Excancosto* would appear to be a local variation of the medieval *ensangosto* (squeezed; anguished); *trasboleado* is unknown but clearly related to the verb *bolear* (to bowl, hence "bowled over" or "spinning") (Corominas, *Diccionario crítico*).

4. Europeans of this time had developed highly ritualized means of expressing social commentary and dissent; Bartolomé's remark about the world upside down carries a large amount of baggage with it. For the Iberian world, see Lafond and Redondo, *L'Image du monde renversé*.

5. In a famous experiment conducted in the 1950s, three men who believed themselves to be Jesus Christ were brought together in the same hospital and were confronted with each other. Like Sánchez, the men defended their delusion by denouncing the other messiahs as false and calling each other insane (Rokeach, *Three Christs of Ypsilanti*).

6. "Monte quaxado de santidad, es llamado 'Carmelo del Mar'" (Santa María, *Historia general profetica*, 55, 59). See Olin, *Catholic Reform*, 51, for an anagogical use of "curdled mountain" by the preacher Egidio da Viterbo.

7. Although the topic remains largely unexplored in Spain, two scholars have surveyed the papers of the Mexican Inquisition to study insanity in the Spanish colony: Sacristán, *Locura e Inquisición*; and Jiménez Olivares, *Psiquiatría e Inquisición*. The books cover virtually the same twenty-five trials, the first focusing on the psychosocial history, the second providing a summary

of each case. In Spain, Tropé reviewed twenty-one cases sent by the tribunal of Valencia to the city's Hospital dels Innocents as part of her study of that hospital (*Locura y sociedad en la Valencia,* 186–206). López Alonso (*Locura y sociedad en Sevilla,* 50–51) mentions that 4.6% of patients in the asylum there were sent by the Inquisition but could not track down their cases, as the trial records of the tribunal are mostly lost.

8. ADC, Inq., leg. 141, no. 1730: "estuvo de vna rezia enfermedad a la qual este testigo le vido estar loco e fuera de juyzio y por tal este testigo se falló con Juan Muñoz vecino de Valsalobre en lo atar e lo ataron las manos e ansi estuvo no sabe quantos dias e despues desta enfermedad este testigo le tiene por tal persona como la por gracia dize en especial unas vezes más que otras segund lo que en él a visto y conoscido."

9. Ibid.: "Le vido de la dicha enfermedad fuera de seso y despues aca le a visto algunas vezes en especial en unas lunas más que en otras fazer e dezir algunos desconciertos tanto que a este testigo le a parescido y pensado que es espiritu o trastornamiento de estomago." See below for a discussion of this statement.

10. Ibid., leg. 229, exp. 2879. Suspended.

11. Literally, the word used was "fatback" (*tocino*). It was a way of questioning a person's Old Christian ancestry. Santaren's statements are interesting also for their homophobic references (*putos bellacos* and *putos judíos*). The abuse recorded here is typical of the period.

12. Ibid., leg. 708, exp. 636, suspended. While no one called Santaren's illness *gota coral,* or epilepsy, one priest suggested "an illness of the heart," which was considered a cause of epilepsy. He also noted that Santaren's expression was changed—all details collected later in Covarrubias y Orozco, *Tesoro de la lengua castellana,* s.v. "gota coral."

13. No one was willing to repeat the exact words that Gonzalo used because they were too obscene, but in effect he had said he wanted to impregnate the Virgin.

14. ADC, Inq., leg. 252, exp. 3410 (1572).

15. AHN, Inq. Toledo, leg. 114, exp. 7.

16. Ibid., audience of Sept. 21, 1541: "porque el dicho Juan Garcia dixo muchas cosas muy esmeras y muy solapadas de tal manera que no se pueden entender el dicho señor inquisidor mandó que lo que quiere dezir que lo diga claramente."

17. Ibid., Oct. 5, 1541. A reference to Our Lady of the Descent, famous for bringing St. Ildefonso his chasuble in the eighth century. A marble sculpture in the Renaissance style marks the place of the miracle (Christian, *Local Reli-*

gion, 78). My thanks to Jean-Pierre Dedieu for drawing my attention to the special aspects of García's case.

18. Ibid., Nov. 22, 1541: "a escogerme da, si quyero ser loco o cient açotes— ¡yo cuerdo y libertado quiero ser!" On the Toledo hospital see Sancho de San Román, "Hospital del Nuncio."

19. Ibid., Nov. 29, 1541: "dezia algunas vezes algunas cosas que pensaba que estaba borracho y que este testigo le tenia por loco y por chocarerro y que algunas vezes parecia que hablaba en seso y siendo preguntado si podria estar en la Casa del Nuncio, dixo que bien trabaja el dicho Juan Garcia, que no lo sabe."

20. Ibid.

21. For example, the 10,000 ducats and palace that García claimed to own were beyond any laborer's wildest dreams. He also said that many daughters of grandees fought over him, and he insisted that Empress Elizabeth had died in September or in January (1539) in Guadalupe, when in fact she had died in Toledo in May. Another odd statement was that a cloud formed over him and followed him wherever he went, which the inquisitors marked.

22. Fernández, *Medicina árabe en España*, 130; italics added.

23. Or in Mexico, for that matter. Sacristán found that witnesses could not define insanity simply on the basis of beliefs (*Locura e Inquisición en Nueva España*, 39). Educated opinion could be more nuanced; echoing Maimonides, in 1623 one Inquisition official warned his colleagues that they could be mistaken in a difficult case because "many persons he said were sane in everything but one topic, on which they were insane" (Lea, *History of the Inquisition*, 3:61).

24. Bigeard, *Folie et les fous littéraires*, 21. Bigeard notes that Lope de Vega uses this medical condition as the cause of one of his characters' insanity. Cervantes's fascination with the topic resulted in the characters of Don Quixote and the Licenciate Vidriera, possibly based on a true story. The word *espíritu* could mean the "energy that vitalizes the [human] organism" by flowing through *vias espirituales* (Mexía, *Silva de varia lección*, 2:113–14).

25. Mexía popularized the Galenic explanation in his immensely successful *Silva de varia lección*, "Del vino."

26. ADC, Inq., leg. 93bis, exp. 1378. Martínez's job was to keep unauthorized livestock out of communal pastures, a position that won him few friends. Despite proving that he drank too much and that many people hated him, Martínez failed to win his case and paid for it with his life. According to witnesses, he had denied the real presence of Christ in the Eucharist. In court, he denied having said the words and was executed as an unrepentant heretic. The

case was tried before all death sentences imposed by local Inquisition tribunals required approval from the Suprema.

27. ADC, Inq., leg. 218, exp. 2664 (1560), suspended. The case went no further than the denunciation, as Mari had previously been declared insane and released by the secular authorities. The Hospital dels Innocents of Valencia admitted several women with similar delusions: the queens of Portugal (1471), Sweden (1474), and Naples (1529) (Tropé, *Locura y sociedad*, 148).

28. The same was true in Mexico (Sacristán, *Locura e Inquisición en Nueva España*, 68).

29. Bigeard, *Folie et les fous littéraires*, 17: "Le mérite essentiel des 'encyclopédies' médicales du XVIe siècle est d'avoir redécouvert le rôle primordial du cerveau dans les maladies mentales."

30. Lisón Tolosana, *Demonios y exorcismos*, 103–7. Lisón quotes Castañega: "Otros hay que son enfermos de enfermedades naturales no conocidas de los medicos de la tierra, ni destos hay tantos hombres como mujeres, que son enfermas como de alguna especie de mania o flaqueza de celebro o pusilanimidad y desfallecimiento del corazon; o semejantes pasiones ocultas, que muchas veces por no poder conocer la causa de la enfermedad, ni saberles poner el remedio natural que se requiere, dicen que tienen espiritus o demonios . . . ; mas el buen filosofo natural (cual se rrequiere que sea el medico) conoce como todas estas cosas son enfermedades y pasiones naturales. . . . Y el remedio . . . por via natural se ha de procurar con medicinas naturales" (104). See also L. S. Granjel, "Aspectos médicos," 113–78; and Homza, "To Annihilate Sorcery."

31. Certain sanctuaries gained a reputation for curing the insane. Several in Germany are studied in detail by Midelfort, *History of Madness*, chap. 6. In the district of Moya, Nuestra Señora de Texeda was the most potent shrine, with two miraculous cures of the insane to its credit (Ponce de León, *Milagros y loores confirmados*, 238, 239).

32. On this point see Foriers, "Condition des insensés," 31–32; Gómez, *Commentariorvm*, f. 339v; and Dedieu, "Modèle religieux," 252–54. From the few cases described, the Spanish Inquisition seems to have been somewhat more understanding of these extreme cases than the French courts.

33. Menéndez Pelayo, *Historia de los heterodoxos españoles*, 1:519.

34. Eimeric and Peña, *Manual de los inquisidores*, 150.

35. On millennial preachers in Italy see Niccoli, *Prophecy*, chap. 5; and Weinstein, *Savonarola and Florence*. "Barba" was a Waldesian term for prophet.

36. Menéndez Pelayo, *Historia de los heterodoxos españoles*, 1:582–83. More is recorded of this case; the early sixteenth-century archivist of the Crown of Aragon extracted large portions of the trial, which are in included in

the *Colección de documentos inéditos*, vol. 28, pt. 2, pp. 221–35. At this time (1500) Barcelona had close connections with Italy.

37. Gerson, *Tractatus*, 576.

38. Aquinas, *Summa Theologiae*, "De prophetia" (Q. 172.4), 447–51.

39. Gerson, *De probatione spirituum*, 533–34. Gerson introduces social prejudice as well, however, by suggesting that the uneducated laity, women in particular, should be evaluated with extra caution, as they are more emotional and susceptible to the devil's influence.

40. See Midelfort, "Sin, Melancholy, Obsession" and "Johann Weyer."

41. Gerson, *Tractatus*, 582.

42. Luis de San Pablo (discussed in chap. 5) is a perfect example of what Gerson warned against: excessive penances that undermined the individual's physical health, thereby opening the door to mental collapse and the devil's interference. On religious women, see Weber, "Between Ecstasy and Exorcism" and "Spiritual Administration."

43. Kagan, *Lucrecia's Dreams*, 39–40.

44. Monter, *Frontiers of Heresy*, 255–75; Caro Baroja, *World of Witches*.

45. Tropé, *Locura y sociedad*, 31–32; Fernández, *Medicina árabe*, 199.

46. A popular survey is González Duro, *Historia de la locura*.

47. The "locos" received about 3 ounces of meat daily plus the least desirable parts of the animal, such as feet, viscera, and heads, while other patients received 6 ounces of good meat every day. The most complete study of the hospital is Baquero, *Bosquejo histórico*; chap. 3 describes the hospital in the sixteenth century. Also used for this description is *Antigua descripción de Zaragoza*, based on a manuscript from the late sixteenth century, and Murillo, *Fundación Milagrosa*. The hospital was destroyed in the War of Independence (1808–12).

48. Proceso, f. 160r.

49. Baquero, *Bosquejo histórico*, 51. The participation of the city's madmen and -women in Corpus Christi festivals is noted in Valencia and Toledo as well.

50. Ibid.

51. Proceso, f. 163v.

Conclusion

1. The petition is preserved as ADC, Inq., Papeles sueltos, 761: 906. Sánchez is mentioned ibid., leg. 217, exp. 2644, contra Miguel Torralba, mesonero de Cardenete, suspended.

2. Carrasco, "Inquisición 'por de dentro,'" 252–53. These charges sound

like malicious gossip, but they are presented without comment or challenge. When one sees the quantity of paperwork Ybaneta drafted, it is hard to believe he could have found time to weave cloth!

3. AHN, Inq., Cuenca, leg. 1933, exp. 1.

4. Carrasco, "Inquisición 'por de dentro,'" 254. Serrano eventually became vicar general and a canon in Toledo; he died in Madrid in 1595 (marginal note in ADC, Inq., L-349, "Registro de provisiones," Aug. 2, 1555, entry recording the appointment of Bachiller Serrano to the tribunal).

5. Scandella, *Domenico Scandella.*

6. Apparently a misunderstanding of the cult of Nuestra Señora de la Palma in southern Spain. Generally, the inquisitors tried to maintain a strict distinction between superstition and heresy, and regarded superstition as the bishop's responsibility.

7. A brief description is in Nalle, *God in La Mancha*, 183.

8. See ADC, Inq., leg. 36, exp. 611, Andrés Borrachero, Huete, 1500. Andrés clearly did believe that the soul survived the death of the body, despite his first statement. On later examples of religious skepticism, see Griffiths, "Popular Religious Scepticism." Belief in the transmigration of souls into the bodies of other beings, where they would be reincarnated according to their sins, was widely diffused in the ancient Mediterranean world.

9. While historians have ignored the topic, the anthropologist Carmelo Lisón Tolosana has published a study of contemporary belief in the ancient hordes titled *La Santa Compaña;* and the literary historian Augustin Redondo has surveyed the literary evidence in "Tradiciones hispánicas."

10. To begin, see Ginzburg, *Night Battles.* Also Niccoli, *Prophecy and the People*, chap. 3; Le Roy Ladurie, *Montaillou*, 288–90, 345–51; and Behringer, *Shaman of Oberstdorf.*

11. "Vio a poco d'ora venir mui grandes yentes / con ciriales en manos e con cirios ardientes con su rei en medio feos ca non luzientes (Berceo, *Milagros de Nuestra Señora*, verses 73–74).

12. "Y ven los moradores encontrarse por el aire esquadrones; oyense voces como de personas que acometen: *estantiguas* llama el vulgo español a semejantes apariencias o fantasmas" (Mendoza, *Guerra de Granada*, bk. 3, p. 124). *Estantiguas* is a contraction of *huestes antiguas* (ancient hordes), found in medieval accounts. Mendoza's comment (about a battle dating from Roman times) is intriguing, but while in Italy he may have seen printed reports of precisely such a fantastic battle that reputedly took place in northern Italy in 1518. For Mendoza's biography, see Spivakovsky, *Son of the Alhambra.*

13. A general study is Bourseiller, *Faux messies.* The general phenomenon of messianism in the Iberian world has been studied by Castro, *Aspectos del*

vivir hispánico; Lafaye, *Mesías, cruzadas, utopías;* and Delgado, *Metamorpho-sen des Messianismus.*

14. Much more material becomes available on the likes of the seventeenth-century self-declared messiahs Sabbatai Sevi, Simon Morin, and James Naylor. An exemplary study is Scholem, *Sabbatai Sevi.* Sevi was regarded by many Jews of the time as the true Messiah.

15. On El Encubierto, begin with Milhou, "Chauvre-souris," and García Cárcel, *Germanías de Valencia,* 132–38. On David Reubeni and Luis Dias, see Lipiner, *O Sapateiro de Trancoso.*

BIBLIOGRAPHY

Primary Sources

Archival Sources

Archivo Catedralicio de Cuenca
    Rentas de la Mesa Capitular
Archivo Diocesano de Cuenca
    Inquisición
    Parroquías
Archivo General de Simancas
    Cámara de Castilla
    Registro General de Sellos
Archivo Histórico Nacional, Madrid
    Consejos Suprimidos, Inquisición
    Sección Nobleza, Toledo
Archivo Histórico Provincial de Cuenca
    Protocolos
Archivo Municipal de Cuenca
    Libros de Actas
Archivo Municipal de Requena
    Libros de Actas
Archivo Real de la Chancillería, Granada
    Sección de Pleitos

Printed Primary Sources

Alba, Ramón. *Acerca de algunas particularidades de las Comunidades de Castilla tal vez relacionadas con el supuesto acaecer Terreno del Milenio Igualitario.* Madrid: Editora Nacional, 1975.
Antigua descripción de Zaragoza. Ed. "Kirón." Madrid, 1940.

Aquinas, Thomas. *Summa Theologiae: A Concise Translation.* Ed. Timothy McDermott. London: Eyre & Spottiswoode, 1989.

Berceo, Gonzalo de. *Los milagros de Nuestra Señora.* Ed. Brian Dutton. London: Tamesis Books, 1971.

Blanco Sánchez, A. "Inventario de Juan de Ayala, gran impresor toledano (1556)." *Boletín de la Real Academia Española de Historia* 62 (1987): 207–50.

Colección de documentos inéditos del Archivo de la Corona de Aragón. Barcelona: Impreso del Archivo, 1865.

Covarrubias y Orozco, Sebastián. *Tesoro de la lengua castellana o española.* (1611.) Madrid: Turner, 1977.

Cruz, Francisco de la. *Inquisición, Actas I, II-1.* Ed. Vidal Abril Castelló and Miguel J. Abril Stoffels. Madrid: CSIC, 1992–96.

Dánvila y Collado, Manuel. *Historia crítica y documentada de las comunidades de Castilla.* 6 vols. Madrid: M. Tello, 1897–99.

Eimeric, Nicolau, and Francisco Peña. *El manual de los inquisidores.* Trans. (into French) Louis Sala-Molins; trans. (from French into Spanish) Francisco Martín. Barcelona: Muchnik, 1983.

Ferrazzi, Cecilia. *Autobiography of an Aspiring Saint.* Trans. and ed. Anne J. Schutte. Chicago: University of Chicago Press, 1996.

Gerson, Jean. *De probatione spirituum.* In *Opera,* ed. Edmond Richer, 529–34. Paris: n.p., 1606.

———. *Tractatus de distinctione verarum visionum a falsis.* In *Opera,* ed. Edmond Richer, 575–93. Paris: n.p., 1606.

Gómez, Antonio. *Commentariorvm, variarvmque, resolvtionvm ivris civilis communis, et regii.* Venice: Ad candentis Salamandrae insigne, 1572.

Guevara, Antonio de. *Menosprecio de corte y alabanza de aldea.* (1539.) Ed. Asunció Rallo. Madrid: Cátedra, 1984.

Horas de nuestra señora en romance: segun el vso romano muy cumplidas segun se vera por la tabla. Toledo: Juan de Ayala, 1565.

Huarte de San Juan, Juan. *Examen de ingenios para las ciencias.* Ed. Guillermo Serés. Madrid: Cátedra, 1989.

Hurtado de Mendoza, Diego. *Guerra de Granada.* Ed. Bernardo Blanco-González. Madrid: Castalia, 1970.

The "Libro de las profecías" of Christopher Columbus. Ed. Delno C. West and August Kling. Facs. ed. Gainesville: University of Florida Press, 1991.

Mexía, Pedro. *Silva de varia lección.* (1550.) Ed. Antonio Castro. 2 vols. Madrid: Cátedra, 1989.

Murillo, Diego. *Fundación Milagrosa de la Capilla Angélica y apostólica de la*

Madre de Dios del Pilar y Excellencias de la imperial ciudad de Çaragoça. Barcelona: Mateaud, 1616.

Pinel y Monroy, Francisco. *Retrato del buen vasallo, copiado de la vida, y hechos de D. Andrés de Cabrera, Primero Marqués de Moya.* (1677.) Moya: Asociación Amigos de Moya, 1992.

Ponce de León, Fr. Pedro. *Milagros y loores confirmados con mvchos exemplos de la soberana emperatriz de los cielos, santa Maria de Texeda.* Valencia: Gerónimo Vilagraía, 1663.

La Santa Biblia: Antiguo y Nuevo Testamentos. Casiodoro de Reina translation, 1569, rev. 1602, 1960. Mexico City: Sociedad Biblia, 1992.

Santa María, Francisco de. *Historia general profetica de la orden de Nuestra Señora del Carmen.* Madrid: Francisco Martínez, 1630.

Scandella, Domenico. *Domenico Scandella Known as Menocchio: His Trials Before the Inquisition (1583–1599).* Ed. Andrea Del Col. Trans. John and Anne C. Tedeschi. Binghamton, N.Y.: Medieval and Renaissance Texts and Studies, 1996.

Simancas, Diego de. *De Catholicis Institutionibus. Liber ad praecavendas et extirpandas herese admodum necessarius.* (1552.) In *Tractatus Illustrium in vtraqve tum pontificii, tvm caesari iuris facvltate Iurisconsultorum.* Vol. 11, pt. 2, *De Iudicijs Criminalibus S. Inquisitionis.* Venice: Franciscus Zilettus, 1584.

Secondary Sources

Alcalá-Zamora, José N., dir. *La vida cotidiana en la España de Velázquez: El retrato vivo y contradictorio de un imperio que inicia su decadencia.* Madrid: Temas de Hoy, 1994.

Alvarez Delgado, Yasmina. "Repoblación y frontera en la Sierra baja de Cuenca." In *Primer Congreso Castilla–La Mancha: Actas,* 5:145–51. Toledo: Junta de Comunidades Castilla–La Mancha, 1988.

Appleby, Joyce, and Lynn Hunt. *Telling the Truth about History.* New York: Norton, 1994.

Asensio, Eugenio. "Fray Luis de Maluenda, apologista de la Inquisición, condendado en la Índice inquisitorial." *Arquivos do Centro Cultural Português* 9 (1975): 87–100.

Baquero, Aurelia. *Bosquejo histórico del Hospital Real y General de Nuestra Señora de la Gracía de Zarugoza.* Zaragoza: Seccíon de Estudios Médicos Aragoneses, Institución "Fernando el Católico," 1952.

Behringer, Wolfgang. *Shaman of Oberstdorf: Chonrad Stoeckhlin and the*

Phantoms of the Night. Trans. H. C. Erik Midelfort. Charlottesville: University Press of Virginia, 1998.

Beltrán de Heredia, Vicente. *Las corrientes de espiritualidad entre los dominicos de Castilla durante la primera mitad del siglo XVI.* Salamanca: n.p., 1941.

Bigeard, Martine. *La folie et les fous littéraires en Espagne, 1500–1650.* Paris: Centre de Recherches Hispaniques, 1972.

Bourseiller, Christophe. *Les faux messies: Histoire d'une attente.* Paris: Fayard, 1993.

Caro Baroja, Julio. *The World of Witches.* London: Weidenfeld & Nicolson, 1968.

Carrasco, Rafael. "La Inquisición 'por de dentro': La visita del inquisidor Padilla al oficio de Cuenca (1559)." In *Primer Congreso de Historia de Castilla–La Mancha: Actas,* 7:249–59. Toledo: Junta de Comunidades de Castilla–La Mancha, 1988.

Castro, Américo. *Aspectos del vivir hispánico: Espiritualismo, mesianismo, actitud personal en los siglos XIV al XVI.* Santiago de Chile: Cruz del Sur, 1949.

Cátedra, Pedro M. *Sermón, sociedad y literatura en la Edad Media: San Vicente Ferrer en Castilla (1411–1412): Estudio bibliográfico, literario y edición de los textos inéditos.* Valladolid: Junta de Castilla y León, 1994.

Cervera Vera, Luis. *Francisco de Eiximenis y su sociedad urbana ideal.* Madrid: Swan, 1989.

Chartier, Roger. *On the Edge of the Cliff: History, Language, and Practices.* Trans. Lydia G. Cochrane. Baltimore: Johns Hopkins University Press, 1997.

Christian, William A., Jr. *Apparitions in Late Medieval and Renaissance Spain.* Princeton: Princeton University Press, 1981.

———. *Local Religion in Sixteenth-Century Spain.* Princeton: Princeton University Press, 1981.

Contreras, Jaime. *Sotos contra Riquelmes: Regidores, inquisidores y criptojudíos.* Madrid: Anaya & Muchnik, 1992.

Cooper, Edward. *Castillos señoriales en la Corona de Castilla.* 2 vols. Madrid: Fundación Universitaria Española, 1980–1981.

———. "Nueva aproximación a la historia de la fortaleza de Cardenete." In *Moya: Estudios y documentos I,* 89–92.

Corominas, Juan. *Diccionario crítico etimológico castellano e hispánico.* 6 vols. Madrid: Gredos, c. 1980–91.

Davis, Natalie Zemon. *The Return of Martin Guerre.* Cambridge: Harvard University Press, 1983.

Dedieu, Jean-Pierre. "Le modèle religieux: Les disciplines du langage et de l'action." In *L'Inquisition Espagnole, X^{ve}–XIXe siècle,* ed. Bartolomé Bennassar, 241–67. Paris: Hachette, 1979.

Delgado, Mariano. *Die Metamorphosen des Messianismus in den iberischen Kulturen.* Freiburg: Immensee, 1994.

Domínguez Ortiz, Antonio. *La clase social de los conversos en Castilla en la edad moderna.* Madrid: CSIC, 1985.

Edwards, John. "The Conversos: A Theological Approach." *Bulletin of Hispanic Studies* 62 (1985): 39–49.

———. "Elijah and the Inquisition: Messianic Prophecy among *Conversos* in Spain, c. 1500." *Nottingham Medieval Studies* 28 (1984): 79–94.

Fajardo Spínola, Francisco. *Hechicería y brujería en Canarias en la Edad Moderna.* Las Palmas: Ediciones del Cabildo Insular, 1992.

Fernández, Fidel. *La medicina árabe en España.* Barcelona: Juventud, 1936.

Flecniakoska, Jean-Louis. "La propagation des idées protestantes par les français en Espagne et l'Inquisition de Cuenca (1554–1578)." *Bulletin de la Société de l'Histoire du Protestantism Français* 120 (1974): 532–54.

Flynn, Maureen. *Sacred Charity: Confraternities and Social Welfare in Spain, 1400–1700.* Ithaca: Cornell University Press, 1989.

Foriers, P. "La condition des insensés à la Renaissance." In *Folie et déraison à la Renaissance,* 27–39. Brussels: Editions de l'Université de Bruxelles, 1976.

Foucault, Michel. *Madness and Civilization: A History of Insanity in the Age of Reason.* Trans. Richard Howard. New York: Vintage Books, 1973.

Fuster, Joan. *Rebeldes y heterodoxos.* Barcelona: Ariel, 1972.

García Cárcel, Ricardo. *Las germanías de Valencia.* 2nd ed. Barcelona: Península, 1981.

García y García de Castro, Rafael. *Virtudes de la Reina Católica.* Madrid: CSIC, 1961.

Ginzburg, Carlo. *The Cheese and the Worms: The Cosmos of a Sixteenth-Century Miller.* Baltimore: Johns Hopkins University Press, 1980.

———. *The Night Battles: Witchcraft and Agrarian Cults in the Sixteenth and Seventeenth Centuries.* Trans John and Anne Tedeschi. New York: Penguin, 1985.

González Duro, Enrique. *Historia de la locura en España.* 2 vols. Madrid: Temas de Hoy, 1994.

Granjel, L. S. "Aspectos médicos de la literatura antisupersticiosa española de los siglos XVI y XVII." In *Humanismo y medicina,* 113–78. Salamanca, 1968.

Griffiths, Nicholas. "Popular Religious Scepticism and Idiosyncrasy in Post-Tridentine Cuenca." In *Faith and Fanaticism: Religious Fervour in Early Modern Spain,* ed. Lesley K. Twomey, 95–126. Aldershot:Ashgate, 1997.

Gutiérrez Nieto, Juan Ignacio. *Las Comunidades como movimiento antiseñorial: La formación del bando realista en la guerra civil castellana de 1520–1521.* Barcelona: Planeta, 1973.

Haliczer, Stephen. "The Jew as Witch: Displaced Aggression and the Myth of the Santo Niño de La Guardia." In *Cultural Encounters: The Impact of the Inquisition in Spain and the New World,* ed. Mary Elizabeth Perry and Anne J. Cruz, 146–56. Berkeley: University of California Press, 1991.

Hamilton, Alastair. *Heresy and Mysticism in Sixteenth-Century Spain: The Alumbrados.* Toronto: University of Toronto Press, 1992.

Harvey, L. P. *Islamic Spain: 1250 to 1500.* Chicago: University of Chicago Press, 1990.

Herrero Salgado, Félix. *La oratoria sagrada española de los siglos XVI y XVII.* Madrid: Fundación Universitaria Española, 1996.

Homza, Lu Ann. "To Annihilate Sorcery and Amend the Church: A New Interpretation of Pedro Ciruelo's *Reprobación de las supersticiones y hechicerías.*" In *Religion, Body, and Gender in Early Modern Spain,* ed. A. Saint-Saëns, 46–64. San Francisco: Edwin Mellen, 1991.

Jiménez Monteserín, Miguel. "Los hermanos Valdés y el mundo judeoconverso conquense." In *Política, religión e inquisición en la España moderna: Homenaje a Joaquín Pérez Villanueva,* 379–400. Madrid: UAM, 1996.

———. "Los luteranos ante el tribunal de la Inquisición de Cuenca, 1525–1600." In *La Inquisición española: Nueva visión, nuevos horizontes,* ed. Joaquín Pérez Villanueva, 689–736. Madrid: Siglo Veintiuno, 1980.

Jiménez Olivares, Ernestina. *Psiquiatría e Inquisición: Procesos a enfermos mentales.* Mexico City: Facultad de Medicina, UNAM, 1992.

Kagan, Richard L. *Lucrecia's Dreams: Politics and Prophecy in Sixteenth-Century Spain.* Berkeley: University of California Press, 1990.

Kamen, Henry. *The Spanish Inquisition: A Historical Revision.* London: Weidenfeld & Nicolson, 1997.

Kinder, A. Gordon. "'Ydiota y sin letras': Evidence of Literacy among the *Alumbrados* of Toledo." *Journal of the Institute of Romance Studies* 4 (1996): 37–49.

Lafaye, Jacques. *Mesías, cruzadas, utopías: El judeo-cristianismo en las sociedades ibéricas.* Mexico City: Fondo de Cultura Económica, 1984.

Lafond, Jean, and Augustin Redondo, eds. *L'Image du monde renversé et ses representations littéraires et para-littéraires de la fin du XVIᵉ siècle au milieu du XVIIIᵉ.* Paris: Université de Tours, 1979.

Lea, Henry Charles. *A History of the Inquisition of Spain.* 4 vols. New York: AMS Press, 1988.

León Tello, Pilar. *Archivo de los duques de Frias.* 3 vols. Madrid: Dirección General de Archivos y Bibliotecas y Casa de los Duques de Frías, 1973.

Le Roy Ladurie, Emmanuel. *Montaillou: The Promised Land of Error.* Trans. Barbara Bray. New York: George Braziller, 1978.

Lipiner, Elias. *O Sapateiro de Trancoso e o Alfaiate de Setúbal.* Rio de Janeiro: Imago, 1993.

Lisón Tolosana, Carmelo. *Demonios y exorcismos en los siglos de oro.* Madrid: Akal, 1990.

———. *La Santa Compaña: Fantasías reales, realidades fantásticas.* Madrid: Akal, 1998.

López Alonso, Carmen. *Locura y sociedad en Sevilla: Historia del hospital de los inocentes (1436?–1840).* Seville: Diputación Provincial, 1988.

Lorenzo Cadarso, P. L. "Esplendor y decadencia de las oligarquías conversas de Cuenca y Guadalajara (siglos XV–XVI)." *Hispania* 54 (1994): 53–94.

Márquez, Antonio. *Los alumbrados: Orígenes y filosofía, 1525–1559.* Madrid: Taurus, 1972.

Martz, Linda. *Poverty and Welfare in Habsburg Spain: The Example of Toledo.* Cambridge: Cambridge University Press, 1983.

McKendrick, Geraldine, and Angus MacKay. "Visionaries and Affective Spirituality during the First Half of the Sixteenth Century." In *Cultural Encounters: The Impact of the Inquisition in Spain and the New World,* ed. Mary Elizabeth Perry and Anne J. Cruz, 93–104. Berkeley: University of California Press, 1991.

Menéndez Pelayo, Marcelino. *Historia de los heterodoxos españoles.* 3rd. ed. Madrid: BAC, 1978.

Midelfort, H. C. Erik. *A History of Madness in Sixteenth-Century Germany.* Stanford: Stanford University Press, 1999.

———. "Johann Weyer and the Transformation of the Insanity Defense." In *The German People and the Reformation,* ed. R. Po-Chia Hsia, 234–62. Ithaca: Cornell University Press, 1988.

———. "Sin, Melancholy, Obsession: Insanity and Culture in Sixteenth-Century Germany." In *Understanding Popular Culture: Europe from the Middle Ages to the Nineteenth Century,* ed. Steven L. Kaplan, 113–46. New York: Mouton, 1984.

Milhou, Alain. "La chauvre-souris, le nouveau David et le Roi Caché (trois images de l'empereur des derniers temps dans le monde ibérique)." *Mélanges de la Casa de Velázquez* 18 (1982): 61–79.

———. *Colón y su mentalidad mesiánica en el ambiente franciscanista español.* Valladolid: Universidad de Valladolid, 1983.

Monter, William. *Frontiers of Heresy: The Spanish Inquisition from the Basque Lands to Sicily.* Cambridge: Cambridge University Press, 1990.

Moya: Estudios y documentos I. Ed. Grupo de Investigación de Moya. Cuenca: Diputación Provincial, 1996.

Nalle, Sara T. *God in La Mancha: Religious Reform and the People of Cuenca, 1500–1650.* Baltimore: Johns Hopkins University Press, 1992.

———. "Literacy and Culture in Early Modern Castile." *Past & Present* 125 (1989): 65–96.

———. "The Millennial Moment: Revolution and Radical Religion in Sixteenth-Century Spain." In *Toward the Millennium: Messianic Expectations from the Bible to Waco,* ed. Peter Schäfer and Mark Cohen, 153–73. Leiden: Brill, 1998.

———. "Moya busca nuevo señor: Aspectos de la rebelión comunera en el marquesado de Moya." In *Moya: Estudios y documentos I,* 93–102.

———. "Printing and Reading Popular Religious Texts in Sixteenth-Century Castile." In *Culture and the Formation of the State,* ed. Thomas Lewis and Francisco J. Sánchez, 123–53. New York: Garland, 1999.

Niccoli, Ottavia. *Prophecy and the People in Renaissance Italy.* Trans. Lydia Cochrane. Princeton: Princeton University Press, 1990.

Nieto, José C. *Juan de Valdés and the Origins of the Spanish and the Italian Reformation.* Geneva: Droz, 1970.

Olin, John C. *Catholic Reform from Cardinal Ximenes to the Council of Trent, 1495–1563.* New York: Fordham University Press, 1990.

Ortega, Milagros. "Las proposiciones del Edicto de los Alumbrados: Autores y calificadores." In *Cuadernos de Investigación Histórica* 1:23–36. Madrid: Fundación Universitaria Española, 1977.

Pérez Ramírez, Dimas. "El Archivo de la Inquisición de Cuenca: Formación, vicisitudes, estado actual." In *La Inquisición española: Nueva visión, nuevos horizontes,* ed. Joaquín Pérez Villanueva, 855–75. Madrid: Siglo Veintiuno, 1980.

———. *Catálogo del Archivo de la Inquisición de Cuenca.* Madrid: Fundación Universitaria Española, 1982.

Pérez Villanueva, Joaquín, ed. *La Inquisición española: Nueva visión, nuevos horizontes.* Madrid: Siglo Veintiuno, 1980.

Pou y Martí, J. M. *Visionarios, beguinos y fraticelos catalanes (siglos XIII–XV).* 2nd. rev. ed. Madrid: Colegio "Cardenal Cisneros," 1991.

Rábade Obradó, M. P. *Una élite de poder en la Corte de los Reyes Católicos: Los judeoconversos.* Madrid: Sigilo, 1993.

Redondo, Augustin. *Antonio de Guevara (1480?–1545) et l'Espagne de son temps.* Geneva: Droz, 1976.

———. "Las tradiciones hispánicas de la 'estantigua' ('cacería salvaje' o *mesnie hellequin*) y su resurgencia en el *Quijote*." In *Otra manera de leer el "Quijote": Historia, tradiciones culturales y literatura*, 101–19. Madrid: Castalia, 1997.

Reeves, Marjorie. *The Influence of Prophecy in the Later Middle Ages: A Study in Joachimism*. Notre Dame: University of Notre Dame Press, 1993.

Rodríguez-Moñino, Antonio. *Diccionario de pliegos sueltos poéticos (siglo XVI)*. Madrid: Castalia, 1970.

Rokeach, Milton. *The Three Christs of Ypsilanti: A Psychological Study*. New York: Knopf, 1964.

Rokiski Lázaro, María Luz. *Arquitectura del siglo XVI en Cuenca*. Cuenca: Diputación Provincial de Cuenca, 1985.

Sacristán, María Cristina. *Locura e Inquisición en Nueva España, 1571–1760*. Mexico City: Fondo de Cultura Económica, 1992.

Sainz Rodríguez, Pedro. *La siembra mística del cardenal Cisneros y las reformas en la Iglesia*. Salamanca: Universidad Pontificia de Salamanca, 1979.

Salomon, Noël. *Lo villano en el teatro del Siglo de Oro*. Madrid: Castalia, 1985.

Sánchez Gil, Víctor. "El tribunal de la Inquisición de Cuenca." *Archivo-Ibero-Americano* 40 (1980): 3–36.

Sancho de San Román, Rafael. "El hospital del Nuncio de Toledo en la historia de la asistencia psiquiátrica." *Anales Toledanos* 17 (1983): 55–71.

Schama, Simon. *Dead Certainties (Unwarranted Speculations)*. New York: Vintage Books, 1992.

Scholem, Gershom. *Sabbatai Sevi: The Mystical Messiah, 1626–1676*. Trans. R. J. Zwi Werblowsky. Princeton: Princeton University Press, 1973.

Spiegel, Gabrielle M. *The Past as Text: The Theory and Practice of Medieval Historiography*. Baltimore: Johns Hopkins University Press, 1997.

Spivakovsky, Erika. *Son of the Alhambra: Diego Hurtado de Menodza, 1504–1575*. Austin: University of Texas Press, 1970.

Tropé, Hélène. *Locura y sociedad en la Valencia de los siglos XV al XVII*. Valencia: Diputación de Valencia, 1994.

Vassberg, David E. *The Village and the Outside World in Golden Age Castile: Mobility and Migration in Everyday Rural Life*. Cambridge: Cambridge University Press, 1996.

Weber, Alison. "Between Ecstasy and Exorcism: Religious Negotiation in Sixteenth-Century Spain." *Journal of Medieval and Renaissance Studies* 23 (1993): 221–34.

———. "Spiritual Administration: Gender and Discernment in the Carmelite Reform." *Sixteenth Century Journal* 31 (2000): 127–50.

Weinstein, Donald. *Savonarola and Florence: Prophecy and Patriotism in the Renaissance.* Princeton: Princeton University Press, 1970.

Windschuttle, Keith. *The Killing of History: How Literary Critics and Social Theorists are Murdering Our Past.* New York: Free Press, 1997.

Wunderli, Richard. *Peasant Fires: The Drummer of Niklashausen.* Bloomington: Indiana University Press, 1992.

INDEX

Page numbers in italic refer to illustrations

Quaternity, 29, 64. *See also* Trinity

Ramírez de Vergara, Dr. Alonso, 75,
77, 78, 84, 95, 98, 100, 101, 119,
125, 128, 130, 131, 136, 142, 163,
168
realgar, 88, 199 n. 36
Requena, 66, 143
Reubeni, David, 168
Riego, Dr. *See* García del Riego,
Dr. Diego
River of Stones (*rio de las piedras*),
131, 132, 133, 138, 143
Roa, Ana la, trial of (1554), 111–12
Ruiz, Francisco, 22
Ruiz de Alarcón, Jorge, lord of Val-
verde, 195 n. 9

Sacedón, 111
Sánchez, Alonso, notary, 121, 124, 135
Sánchez, Bartolomé: breakdown, 9–
10, 15–21; converso links, 68, 71,
197 n. 43; escape to Cardenete, 116–
18; family history, 10–11, 76; hospi-
talized as insane, 136, 160; pilgrimage to Guadalupe, 133; prayers of,
74, 76, 77, 78, 142; property of, 25;
Scripture, used by, 33, 35–36, 50,
132, 189 n. 17, 190 n. 5, 191 n. 20,
193 n. 28, 197 n. 10; symptoms of
illness, 140, 144; vision of, 16, 102,
104, 139
Sánchez, Bartolomé, and the Inquisition: auto de fe of, 97–100; demands own lawyer, 31; indictment
of, 80; insanity hearings, 90–92,
125–27; reconciliation of, 108;
threats against the Holy Office, 38,
47, 49. *See also* baptism; confession; Elijah-Messiah; Eucharist;
faith; grace; idols; indulgences; Messiah, the; Pope, the; Quaternity;
Trinity

Sánchez, Bartolomico, 20
Sánchez, Juan, 111
Sánchez, Martín, 62
Sánchez, Mateo, priest, 116
San Clemente, 66
San Pablo, Luis de, trial of (1549), 88,
156, 209 n. 42
Santaren, Juan de, trial of (1582), 146–
47, 152
Santiago de Compostela, 10
Scandella, Domenico, 72, 165
sermons, 64, 66–67, 68, 69, 140
serpent, 108, 201 n. 32
Serrano, Bachiller, 125, 126, 128, 130,
165, 210 n. 4
shrines of the Virgin Mary: Our
Lady of the Bridge (Cuenca), 113,
115; Our Lady of the Candles (Monteagudo), 16; Our Lady of the Descent (Toledo), 150; Our Lady
of Guadalupe (Guadalupe), 134;
Our Lady of Texeda (Moya),
208 n. 31
Sigüenza, 26, 28, 113
sin, 32, 40, 45, 49, 53; mortal v. venial, 33
Son of God. *See* Jesus Christ
Son of Man, 69, 120, 140. *See also*
Messiah, the; messianism
soul, beliefs about, 15, 73, 74, 82, 166,
167

Tapia, Diego de, 80, 81, 82, 87, 90, 101,
107, 127
Tebar, 145
Toledo, 61, 68, 149. *See also* hospitals
for the insane, Toledo
Tordesillas, Junta de, 58
torture. *See under* Inquisition of
Spain
transubstantiation, 40, 41
Trinity, beliefs about, 22, 29, 30, 46,
64. *See also* Quaternity

Urbano, Mossen, trial of (1507), 155–56

Valencia: city, 158; kingdom, 13, 58
Valhermosa, 145
Valverde, 66
Vélez, Luis, 91, 93
Verdugo, Lucas, 153
Vergara, Dr. *See* Ramírez de Vergara, Dr. Alonso
Villaescusa de Haro, 153
Villamalea, 14, 40
Villanova, Arnold of, 68, 155
Villar de Saz de Arcas, 116
Villena, marquises of, 58
Víllora, lord of, 14

Virgin Mary, 113, 114, 120; Coronation of the Virgin, *18, 64. See also* shrines of the Virgin Mary; Quaternity

witchcraft, 110, 157, 158
world turned upside down, motif of, 9, 141, 205 n. 4

Ybaneta, Juan de, court recorder, 5, 105, 136, 164; statement for the record, 128–30
Yémeda, Vega de, 14, *14*

Zomeño, Hernán, 17, 63